Co-Creation in Higher Education

CREATIVE EDUCATION BOOK SERIES

Volume 6

Scope

The knowledge, learning and creative economies manifest the changing significance of intellectual capital and the thickening connections between economic growth, knowledge and creativity. Increasingly economic and social activity is comprised by the 'symbolic' or 'weightless' economy with its iconic, immaterial and digital goods. This new digital knowledge economy includes new international labor that rely on developments in information and communication technologies (ICTs) that are changing the format, density and nature of the exchange and flows of knowledge, research and scholarship. Delivery modes in education are being reshaped. New global cultures of knowledge and research networks are spreading rapidly. New forms of openness and networking, cross-border people movement, flows of capital, portal cities and intensive development zones all are changing the conditions of imagining and producing and the sharing of creative work in different spheres. At the centre of is the economy/ creativity nexus. But are education systems, institutions, assumptions and habits positioned and able so as to seize the opportunities and meet the challenges? This new series investigates all the aspects of education in (and as) the creative economy in order to extend the dialogue about the relationship between contemporary higher education and the changing face of contemporary economies.

Co-Creation in Higher Education

Students and Educators Preparing Creatively and Collaboratively to the Challenge of the Future

Edited by

Tatiana Chemi and Lone Krogh
Aalborg University, Aalborg, Denmark

SENSE PUBLISHERS
ROTTERDAM/BOSTON/TAIPEI

A C.I.P. record for this book is available from the Library of Congress.

ISBN: 978-94-6351-117-9 (paperback)
ISBN: 978-94-6351-118-6 (hardback)
ISBN: 978-94-6351-119-3 (e-book)

Published by: Sense Publishers,
P.O. Box 21858,
3001 AW Rotterdam,
The Netherlands
https://www.sensepublishers.com/

All chapters in this book have undergone peer review.

Printed on acid-free paper

TABLE OF CONTENTS

TATIANA CHEMI AND LONE KROGH

SETTING THE STAGE FOR CO-CREATION IN HIGHER EDUCATION

RETHINKING CO-CREATION

With this introductory chapter we wish to set the stage for the perspectives behind the present contribution. The broad field to which our research studies ascribe will be presented and the structure of the book unfolded. Our ambition is not to review exhaustively the many – and still growing in number – contributions that have been dedicated to the investigation of co-creative practices. Rather, we wish to make visible and explicit the common thread among the different chapters, as well as to relate our contributions to a specific field of studies and a specific need for knowledge. First of all, we should spend some words to clarify the concept of co-creation.

Contributions on co-creation have so far touched upon specific themes, such as:

- design thinking
- product innovation
- organisational development
- social innovation/management research
- student direction
- conceptual research in general

Contributions that make use of the concept of co-creation are primarily design and business oriented. Prahalad and Ramaswamy (2004) are often mentioned as the initiators of co-creative discourses. However, their perspective on co-creation is confined to the market discourse. In their understanding, co-creation is related to the value creation that customers-market relations can generate bringing new values into the market. Their ground-breaking role is recognised, probably on the grounds that they were the first to write about optimising customer experiences through co-creation (co-opting).

Degnegaard's review (2014) considers a wide range of disciplines in his specification of the concept and we consider this as a good place to start. We refer to his review for a thorough conceptual stage setting. Sanders and Stappers (2008), instead, represent one of the major research areas in co-creation: design thinking. Voorberg et al. (2014) contribute with a review that is focused on social innovation. Camargo-Borges and Rasera (2013) represent a second direction within co-creation: a social constructivist perspective on organisational development. As Degnegaard

(2014, p. 99) clearly illustrates, business and social studies are the areas that have mostly contributed to reflections on and applications of the concept of co-creation. He therefore concludes that "there is very little research-based literature so far on how the field of co-creation has developed, and of how the concept is being established and on the future trajectory of the concept of co-creation" (Degnegaard, 2014, p. 96). Regarding the design thinking perspective, we refer to Liedtka's extensive work (2014) and her collaboration with Ogilvie (Liedtka & Ogilvie, 2011).

Our anthology focuses on approaches to teaching and learning in Higher Education (HE) with a special focus on collaborative, co-creative and distributed perspectives. As such, it aims to follow up on research in the area of co-creation and to apply it in the new context represented by Higher Education. With this collection of articles, we wish to show the diversity of approaches to co-creation, on the one hand and, on the other, we intend to give a specific direction to these studies, which is humanistic, sociological, creative and pedagogical – a direction that is still in need of further investigation and research into co-creative practices. In accordance with our purpose, we look at co-creation as the process of creative (original and valuable) generation of shared meaning and development.

HIGHER EDUCATION: CHALLENGES

HE institutions are here seen in the light of the societal developments and of recent directions in academic workplaces, nationally and internationally. The academic labour market has been changing rapidly during recent decades and new developmental tendencies in how to handle the development and its challenges have led to the fact that higher educational pedagogies are emerging (Krogh, 2013). Educating students to be able to develop skills that will prepare them to manage personal as well as social and occupational challenges in ever-changing, global and technology-based settings is progressively becoming the aim of educational institutions. According to the transformations in society, HE institutions are changing their very roles, from focusing on research and teaching to having focus on research, teaching and more effective learning. This includes keeping their attention on the emotional, sensory, affective and psychological sides of learning and teaching, together with a general approach to curriculum development that is creative and innovative. At the same time, these ideals have to face a harsh reality: the number of students is increasing more and more. This makes motivational, relational and affective issues even more relevant. We have to ask ourselves, are the students increasingly unengaged and detached? And are the HE institutions able to engage and challenge students optimally? However, we know from research and experiences (Aarup Jensen, 2015) that students seem to react according to the structures, culture, and human beings (staff) they meet in the educational systems, if we as educators invite and allow them to do so. Therefore, we must not underestimate the influence that the institutional system and staff have on the students' learning and development. If we wish to prepare our students for a yet unknown future, we must work on academic excellence, as well as psycho-affective readiness (mindfulness, resilience, collaborative processes, creativity). How can the HE institutions of the future prepare for this educational task?

We know a great deal about what makes learning happen (Ramsden, 2003; Gibbs & Tang, 2007), and in HE institutions a large number of teachers carry out experiments that approach and involve the students in such a way that they learn skills and abilities to meet future challenges.

In Denmark, principles of collaborative and co-creative learning have found their institutional places. Aalborg and Roskilde universities have for years been organising their pedagogy based on principles such as problem-based learning (PBL), student-led directions and participation, students taking on responsibilities and teachers as supervisors, facilitators (Bovill, 2011). At other institutions (e.g. UCN[1] in Denmark, Uppsala University/CEMUS[2] in Sweden), principles such as learner-led (Iversen et al., 2015) and co-creation processes in teaching activities have resulted in increased student engagement and involvement, and high-level learning outcomes.

It is not simple to change educational cultures. Many diverging interests, traditions, values, and emotions are influencing these changes and the very possibility of them happening.

This book will cover and document new research within aspects of working with teaching and learning approaches aimed at empowering students to handle their lives during their education and towards an occupational life.

There is not one way of doing this, all kinds of teaching strategies must be based on very essential curricular arguments for making the relevant choices for doing it. We refer here to the principles of alignment (Biggs & Tang, 2007) or the educational design (Dale, 1999; Jank & Meyer, 2006).

The basic themes we are interested in researching are:

- Problem-based learning (PBL)
- Co-creation
- Learner-led teaching
- Student-centred approaches
- Assessment
- Arts-based methods
- Collaborative dynamics
- Interconnection of cognition/emotion
- Creativity in HE

WHY CO-CREATION?

The relevance of investigations and research on the concept and practices of co-creation is many-sided. The concept is intuitively perceived and understood, as is the experience of shared values across different stakeholders. Not as intuitive, though, are the ways in which individuals and groups can develop awareness of the practices that are linked to co-creative experiences.

Within the framework of Higher Education this is even more relevant: for a future that needs to strengthen human relationships and practices of sharing, the ability (or disposition) of creating a shared value in spite of differences is strategically fundamental.

Can we envision and describe co-creation as deliberate research strategy for the future? Can we imagine a future where co-creation is a deliberate pedagogical strategy?

Often educators work with co-creation in their teaching but lack a context to reflect, analyse and conceptualise their co-creative practices. With this book based on our research in different HE areas, we wish to engage in a conversation with scholars, researchers and practitioners, and we wish to think together with educators *about* co-creation, as a framework that can explain relational dynamics in Higher Education for society in the future.

Our target group is an international community of scholars, researchers, educators, artists, leaders and consultants at Higher Education institutions. Our book is primarily aimed at an academic reader. However, reflective practitioners within adult education in a broader sense might be interested in the topic, especially if their profession involves educational or organisational tasks (adult learning or life-long learning). Moreover, the book is meant as inspiration for educators, facilitators and leaders, who are interested in the concept of co-creation and its applications in different HE educational areas. At academic level, we believe that several graduate and postgraduate courses can actively use the book, as a teaching or inspiration resource.

We suggest that attention to co-creative processes is a trend that is going to grow in the future, together with the growing of interest in creative solutions for future education and organisation. With the global focus on our main and intertwined themes, we intend to address an international audience of scholars in the Western world as well as countries with growing economies. Where, globally, countries have conceptualised and formulated a strategic interest in the field of Higher Education, we can offer original and relevant research.

It is our hope that this book will inspire a large target group from the fields of education, pedagogy, leadership, consulting and development. Last but not least, we wish to contribute meaningfully to the future development of these fields, opening up new debates on co-creation and on how to prepare our students in the best way to handle academic tasks and challenges in the future.

BOOK STRUCTURE

The present volume is the product of a co-creative process that the authors went through and that we, as editors, facilitated. The chapters cover a variety of topics and interventions within Higher Education. Their authors have worked collaboratively, giving each other feedback and suggestions. This generated internal conversations that – hopefully – generated a shared value for all.

In Chapter 1, *Re-thinking curriculum for 21st-century learners – Examining the advantages and disadvantages of adding co-creative aspects to Problem-Based Learning*, Annie Aarup Jensen and Lone Krogh discuss an experiment of changing curriculum in the direction of students, to a greater degree, becoming 'leaders' of their own learning processes and how this can be done within the formal framework of an educational programme. They argue that the Problem-Based Learning (PBL) principles as they are practiced at Aalborg University with focus on concepts such as student direction, problem solving, peer feedback and teachers facilitating the learning processes and the competence development can be transferred to other teaching areas. The case in point is a 1st year BA in Organisational Learning, where an experiment was carried out. Students were offered the possibility of participating in co-creative and collaborative processes with the teachers as far as the formal framework of the programme allowed. Some of the results of the experiment are presented. Among other things they show that most students wish to be a part of the co-creation processes regarding teaching activities. However, some also seem to prioritise more traditional teaching forms. From the results they also see that introducing these kinds of change in an educational institution is not necessarily an easy task for neither teachers nor students, as it entails a shift in roles for both.

In Chapter 2, *Co-creating knowledge – students and teachers together in a field of emergence*, Ann-Merete Iversen and Anni Stavnskær Pedersen introduce co-creative processes as a means to re-inventing teaching in Higher Education. A methodological approach is presented in which significant parts of knowledge production and knowledge exchange are based on co-creative generative dialogue between students and teachers. It is argued that co-creative methodology enhances the societal relevance of education and at the same time prepares students for becoming 21st-century knowledge workers.

Chapter 3, *Facilitating reflective learning and co-creative teaching by portfolios in problem-based learning (PBL)*, will mainly focus on how the development of teaching portfolios can facilitate new teaching staff's reflective capability in a PBL environment. Chunfang Zhou, Ole Ravn, and Xiangyun Du look at the social theories of learning that regard a co-created curriculum model as a basis for developing a community of practice, as in PBL, where all learners and teachers are reflective partners who contribute to a joint enterprise, a shared repertoire and mutual engagement. One of the authors of this chapter describes how reflective didactic experiences were developed by her teaching portfolio through participation in the university pedagogy programme at Aalborg University (AAU), Denmark. The discussion of this case leads to the following findings: (1) the teaching portfolio is an effective means of facilitating new staff's self-enhancement and shaping professional identity towards being a reflective teacher, and (2) the teaching portfolio is an effective means of building reflective conversations for oneself and between supervisors in a PBL staff development programme, and of developing the value of co-creation in a PBL environment.

In Chapter 4, *Teaching co-creation in higher education through dance exercises*, Claus Springborg explores how to use exercises from improvised couples dances, such as tango and contact improvisation, to teach four co-creation capabilities: Voicing, listening, respecting, and suspending (Isaacs, 1999). He first looks at the challenge of teaching these co-creation skills from two related perspectives: deutero-learning (Bateson, 1972a) and embodied neural metaphors (Lakoff, 2012; Springborg, 2015). The perspective of deutero-learning highlights that an important part of learning co-creation skills is the process of internalising the structure of the learning context itself. The perspective of embodied neural metaphors highlights the importance of considering which sensory-motor experiences students are exposed to within the learning context and whether these can be used as embodied metaphors for the more abstract co-creation skills and concepts taught. The author proposes how exercises elsewhere used to teach improvised couples dance can provide both a learning environment structure and direct sensory experiences, useful for the teaching of co-creation skills, such as voicing, listening, respecting, and suspending.

In Chapter 5, *Co-creation in PBL project work*, Ole Ravn uses the notion of co-creation in the particular context of higher education where the teaching by supervisors and the learning processes of students are entangled in a co-creative process in a PBL setting. The scenario is the situation where the teaching process is developed continuously during meetings with students and the specific content is what students bring into the teaching and learning situation. And the students' learning processes and knowledge production are shaped and formed by a co-creative process, fuelled by their own and the supervisor's contributions. Based on the above reflections on the key elements in the area of teacher-student co-creation, this chapter takes as its problem formulation: how can a supervisor establish an open space for a co-creative process between supervisor and a group of students?

The approach to developing a vocabulary about this open space for co-creativity falls into three steps. First, the idea is to pinpoint more clearly how we can conceptualise the open space for co-creative processes in education. Here the framework developed by Helle Alrø and Ole Skovsmose in their study of dialogical processes in education is discussed. Their work builds, among other sources, on Paulo Freire's ideas of dialogical pedagogy.

Secondly, the idea is to look into supervision approaches and discuss how they relate to the developed co-creative process space. Finally the chapter establishes some reflections on how to open the co-creative space in a fruitful way.

In chapter 6, *A cogenerative dialogue: reflecting on education for co-creation*, Henrik Find Fladkjær and Kathrin Otrel-Cass utilise Roth & Tobin's method of cogenerative dialogue (2001) to co-construct and analyse a teaching innovation. The teaching innovation was based on the principle of peer learning and involved students going through cycles of evaluating, critiquing and co-constructing their learning. More specifically, students discussed first in groups with a more senior peer, then paired up with an opponent student to discuss each other's projects, not only to share feedback but also to come up with solutions. The authors' cogeneration foregrounded different insights and voices and how they have come together to formulate a joint product, this chapter.

In Chapter 7, *Theatre as co-creative space and as inspiration for higher education*, Tatiana Chemi and Pierangelo Pompa look at collaboration in the theatrical creative process, which defines a very interesting and fertile paradigm for all kind of co-creative dynamics. Theatre can be co-creative or not. Theatrical co-creation implies structurally a pedagogical and ethical process, since it is founded on the development of embodied skills and values, which are always, by their own technical nature, relational and social. In the extra-daily time and space of theatre laboratory work, the traditional notion of authoriality is abandoned, and a collective body-mind arises as an unforeseeable discovery for each individual.

In Chapter 8, *Co-creating the joy of writing: creative analytical writing practices*, Charlotte Wegener suggests a way to think about and teach creative co-created writing practices that makes writing a key to both learning and identity building for students. It suggests ways in which writing becomes a way of thinking, learning and being in the world, and allows for joy. The chapter presents examples from writing supervision based on a model of three drivers for creative co-created writing called 'the Toolbox', 'the Building Materials' and 'the Building'.

The purpose of Chapter 9, *Co-creating meaning through Artful Inquiry*, is to point out the need for aesthetic and artful methods for reflection, learning and co-creation. The context is management education focused on developing innovation competency. The data derive from action research, observations and written reports. The main contribution of this chapter is the introduction of a model for Artful Inquiry, which involves constructing powerful questions and finding appropriate artistic methods for reflecting and for co-creating with people or with artistic material. Lotte Darsø argues that Artful Inquiry can access deeper layers of knowing, which would otherwise remain tacit and non-conscious. The findings show how new insights can be obtained through drawing with dominant and non-dominant hands and through reflecting with artistic processes. The material 'speaks back' in surprising ways, metaphorically and symbolically. Also the impact of leadership icons, as well as co-creating with tangible materials, can give rise to new meaning and transformational learning.

In Chapter 10, *Arts-involving Burning Man festival as co-creation in social education studies*, Julie Borup Jensen addresses the topic of co-creation in student learning processes concerning democracy and citizenship in social education studies at the Danish University College, Northern Jutland. The co-creational effects of experimenting with an arts-involving festival, inspired by the new Nevada Desert event *Burning Man*, in collaboration with pedagogical staff and residents of local refugee and immigrant institutions and local communities, are investigated by means of socio-cultural and cultural-psychological perspectives on learning processes. Original data is drawn from a qualitative action research project that aimed at developing practice and knowledge about arts involvement in the local social education programme. The study revealed potential and challenges in respect of using artistic and aesthetic expressions, methods and activities as a way of framing the co-creational aspects of student learning within the area of democracy and citizenship. The findings show that working with co-creation in teaching may lead to community building, building of relationships within the local community, visibility in society and, last but not least, student learning and development of understanding of democracy in practice. The findings also indicate that there are challenges in respect of scaffolding a co-creational process that requires a great deal of negotiation of responsibility and participation.

In Chapter 11, *Bizchange: co-design meetings to enable stakeholder-supported design moves*, Sune Gudiksen, Søren Bolvig Poulsen et al. take their point of departure in co-creation as a design negotiation endeavour. Through an engaged scholarship approach and in a four-month course *BizChange,* they describe a series of co-design meetings in three different digital media student-company cases. In particular, they explore in what way the students manage to get across perspectives, ideas and concepts to decision makers and stakeholders. This includes how to approach stakeholder involvement and associated constraints, the inclusion of experienced peers to spot blind spots and the use of co-design negotiation tools as a means of involving a circle of stakeholders.

In Chapter 12, *Teaching co-creation: paradoxes in rock and pop ensemble classes*, Turid Nørlund Christensen looks at the domain of arts-based rock and pop music, where co-creative processes are essential in the artistic formation of an authentic and original band expression. However, methods for teaching the tacit knowledge of these artistic co-creative competences in Higher Education have yet to be developed. Teaching ensemble playing from an artistic co-creative perspective was researched from an instructor's point of view in a pedagogic development project at the Royal Academy of Music, Aarhus (RAMA). An ensemble course was designed and facilitated through problem-finding group improvisations, mimicking the exploratory process of co-creative rock bands. Experience-based group reflections were facilitated, aiming at identifying and transforming the domain-specific tacit knowledge to propositional knowledge from a social constructivist perspective. The didactics and methodology were conceptualised from a pragmatic approach to interdisciplinary research in co-creation, co-design, social systems, cultural sociology, psychology, educational theory, dramaturgy, and domain-specific aesthetic and educational studies, and researched using audio recordings, feedback from students, class notes and self-observations.

Two main contributions resulted:

- Structures for a co-creative educational design approach, incorporating the informal educational characteristics of rock and pop ensembles and corresponding learning objectives.
- A mapping of the structural elements of the educational co-design approach and corresponding co-creative competences, derived from the aesthetic characteristics of rock and pop ensembles.

In Chapter 13, *Designing learning for co-creation – conceptual and practical considerations*, Dorina Gnaur and Inger Marie Larsen-Nielsen explore the practical implications of the concept of co-creation in a professional context from an educational point of view. The question they are posing themselves is: how can higher and further education (HE) educate for co-creation, that is, provide educational frameworks that respond to the societal demand for co-creation, particularly within the public welfare sector? First, they focus on which organisational and individual requirements an HE learning design should take into account in order to support the diffusion of co-creation competences. Then they argue for the need to integrate these considerations in the learning design and demonstrate a practical application in the form of a didactical design. They call this a hybrid learning design, in that it takes advantage of technological developments to mediate co-creative learning in multiple learning environments.

NOTES

1 University College North Jutland.
2 The Centre for Environment and Development Studies.

REFERENCES

Biggs, J., & Tang, C. (2007). *Teaching for quality learning in university*. The Society for Research into Higher Education.

Bovill C., Cook-Sather. A., & Felten, P. (2011). Students as co-creators of teaching approaches, course design and curricula: For academic developers. *International Journal for Academic Development, 16*(2), 133–145. ISSN 1360-144X

Camargos-Borges, C., & Rasera, E. F. (2013). Social constructionism in the context of organization development: Dialogue, imagination, and co-creation as resource of change, *SAGE Open*, April June, 2013, 1–7.

Dale, E. L. (1999). *Pædagogisk filosofi*. Aarhus: Klim.

Degnegaard, R. (2014). Co-creation, prevailing streams and future design trajectories. *CoDesign, 10*(2), 96–111.

Jank, W., & Meyer, H. (2006). *Didaktiske modeller*. Gyldendals Lærerbibliotek.

Krogh, L. (2013). The aalborg PBL model and Employability. In L. B. Henriksen (Ed.), *What did you learn in the real world today: The case of practicum in university education*. Aalborg: Aalborg University Press.

Iversen, A. M., Pedersen, A. S., Krogh, L., & Jensen, A. A. (2015). Learning, leading, and letting go of control: Learner-led approaches in education. *Sage Open, 5*(4), 1–11.

Liedtka, J. (2014). Linking design thinking to innovation outcomes: The role of cognitive bias reduction. *Academy of Management Proceedings, 2014*(1), p. 10628. Academy of Management.

Liedtka, J., & Ogilvie, T. (2011). *Designing for growth*. New York, NY: Columbia Business School.

Prahalad, C. K., & Ramaswamy, V. (2004). Co-creation experiences: The next practice in value creation. *Journal of interactive marketing, 18*(3), 6–14.

Sanders, E. B., & Stappers, P. J. (2008, March). Co-creation and the new landscapes of design. In *CoDesign, 4*(1), 5–18.

Voorberg, W. H., Bekkers, V. J. J. M., & Tummers, L. G. (2014). A systematic review of co-creation and co-production: Embarking on the social innovation journey. *Public Management Review*, 2014. Retrieved from www.tandfonline.com

Ramsden, P. (2003). *Learning to teach in higher education*. Routledge.

Aarup Jensen, A. (2015). How does it feel to become a master's student? Boundary crossing and emotions related to understanding a new educational context. In B. Lund & T. Chemi (Eds.), *Dealing with emotions: A pedagogical challenge to innovative learning*. Rotterdam, the Netherlands: Sense Publishers.

Tatiana Chemi
Department of Learning and Philosophy
Aalborg University

Lone Krogh
Department of Learning and Philosophy
Aalborg University

ANNIE AARUP JENSEN AND LONE KROGH

1. RE-THINKING CURRICULUM FOR 21ST-CENTURY LEARNERS

Examining the Advantages and Disadvantages of Adding Co-Creative Aspects to Problem-Based Learning

> Through whom is Denmark going to live in the future? We must live by our children. We do not know what they are going to do. But we know that they are the ones who will drive everything. And the best we can do for them is to prepare them for a future that no one knows what it will look like. Therefore, what is happening in the education system, public and private, is paramount. For this is where the preparation for to the unknown and unpredictable happens. This is where our children can be fired with self-awareness, competences and confidence. With perceptions of what talents they carry. With professional skills to think and act, academically and creatively. And with confidence to meet the unpredictable future with the belief that precisely what they personally have to offer is worth something. That precisely their contribution can help to change things, and not only to be victims of change.
>
> (Claus Buhl, Nyhedsbloggen *Information* 13. January 2012. Translated from Danish by the authors)

INTRODUCTION

Why is it relevant to re-think curriculum in Higher Education? Society and the labour markets have in many ways been undergoing dramatic changes during past decades. This has been explained as being a change from the industrial society to the information society, the knowledge society, and even to the learning economy and society (Lundval, 2008). Academic working life – whether we talk about the private or public sector – has become more complex and unpredictable, technologically as well as in terms of work functions, qualifications, competencies, values and attitudes among employers and employees. The changes have had an impact on jobs, work functions and company structures, as well as on industrial dynamics. However, they have also had an important impact on everyday social life and on the dynamics of the economy and society (Sennett, 2006). The changes not only have an impact on society in general and on firms and institutions as such. They also seem to affect relationships between people in all their mutual activities.

T. Chemi & L. Krogh (Eds.), Co-Creation in Higher Education, 1–14.

These tendencies influence the requirements for professional and personal competencies of academic and scientific staff. Relating to the professional foundation of disciplines within the individual subject area and profession, there is a demand for abilities in development, planning, knowledge processing, theoretical reflection and problem solving (Globalisation Council, 2006).

Regarding the student perspective, an international Education Advisory Board (Learning in the 21st Century) has been bold enough to come up with some suggestions regarding how to name 21st-century student (the millennials). These students represent the generation born during the previous century. At a general level they seem – according to investigations done by the Education Advisory Board – to be able to react and act according to changes in society. In the paper, they characterise this generation of students in general terms as follows,

- They like to be in control, but they do not want to be bound by traditional schedules, and they do not necessarily want to sit in a classroom to learn. Instead, they prefer to use technology to study at any time of the day or night, … and they want to define "balance" in that in their own individual ways.
- They like choices. In project-based environments, they use technology to complete tasks in new and creative ways. They are group-oriented and social. Relentlessly exposed to the world through the media.
- They are highly collaborative; sharing what they learn with others actually helps them in creating their own personal identities.
- They are inclusive, because their generation has been taught to be tolerant of all kind of races, religions and sexual orientations.
- They are users of digital technology, as ICT has always been part of their lives.
- They think differently. They simply accept technology, adapt to it and use it.
- They are more likely to take risks.
- They value time off because they consider life as being uncertain.

We might assume that the developments they are experiencing regarding changes in society, in IT, in internationalisation and global conflicts, in their personal and school lives so far have put them on track to meet the challenges for their future in societies undergoing continuous changes. However, it is important to be aware that we also see many young students having difficulties in handling all these challenges. This only emphasises the importance of focusing to a much greater degree on the individual student's prerequisites in educational settings.

According to Ananiadou and Claro (2009) developments in society and economy require educational systems to support young people in acquiring the skills and competencies that allow them to benefit from emerging new forms of socialisation and to contribute actively to economic development in a system where the main asset is knowledge. These skills and competencies are often referred to as 21st-century skills and competencies, in order to indicate that they are more related to the needs of the emerging models of economic and social development than to those of the past century, which were primarily suited to an industrial mode of production. Comparing the above-mentioned characteristics of 21st-century learners with the demands for 21st-century skills and competencies, it seems that students, generally speaking, not only are ready to acquire and develop these types of skills, but also expect a change from traditional teaching and learning methods in the direction of more innovative methods. They are collaborative risk takers and media literates, and they are already themselves practicing new and alternative ways of informal learning.

Back in 1998, Boud and Marton emphasised in their research that Higher Education (HE) institutions have the responsibility to ensure students become prepared for an unknown future. HE institutions have, according to the two researchers, to make sure that students learn the basic academic skills in order to continuously be able to solve unforeseen problems in a diversity of professional and private situations. Their answer to the demands of the unknown future was thus focused on students learning basic academic skills, and they recommended learning these skills during education through innovative teaching and learning strategies and methods.

Continuously developing curriculum is the foundation for building education that will meet the demands of society and the workplace. But there is no doubt that, when the politicians cut investment in a system and regulate the financial resources spent on education, this is the ultimate reason for the HE[1] system to change. The huge access to HE by students during the last decade (education in Denmark is free), together with the reduction in finances, have become the driving force to re-think education in HE institutions. Furthermore, the Danish government has increased its focus on the quality of education and teaching, to ensure that economic resources are spent as intended and that the amount spent is worthwhile. Here, an important question is how the government defines quality. Some of their focus is centred on issues such as transparency, students' experience of meaningfulness, relevance, and employability. The Expert Committee on Quality in Higher Education in Denmark established by the Danish Government (2014) published two reports, in Winter 2015 and Spring 2016, in which several of the above-mentioned quality issues were pointed out. Furthermore, the Danish Accreditation Institution published an analysis report in 2015, based on knowledge from the accreditation process at the Danish Accreditation Institution, supplemented by interviews with selected informants and stakeholders from the educational sector. The analyses showed that, despite the varied and comprehensive work being done by the educational institutions to ensure the relevance of their programmes, it is important to improve the match between graduate competencies and demands from labour markets.

From the above-mentioned arguments, and from the focus of politicians and stakeholders, it follows that we need to reconsider how study programmes are organised and how resources are used in order to be able to educate our students for society and for the future academic and scientific labour market, in the most relevant ways.

In this chapter we investigate how and to what extent an existing pedagogical model based on problem orientation and student direction may be further developed to take into account the above-mentioned factors and meet the expectations of the 21st-century learner. We will do this by first presenting the existing pedagogical model (Problem-based Learning – PBL) and what it requires of students to participate. Based on this, we analyse an experiment that aimed at increasing student contribution and responsibility through co-creative processes. The results are related to the concepts of co-creation, learning conditions and the 21st-century learner.

THE PEDAGOGICAL MODEL – PROBLEM-BASED LEARNING

The pedagogical framework of the experiment is problem orientation and student-directed learning based on the principles of the Aalborg University PBL model. Problem-based learning, project work, etc. are concepts that are used widely and with different meanings, integrated into varying educational designs and with different kinds of goals. The original idea and theoretical foundation of problem-based project work, in a Danish context, were formulated by the Danish researcher K. Illeris (1974) in his seminal book, *Problem orientation and participant direction: An introduction to alternative didactics*. The PBL pedagogies at Aalborg University have been developed from these original principles since the 1970s. Exemplarity, open curriculum, interdisciplinary and experience-based learning, peer learning, and collaborative learning in groups are important concepts (Aarup Jensen & Krogh, 2013). These concepts will be further explained in the following sections.

Basic Principles of Problem-Based Project Work

Illeris lists three categories of qualifications which appeared to be necessary for the development of society at that time: (1) skills which can be defined in direct relation to a given task or work process, (2) adaptive qualifications of a general character and comprising attitudinal characteristics (e.g. diligence, perseverance, vigilance etc.) – combined with a willingness to apply these characteristics in relation to work, to accept and adapt to existing work processes, (3) creative/innovative qualifications that may be divided into qualifications for scientific, innovative work and qualifications for continuous renewal and the ability to collaborate (Illeris, pp. 32–35). Referring to Piaget, Illeris understands accommodative learning processes as a prerequisite for creativity. From this point of departure, he describes an expedient learning process that allows for the development of skills, adaptive ability and creativity in a process which alternates between accommodative processes (the creation of new cognitive structures) and assimilative processes (the incorporation of new material in the individual's existing structures). Such alternating processes are a precondition of students' ability to acquire holistic competencies that comprise skills, an adaptive ability and creative qualifications (Illeris, pp. 76–77).

Illeris developed these ideas further, suggesting an alternative didactic concept – problem-oriented project work, characterised by:

- *Problem orientation*, which means that the point of departure is the subject-related knowledge, methods and theories relevant to the specific problem, rather

than a narrow discipline-bound theme or task. Consequently, interdisciplinarity becomes a core principle.
- *Participant direction*, which means that the students define the problem and choose the work methods.

These are important principles for the creation of possibilities for the accommodative learning processes, which are necessary for developing creativity and flexibility. This is important to emphasise, because if teachers or the educational system determine the problems for students to work on, and how students are supposed to work with problems, there may be a transgression of the traditional borders between disciplines, but new political agendas may delimit and constrict the students' work in the same way as the traditional disciplinary borders would do, thus hindering students' accommodative learning processes (Illeris, 1982). In other words, the possibility of creativity and innovation relies on students' ownership of their projects and their freedom and responsibility to find and define the problem to research. With this freedom and responsibility also comes a demand for academic skills, such as analytical skills, critical reflection and communicative and cooperative skills. These are examples of the accommodative learning processes that students (are expected to) go through during their collaborative work on the project. Accommodative learning processes are demanding and will only take place in situations of significance for the individual student, where something is at stake. Otherwise, the individual student will dismiss the problem or assimilate it, i.e. integrate it into already established cognitive structures (Illeris, pp. 82–83). Therefore it is important that the individual student is motivated and engaged in the problem and the process of researching it.

The principles are:

- *Exemplarity*, which means working with the important and representative aspects, which exemplify the area of the discipline in question.
- *Group work.* Students collaborate in groups on problem finding and problem solving. In this way they learn the difficult art of collaboration, communication and project leadership.

Practicing the PBL Project Work

Typically, the problem-based project work will go through the following phases,

- Selection of the subject and the first reflections on relevant problems;
- Problem formulation of the project – a dynamic process which continues throughout the project period;
- Methodological reflections and decisions on how to research and solve the questions raised in the problem formulation;
- Project work (i.e. theoretical and empirical work, perhaps involving experiments);

- Production of project report (sometimes involving descriptions of reflections on work processes); and
- Product evaluation and if necessary – product adjustment.

The role of the teachers is to act as supervisors/facilitators and to offer the students formative assessment and feedback during their project work in order to provide valuable input in the process. Sometimes fellow students give feedback, organised as opponent seminars.

Problem-based project work may be interpreted and implemented in a number of different ways, according to educational institutions, disciplines, subjects, and learning goals. There may be varying degrees of free choice regarding the specific problem, subject area, and method, and the project work may differ in size (ECTS[2] points), i.e. the students' workload per semester. At Aalborg University problem-oriented project work generally accounts for 50% of the study activities. The remaining 50% consists of course work, lectures, workshops, assignments etc. The study activities should support and inspire students in their project work.

During the project work the groups are assigned a supervisor with whom they discuss their problem formulation/research questions, progression of their work and the chapters of the project report. This report will be the final documentation of their work over the project period and form the basis of their oral examination, which will take place with all group members present. The role of the supervisor/facilitator is important both as discussant for the group and as controller/representative of the study programme, in terms of ensuring that the subject area of the project lies within the framework of the formal study regulation. The role as discussant also means asking critical questions, turning the students' attention to weak or questionable points in their work as well as commending the good points. Furthermore, the supervisor/facilitator may recommend literature, theories, methods of research etc. It is, however, essential to mention that the supervisor does not take over the project, but that the students remain the 'owners' of the project and make their own decisions.

Some elements of PBL are key points that we consider relevant to transfer into other kinds of learning arenas. The elements in question are:

- student direction, where students are the owners and the managers of their own research and learning processes in investigating subject-relevant problems,
- students defining and leading the learning processes towards defining methods of finding solutions for the problems, and
- teachers as collaborative partners, not taking ownership of the students' work, but instead having the role of facilitating their learning processes.

National and international research has documented that most students are well motivated and curious when they start on HE programmes (Ramsden, 2003; Biggs & Tang, 2007, Iversen et al., 2015).

We also know from working with and doing research in relation to the pedagogies in the Aalborg PBL model (Problem-based Learning), that most students can manage individual as well as collaborative learning processes, when it is expected of them and clearly signalled to them, although they may be collaborating with fellow students with diverse backgrounds. However, we also realise that many students lose motivation and interest for the study if they experience teaching activities and a culture where they are not taken seriously and if the culture signals distance and academic arrogance (Ramsden, 2003, Biggs & Tang, 2007).

The learning processes involved for the students in the Aalborg PBL model as described regard both the subject-related content of the project work, and the basic academic skills of finding the (right) problem to investigate/the right research question, doing research, negotiating meaning with peers/fellow students, discussing and arguing, critical thinking, and written communication. These are aspects that are, in a sense, already covered by the pedagogy in the Aalborg PBL model as it has been practiced for years – or should ideally be covered. At the same time, principles such as student direction, collaboration with fellow students and problem solving fit with the characteristics of the 21st-century students aiming at meeting the 21st-century demands described above. Analysing the potentials of the PBL model we decided to expand the principles of this model to cover more aspects of the activities.

CO-CREATION IN EDUCATION

Our inspiration for the concept of co-creation is from the business world, where the concept was introduced by Prahalad and Ramaswamy in 2000 in the article Co-creating Customer Competence (2000) in Harvard Business Review. Here the authors refer to the fact that consumers often seem to be ignored as the factor that most radically transforms the industrial system. In the light of this understanding of co-creation, they were moved out of their role as passive recipients ("audience"), to that of active participants, co-creating about developing products and services. The authors argued that, by doing this, customers are fundamentally changing the dynamics of the marketplace, with marketplaces becoming forums where the consumers play an active role in establishing values.

Although there are contemporary discourses positioning students as customers and universities as marketplaces providing services and products, i.e. education for the marketplace, we will take a different view of the concept of co-creation and move it beyond the business terminology and into the realm of education. The principles we will take from the above-mentioned understanding are the inherent respect for students, the importance of their active participation and openness to their contribution in establishing value in the educational process. From Degnegaard's overview of the development of the concept of co-creation, it appears that the application of the concept may be divided into the following streams (Degnegaard, 2014):

- Co-creating shared meaning (often in a socio-constructivist perspective)

- Co-creating user experience and shared value (marketing and service perspective)
- Co-creating technological solutions (ICT perspective)
- Co-creating ideas and new products and services (related to the concept of innovation)
- Human-centred co-creation (settings for design and research)

We draw on the strands of interest to educationally related issues and terminology. To us, the interesting issue is how to design settings that may support the co-creation of knowledge, shared meaning and peer-to-peer production. Such approaches call for openness to change in the understanding of both teacher and student role.

Based on the overall PBL principles as framework, combined with these principles of co-creation, we designed a pilot period for the first semester of a bachelor study programme in organisational learning, thus taking the PBL model a step further. The rationale behind the experiment was therefore a mix between the pedagogical principles of the PBL learning model applied at Aalborg University, and selected principles of co-creation.

CASE DESCRIPTION

The context of the experiment is first year students at BA level in the study programme of Organisational Learning at Aalborg University. The aim of the programme is to educate students to be able to analyse, support and manage learning and knowledge-based development in private and public organisations in the light of national and international development in society. The subject areas are social science, organisational development and learning at macro, meso and micro level. Within this framework we wished to create learning scenarios where students from day one of their study were expected to involve themselves and participate actively in supporting their own and their fellow students' learning processes.

The Framework of the Programme

The BA degree in Organisational Learning is a 3-year research-based full-time programme, equivalent to 180 ECTS. It aims at giving students an introduction to the social sciences and methods that provide the basis for understanding, analysing, supporting and managing learning and knowledge-based development in private and public organisations. Typical business functions will be as development consultant, quality staff member, innovation employee, occupational health consultant, job consultant and HR consultant. The programme is organised inter-disciplinarily, and is problem-based and practice-oriented, based on organisation theory, learning theory, sociology of knowledge, innovation theory and related disciplines as well as science, methodology and evaluation.

Our research covers the 1st semester where the basis for the content and programme in the whole education is established. The programme follows the PBL model as described above, and a problem-oriented project is the focus of the first semester. In the first semester there are altogether four modules:

Module 1: Problem-Based Learning (PBL I) (5 ECTS)
Module 2: Organisation and Society (15 ECTS)
Module 3: Problem-Based Learning (PBL II) (5 ECTS)
Module 4: Cognition processes and production of knowledge. (5 ECTS)

The students work with two projects. The first project (PBL I), the pilot project, was chosen as the context for the experiment. It was assessed after 4 weeks. This first project forms the basis for the next two modules.

Input for Change

As mentioned, the study programme in question is new. There had been some difficulties the year before with some discontent being voiced and some students dropping out. Based on this, management asked us to take over and to make some changes that might address some of the challenges from the previous year.

Before the summer holiday, meetings were held with 4 more experienced students from the study programme, hired to collaborate with the teacher team in the processes of involving the new students in the study programme in the very best way. During the meetings, they received full information and explanation about the thinking behind and the plans for strengthening the collaboration with students, based on an understanding of concepts such as learner-led teaching and co-creative approaches. It should be mentioned that not all members of the 5-strong teaching team wanted to participate in the experiment, which for some of them represented a pedagogical challenge. 3 of the team agreed to participate, including the coordinator of the programme. This will not, however, be the focus of this chapter.

Based on analyses regarding the content, students' background, the possibilities within the framework of the study regulations and our aim towards more student direction, we had meetings with students from the previous cohort who were appointed tutors to support the new students. Their feedback and evaluation was valuable additional input, and the pedagogical strategy was decided in collaboration with them.

ORGANISING THE EXPERIMENT PEDAGOGICALLY– WHAT DID WE DO?

As a starting point, we argue, based on research and experience (Iversen et al., 2015), that principles such as respect for students and the establishment of study environments where students are offered the role of becoming leaders of their own learning processes are important. Students who act responsibly and have influence on the curriculum while collaborating with teachers (who of course have overall educational responsibility) create good conditions for developing the knowledge and skills which are not only expected and described in the formal study regulations, but also required for the 21st century.

A thematic framework suitable for the project work was decided upon. The theme was "*The university as an organisation: structure and processes*". This theme was chosen with the intention of accommodating students who probably had chosen this course because of their interest in organisations. And one of the most relevant organisations they had to face, at that time, was the university they were just entering. Our plans were that working with a theme that might seem relevant to them would motivate them to work in depth in trying to understand and be able to act pro-actively in their study life within this organisational framework. So we expected that there would be personal, as well as a professional/educational interest and motivation for working with this theme in their first PBL project. Their task was to investigate the phenomenon of the university as an organisational framework for the learning that takes place here at all levels (among students, teachers, principals and so on). They were allowed to choose for themselves which level they wanted to focus on. They could choose different perspectives – society, students, organisation or teachers.

In organising the teaching, several lectures were replaced with teaching and learning forms, where students were the most active partners, within the framework of some rules decided by the teachers and based on their experience and the input of the preparation phase. The principles we followed were those of student direction, problem solving, peer learning and peer assessment, as they were used in PBL project work. They were supplemented with the principles of co-creation, i.e.

- co-creation of knowledge and peer-to-peer production and
- instead of teachers offering feedback on students' work, students gave feedback to each other, supplemented with feedback from the teachers (supervisors).
- instead of teachers lecturing, students prepared and lectured to each other, supplemented by teaching from the teacher.

The overall signal from the teachers was that the students were the most important persons and agents in these feedback and teaching activities.

EMPIRICAL DATA AND RESULTS

There were 36 students representing a diversity of age, gender and educational and cultural background. The gender ratio was approximately 50/50. Most of the students were in the age group between 21 and 30. A few were in their forties. Most of them had some kind of workplace-related experiences, which meant that they knew about working in some kind of organisation. Some of them had an educational background at Diploma or BA level.

The results of the experiment are based on the following empirical data:

- Notes and observations from a 'future workshop', where students were guided through a process where they initially identified and discussed existing challenges

and problems in their education. This is the 'critique phase' and it was followed by the 'dream phase' where students came up with all their wishes without having to consider if they were feasible. The final step was the 'realisation phase' where they had the opportunity to come up with realistic ideas and solutions for dealing with the challenges and problems. The process was facilitated by one of the teachers.
- Reflection papers from 30 students. At the very beginning of the semester they were asked to fill in a reflection paper, where they wrote about their former experiences, their understanding of organisations, their reasons for choosing the course and how they preferred to work in educational settings.
- Notes from classroom observations of the co-creative sessions by the teacher in charge
- Formal evaluation meeting with student representatives
- Formal evaluation done by the school management

Generally, compared with the previous year, there was not much discontent. The students very much enjoyed being active partners, although they also enjoyed high quality lectures from teachers as a supplement.

They wanted even more involvement in planning and practicing the teaching. Students asked for more student teaching and more creative teaching forms in general applied by the teachers. Furthermore, they would also have preferred more teaching together with older fellow students (ref. data from the future workshop).

Their wish for more involvement corresponds with the characteristics of 21st-century students and with what most students write in the reflection paper they are asked to write at the beginning of the semester:

> I partly prefer working individually and partly together with fellow students. I prefer to write under inspiration and feedback from fellow students, so that you get new ideas and thoughts that can move you forwards. (Male, 21 years old).

> I am many-sided, I like to work autonomously and concentrate myself in things, but I definitely also enjoy collaborating with fellow students. (Male, 21 years old)

> I prefer collaborating with fellow students as it provides more angles on the work and because you learn from your fellow students. (Female, 23 years old)

These quotations very much describe the learning approaches of all the students in the class, and they support to a high degree our intentions in organising the semester's teaching as we did. But there are limitations to the extent to which student direction and co-creation can be practiced. One of these limitations is related to the structural conditions. Regarding the planning process, the semester must be planned two months before the start of the semester. This means that a number of decisions have to be made before the students start regarding, for instance, content, literature, or overall frameworks. These conditions pose considerable limitations for co-creating with students in their first semester.

Another challenge is that teachers in a team represent a diversity of values and understandings about how quality teaching has to be unfolded. Such values may be connected with the subject area, with background from different kinds of university teaching cultures and different understandings about how students learn best. In our data we see that students react to these different kinds of approaches and ways of handling teaching and learning situations, – here the degree to which the teachers dare to let go of control and believe that students can do well if goals and expectations to them are transparent and the teacher has prepared the pedagogical framework.

A final limitation is the students' approaches. Although you can read from their expectations stated in the reflection paper at the beginning of the semester that they generally prefer to be in control as active problem solvers with fellow students, when it comes to the actual situation where they are expected to be active and self-directed, old habits from earlier school situations may take over and lead to frustration.

> It would be nice with some nerd teaching (from evaluation with student representatives).

> It would be nice with more teaching, done by senior fellow students (from evaluation with student representatives).

In both cases students ask for more delivery of lectures, which implies a return to a passive role as student.

Our desire to establish a culture where students dared to speak up, ask questions, be active, make decisions, criticise constructively and be professionally responsible for each other's learning processes from the very beginning of their first semester seemed to be successful. They expressed the feeling of having some kind of influence on what was going on and they expressed contentment with that.

However, it is impossible to meet all students' expectations and wishes, and there were also some who expressed a wish for more traditional teaching forms as indicated in the above statements.

CONCLUSION

Based on our experiences of how students engage when they work with PBL projects on self-defined problems/research questions and the principles of co-creation, we aimed at establishing a culture where we involved the students in some of the decision-making processes and expanded the principles of self-definition and self-direction to other types of activities during the semester. Comparing the results of the experiment with the process the year before, the students expressed much more contentment. In that respect we regard the experiment as a success. Relating the results to the characteristics of 21st-century learners we conclude that the pedagogical strategy of co-creation could easily be further strengthened, as the students ask for even more activity, influence and responsibility in relation to teaching.

However, introducing this kind of change in an educational institution is not necessarily an easy task, especially when it entails a shift in roles for teachers. According to a report describing the definitions and foundations of the terms co-creation and co-production in relation to Danish society (Agger & Tortzen, 2015), research shows that professionals within an area may be one of the groups that have the most difficulty in changing their roles, because it challenges their traditional professional culture and understanding of their professional responsibility.

If teachers find that their professional culture and usual approach to pedagogical planning and teaching is questioned or overruled, their response may be resistance or scepticism. Teachers might find that 'the rug is being pulled from under' their professional identity. Another, more pragmatic aspect of change is that, for some teachers, the idea of having to reconsider and rethink an educational element (e.g. a course, a lecture series) might in itself represent a huge work load, which is not always welcomed.

Consequently, while the advantage is that students thrive with the new pedagogical approaches, the disadvantage is that re-thinking curriculum and introducing aspects of co-creation in education may involve daunting aspects for the teachers involved, who are forced to reconsider their role in teaching and learning scenarios, which might lead to resistance to change.

NOTES

1 In Denmark – as in other European countries – there have in recent years been cuts in resources to HE institutions.

2 European Credit Transfer System.

REFERENCES

Aarup Jensen, A., & Krogh, L. (2013). Potentials for further development of PBL strategies at Aalborg University. In L. Krogh & A. A. Jensen (Eds.), *Visions – challenges – strategies, PBL principles and methodologies in a danish and global perspective*. Denmark: Aalborg University Press.

Agger, A., & Tortzen, A. (2015). *Forskningsreview om samskabelse*. University College Lillebaelt. Retrieved from http://samskabelse.ucl.dk/files/2015/02/forskningsreview-om-co-production_samlet-udgave-at-aa-at07115-2.pdf

Ananiadou, K., & Claro, M. (2009). 21st century skills and competences for new millennium learners in OECD countries. *OECD Education Working Papers, 41*, OECD Publishing. Retrieved from http://dx.doi.org/10.1787/218525261154

Biggs J., & Tang, C. (2007). *Teaching for quality learning at university* (3rd Edition). New York, NY: The Society for Research into Higher Education.

Bowden J., & Marton, F. (2006). *The university of learning: Beyond quality and competence*. London & New York, NY: Routledge.

Danish Accreditation Institution. (2015). Retrieved from http://en.akkr.dk/

Degnegaard, R. (2014). *Co-creation, consolidating the field and highlighting new frontiers*. Retrieved from http://openarchive.cbs.dk/xmlui/bitstream/handle/10398/8732/Rex_Degnegaard.pdf?sequence=1 (Download March 2017).

Globalisation Council. (2006). Retrieved from http://www.netpublikationer.dk/um/6648/html/chapter01.htm

Illeris, K. (1974). *Problem orientation and participant direction: An introduction to alternative didactics*. København: Munksgaard.

International Education Advisory Board. (2006). *Learning in the 21st century: Teaching today's student on their terms* (download 12th December 2016). Retrieved from https://www.certiport.com/Portal/Common/DocumentLibrary/IEAB_Whitepaper040808.pdf

Iversen, A.-M., Krogh, L., Aarup Jensen, A., & Stavnskær, A. (2015). Learning, leading, and letting go of control: Learner-led approaches in education. *SAGE Open*, October–December 2015.

Krogh, L. (2013). The aalborg PBL model and employability. In L. B. Henriksen (Ed.), *What did you learn in the real world today: The case of practicum in university educations*. Denmark: Aalborg University Press.

Krogh L., & Jensen, A. A. (2013). The development of PBL-methodologies in Denmark and current challenges. In L. Krogh & A. A. Jensen (Eds.), *Visions – challenges – strategies, PBL principles and methodologies in a danish and global perspective*. Denmark: Aalborg University Press.

Lundvall, B. Å., Rasmussen, P., & Lorenz, E. (2008). Education in the learning economy: A European perspective. *Policy Futures in Education*, *6*(6), 681–700.

Piaget, J. (1954). *The construction of reality in the child*. New York, NY: Basic Books.

Prahalad, C. K., & Ramaswamy, V. (2000). Co-creating customer competence. *Harvard Business Review*, *78*(1), 79–87.

Ramsden, P. (2003). *Learning to teach in higher education*. London & New York, NY: Routledge Falmer.

Sennett, R. (2006). *Den ny kapitalismes kultur*. Viborg: Hovedland.

Sennett, R. (2006). What do we mean by Talent? *The Political Quarterly*, *77*(s1), 163–167.

The Expert Committee on Quality in Higher Education in Denmark. (2015 & 2016). Retrieved from http://ufm.dk/en/education-and-institutions/councils-and-commissions/the-expert-committee-on-quality-in-higher-education-in-denmark

Annie Aarup Jensen
Department of Learning and Philosophy
Aalborg University

Lone Krogh
Department of Learning and Philosophy
Aalborg University

ANN-MERETE IVERSEN AND ANNI STAVNSKÆR PEDERSEN

2. CO-CREATING KNOWLEDGE

Students and Teachers together in a Field of Emergence

> The modern school, at its best, is a satisfying extension of the unreality of societal perception. As we enter the conclusion of an industrializing age, I recognize that, within its walls, lectures are concerned with an abstract dream of future usefulness, while life is happening between classes. Half of the time, and half asleep, teachers and students keep each other caught in a fiction of relevance: Relevance of knowledge to our lives, relevance of the relationships to each other, and relevance to the questions of our time and to the society in which we live.
>
> (Besselink, 2014, p. 92)

Education systems around the world strive to customise methods and practices to fit rapidly changing societal requirements and cultural changes. Education is expected to deliver a highly skilled workforce and the term *employability* is among the parameters used in quality assessment of work done at universities and other higher education institutions. And so the aim of education becomes an ever-changing fixed point.

Preparing students for becoming 21st century knowledge workers, then, entails preparing them for an unknown future. Critical reflection, independent thinking, creativity and a strong sense of navigating in the unforeseen are among the skills required of the individual student. Moravec (2008, 2014) describes the future knowledge worker as "nomadic":

> […] a nomadic knowledge worker – that is a creative, imaginative, and innovative person who can work with almost anybody, anytime, and anywhere. Industrial society is giving way to knowledge and innovation work. Whereas industrialization required people to settle in one place to perform a very specific role or function, the jobs associated with knowledge and information workers have become much less specific concerning task and place. (Moravec, 2014, p. 18)

The point being that, to a large extent, education as we know it is operating in 1.0 mode, out of tune with surrounding cultures and societies, which are operating in mode 3.0. With increasing amounts of accessible knowledge and rapidly changing platforms of learning due to the development in digital media, classical educational

T. Chemi & L. Krogh (Eds.), Co-Creation in Higher Education, 15–30.

institutions are facing the risk of being irrelevant to future generations of students and to society in general terms.

> In university, the focus is on the 1400-page curriculum. In university, the academic assignments must be between 20 and 25 pages. In university, we sit and translate complicated English theoretical texts into Danish, and then write them down in our assignments. Where the hell is the creativity? (Madsen, 2016)

The question is asked by 24-year-old Jonas, a student at the University of Copenhagen, a future knowledge worker, in a direct appeal to his teachers, calling for more creativity, a possibility of independent thinking and translation of theory into practical knowledge in universities.

A quick glance into higher education institutions around the world indicates that the better part of teaching takes place the way it has taken place for centuries (Adler & Hansen, 2012; McWilliam, 2008). The architecture of universities is a good indicator of the didactics performed in the rooms – chairs in rows facing a podium, a blackboard/whiteboard or a screen for the professors to speak and the students to listen.

C. Otto Scharmer, Senior Lecturer at MIT, points to the problem of downloading habits and reproduction of knowledge in teaching; "We probably spend more than 90 percent of our educational resources on lecturing: downloading old bodies of knowledge without self-reflection" (Scharmer, 2007, p. 448). Moreover, he points to the need for a small-scale revolution to transform our education system, so that it becomes up-to-date and able to encourage the individual's resources, creativity, and knowledge: "We need to reinvent our schools and institutions of higher education" (Scharmer, 2007, p. 449).

In this somewhat gloomy future perspective we, as teachers (and researchers), need to ask ourselves: what does it take to re-invent higher education and for teachers to become 21st century educators, especially able to navigate in the unforeseen, instantly designing education in a cross field of societal and cultural change, practical skills and individual relevance?

CO-CREATION IN AN EDUCATIONAL SETTING

The term *co-creation* is used in fields as different as therapy and product innovation (Degnegaard, 2014) although it probably originated in the field of therapy where it is used to describe the shared production of meaning in the therapeutic session. The shared production of something is the common denominator in all the uses of the expression. In the broad field of innovation it denotes a process where different stakeholders are involved in the creation of "the products", be they solutions in the welfare sector or apps for mobile phones. Even though the end goal differs – roughly speaking, the goal is creating solutions within a political system or making money – there is a clear overlap in methods.

The methods applied when working with co-creation are designed to engage the stakeholders in a collective learning process built on emerging awareness and shared commitment. Investigating both the field of intervention and the individual and collective intention is part of this process (Scharmer, 2007, 2014; Hassan, 2014) and requires facilitation, either by the participating stakeholders or by consultants/ facilitators. Frequently-used methods are dialogue, field studies, interviews, log-writing, narratives and a variety of creative methods inspired by the world of design and art (Kahane, 2012; Scharmer, 2007; Darsø, 2004; Hassan, 2014; Belling, 2012; Bason, 2010).

In this chapter, we explore co-creation as an opening towards re-designing and re-inventing the shared space of teaching and learning. The methods suggested in the chapter in some ways suspend the classical concept of teaching and replace it with a structured *co-creative generative dialogue* within which knowledge exchange and knowledge production can take place.

We base the chapter partly on theoretical perspectives, partly on empirical material generated through a series of qualitative interviews with teachers, and on extensive personal experience of teaching in higher education. Our intention is to establish a dialogue between practice and theory. In the interviews, the interviewer did not set out to explore co-creation *per se* but the concept emerged as the interviews progressed. Two main questions were asked; (1) which interdisciplinary, innovation pedagogy can higher education teachers design and use, so that it has the best potential to stimulate the development of innovation and transferability competencies in students? and (2) what does this innovation pedagogy demand of the teacher? (Stavnskær, 2014) In other words, exploring innovation and innovation pedagogy in the interviews led to the emergence of the concept of co-creation. We draw on the descriptions given by the teachers, theoretical perspectives and personal experience in the conceptual framing.

This chapter has two meta-perspectives in its approach to co-creation. One meta-perspective primarily focuses on communication and explores the *term co-creative generative dialogue* and the demands on teachers and students. The other meta-perspective offers a five-phase model to design a co-creative teaching process for students.

IT ALL STARTS WITH COMMUNICATION!

A discovery we made, on analysing the interviews with teachers, was that they brought a focus on communication to their meetings with students, especially with regards to how they listened and asked questions. The teachers described in detail how they listened, how they asked questions, how they meta-communicated with students to create new learning and innovation. Meta-communication in this context is to be understood in the sense originally introduced by Gregory Bateson (1972) as communication about communication "all exchanged cues and propositions about (a) codification and (b) relationship between the communicators". Lotte Darsø, too, highlights the importance of communication: "It is especially important that one is clear about these patterns of dialogue if one wishes to lead processes of change. It is through dialogue that we create the world here and now" (Darsø, 2011, p. 154).

In order to explore the type of communication that facilitates co-creative dialogue between teachers and students we turn to Shaw, who takes her point of departure in complexity theory (Shaw, 2002). Shaw includes a description of the communicative approach to user-driven design, which could be transferred into an educational context (Shaw, 2002, 2005). She describes an open and meaningful type of communication that captures the interest of participants, revolving around what excites or even frustrates them. The dialogue implies a willingness to explore and improvise. The teacher listens closely to what students say and lets associations arise. "I am describing the process of weaving in our actions one with one another to co-create the future" (Shaw, 2002, p. 70).

This implies that the purpose of dialogue between students and teachers is not just the mutual understanding of preconceptions, but also the co-creation of new ideas. The teacher becomes a facilitator in order to encourage lively dialogue and encompass different views, even conflicts, regarding what is going to be taught and how. This requires that teachers and students alike be at ease, with an open approach. Teachers must let go of fixed agendas and be able to help students do the same. "Leading becomes being able to articulate issues and themes as they emerge and transform" (Shaw, 2005, p. 21).

A co-creative dialogue requires the teacher/facilitator to be very conscious of the form of communication used.

Generally speaking, teachers should be good at asking questions and stimulating students to ask questions themselves in order to create lively dialogue. In a quote from the empirical material, one teacher stresses how important it is to listen to the students: "It's important for me to listen to the students and start the process where they are. It is important for me that I can see that they are getting smarter and more competent and that they are empowered" (Stavnskær, 2014). Furthermore, the majority of the teachers focus on listening when facilitating co-creation between teachers and students, as well as in student-student communication. Shaw recognizes that listening is a central competence of the facilitator. The facilitating teacher listens closely to what the students say, and to their associations. Ideas regarding the given task or problem (content and form) should arise out of that listening (Shaw, 2002, p. 5).

This also implies being able to balance different viewpoints and manage conflicts. Students should be encouraged to express explicitly what they think – so that teachers can relate their understanding to other approaches (Iversen et al., 2015).

A co-creative dialogue allows something new and unforeseen to emerge. Stacey puts it this way: "We should expect not to see what we set out to achieve in the way we originally intended" (Stacey, 2007, p. 812).

The majority of teachers emphasised that one has to be able to improvise in the encounter with students, if something new is to arise. One teacher in particular stressed repeatedly in the course of the interview how important improvisation is to her: "Innovative communication consists in being prepared for the unexpected- in being able to improvise. I believe this to be a very important innovative competence. It gives me energy and flow" (Stavnskær, 2014). Similarly, Shaw mentions improvisation in her approach to facilitation: "a more improvisatory way of approaching how we might go on together" (Shaw, 2002, p. 5). The essence is that the facilitator of co-creation, in this case the teacher, should possess the ability to improvise, be ready for it, and have the courage and ability to step into the unknown together with the students.

These teachers' approaches can be seen as similar to the learning processes described by Chris Mowles et al. and Ralph Stacey. In their work, learning is understood as something complex and non-linear, emerging in communication by listening to participants, not by following a path staked out in advance by an expert (Mowles et al., 2008; Stacey, 2007).

It is teachers and students, who know the complexity of their own reality and, on that basis, who can find the way and *create something* together. One of the teachers described something similar: "The most important thing for me is to be a catalyst. Filter whatever the students carry with them, and put it in perspective, while at the same time presenting them with new perspectives" (Stavnskær, 2014). Co-creation is a mutual process amongst teachers and students where both parts contribute, as the teacher here underlines.

However, the demands on teachers and students are not identical. The majority of the teachers interviewed stressed the necessity of connecting with the students 'where they are', so to speak: "Meeting others where they are sounds simple, but it demands a certain didactical knowledge to be able to do it. It's about engaging the students, and getting them to engage themselves. It's like digging for gold" (Stavnskær, 2014). In other words, a precondition for finding gold is meeting students where they are. The majority of teachers interviewed said that they are expected to have a large methodological knowledge they can draw on and adapt to different target groups. They mention that didactics has to be in motion all the time: "It's important that didactics don't stiffen up, that they change to follow who the students are, that they are dynamic" (Stavnskær, 2014). This implies that the teacher has to be able to be flexible and able to create situation-based didactics out of his or her toolbox.

ROLES AND RESISTANCE

Under the title *Unlearning how to teach* Erica McWilliam (2008) introduces what you could call a teacher typology – or a set of positions to describe the relation between student and teacher in current education. Looking at teaching as a social practice, she makes a point in comparing teacher roles and communication strategies in teaching to societal changes and changes in cultural production in general. The point being that relational habits which once served teaching well may be past their expiration date and in need of revision.

McWilliam (2008) outlines three relational positions in teaching: *sage on the stage*, *guide on the side* and *meddler in the middle*, arguing that the latter is a possible equivalent to the unstable and ever-changing cultural conditions teaching is embedded in. In short, *sage on the stage* is a position where the teacher is an expert lecturing primarily one way, a classical auditorium situation. As a *guide on the side*, the teacher is a coach following the learning process on the side. The *meddler in the middle*:

> … positions the teacher and student as mutually involved in assembling and dis-assembling cultural products. It repositions teacher and student as co-directors and co-editors of their social world. […] it means less time giving instructions and more time spent being a usefully ignorant co-worker in the thick of action, less time spent being a custodial risk-minimizer and more time spent being an experimenter and risk-taker; less time spent being a forensic classroom auditor and more time spent being a designer, editor and assembler; less time spent being a counsellor and "best buddy" and more time spent being a collaborative critic and authentic evaluator. (McWilliam, 2008, p. 263)

The apparently paradoxical constellation of being a collaborative critic and an ignorant co-worker makes way for a new interpretation of the relation between teacher and student. This means neither leaving the responsibility of the learning with the student nor placing the responsibility of the teaching on the teacher. It is a position where the social space of teaching and learning is co-created in a cross-field of emergence and control. With the teacher not playing the role of curricular custodian and bearer of answers, knowledge can be regarded, then, as something occurring in a shared space of teaching and learning.

Changing habits, however, requires the will to change. Habits. A somewhat redundant statement, but nevertheless relevant. As teaching is a skill acquired over time, the individual teacher, like all professionals, acquires a level of expertise by doing certain things a great number of times. Changing strategies, consequently, puts the teacher in a potentially vulnerable and anxiety-provoking situation. Otto Scharmer talks about this challenge of not downloading:

> What we do is often based on habitual patterns of action and thought. A familiar stimulus triggers a familiar response. Moving towards a future possibility requires us to become aware of – and abandon – the dominant mode of downloading that causes us to continuously reproduce the patterns of the past. (Scharmer, 2007, p. 119)

Experimenting and taking risks may not be the average state of teaching. And venturing into a space of not knowing is not particularly common either. It is then, in short, something completely "other" that is required by both teachers and students. The challenge is mutual; teachers experimenting are at risk of exposing themselves to disappointed expectations and frustrations on the students' part. Or maybe even anger and aggression. An ability to manage and contain the potential anxiety in students is seen as a central and necessary quality inherent in the role of facilitating co-creative learning processes by most of the teachers we interviewed. One teacher says:

> You should be able to manage the frustrations of students, because [...] you are challenging them. [...] So the contact you will have with them will be closer than if your job was simply to deliver the sum of 2+2. The former approach implies going into a more personal dialogue with them, where you maybe put pressure on them. Some students appreciate it; others find it anxiety-provoking. (Stavnskær, 2014)

Darsø (2011) describes this ability to contain anxiety as essential for something new to emerge: "The teacher must train his ability to 'hold space', space which is characterized by chaos, uncertainty, anxiety, and vulnerability" (p. 12). Another teacher expresses something along the same lines. One should be able to: "contain and manage the students' uncertainty and insecurity. I should be able to handle all the feelings that are circulating in the classroom" (Stavnskær, 2014). And a third teacher adds that it puts a demand on the teacher to navigate on shaky ground, "It requires that you as a teacher "put yourself at risk" (Stavnskær, 2014). As such it takes a great deal of courage to become a 'meddler in the middle' or a co-creating teacher; "Facilitation is not for wimps" (Ghais, 2005, p. 2).

All the teachers interviewed emphasised that when they engaged in the process of facilitation in the search for innovation and co-creation, meeting resistance was part of the process. This resembles the conviction held by Susanne Ghais: "Whereas many books on facilitation treat conflict as an occasional snafu, I consider it as a given" (Ghais, 2005, p. 3). One teacher puts it this way: "You get a few slaps in the face." The courage required is described by another teacher. In a teaching situation she used a new creative method in a course, which led to one student leaving the room in frustration:

> I experienced a student who grabbed her bag and said, "this is simply too much, I'm gone." Then you stand there and hold your breath for 10 or 15 minutes. So you gamble a bit. But always with the idea in mind of creating something new for the students. (Stavnskær, 2014)

One teacher mentions courage explicitly as a necessary element of a co-creative approach. Adler & Hansen, too, identify courage as a central quality in creating change: "Daring to care requires courage—the courage to speak out and to act. Courage transforms convictions and compassion into action" (Adler & Hansen, 2012, p. 2). All this seems to indicate that courage is an essential quality for daring to facilitate transformative processes in students, which means pushing them out of their zones of comfort, as you do when being a co-creative teacher or a *meddler in the middle.* It is clear from these quotes that courage is required if one is to persist with co-creative dialogue when faced with resistance.

THE 'CO' AND THE 'CREATION'

In co-creation both the 'co' and the 'creation' are significant. The 'co' signals that the process is social and the 'creation', that something new appears as a consequence of the process. Taking a closer look at the social aspect in co-creation, inspiration can be found in the writings of Scharmer. He introduces a conceptual approach that combines relation and communication as a set of "social fields" within which different states of attention determine the quality of the communication, which on its part determines the outcome of the situation (Scharmer, 2007). This is conceptualised as a set of different ways in which the 'I' relates to the 'you', both the I and the you being understood as generalised terms. Scharmer names the positions of four different sources of attention from which social action can emerge (Scharmer, 2007, p. 234). Each position combines a state of attention with a mode of communication. The four positions are;

1. The I-in-me: the I relates to the you from a point where the focus is on the I itself. The communication in this state would be a monologue or parallel monologues where communication aims at confirming existing knowledge and perceptions and avoiding relating to the other, who is simply an ear in the periphery of attention.
2. The I-in-it: the I directs the attention to the outer world. From a position of not necessarily wanting to change, the attention is directed towards seeing the world as it really is. The mode of communication is discussion and critical scrutiny.
3. The I-in-you: the I relates to the you with the intention of understanding beyond the boundaries of the preconceptions of the I. Emphatic listening, dialogue, and reflective inquiry characterise the communication of this position.
4. The I-in-now combines introspective self-awareness of the I with listening beyond the I and entering a collective field of emergence. It is listening to both the intention and preconceptions of the I and being part of a shared generative space. The mode of communication is *presencing* – a hard to define term, which we choose to name generative dialogue, partly for lack of a better expression and partly inspired by earlier writings of Scharmer and Kaüfer (2000).

Most of the teachers interviewed describe how they establish a dialogue with the students, and how their field of attention moves away from themselves towards the domain of 'I-in-you': "Creating this kind of attentiveness and closeness is not so simple. One needs to have both knowledge and the opportunity of training the skills involved in practicing this kind of dialogue".

Above and beyond listening and dialogue is the 'I-in-now' position, which is a creative field of generative listening. The distance between teacher and student is dissolved, and a process of co-creation arises:

> The relationship with the students is more equal and more a co-creation process. As a teacher I have more knowledge that I contribute to the shared knowledge – where students also contribute. The knowledge I contribute and

> what the students bring is made into one collective pool of knowledge. It is a broader and more diverse perspective on the new knowledge that emerges between us. (Stavnskær, 2014)

It is neither clear nor important who contributes what in the dialogue, but something new arises among the participants and the learning process is mutual. "Being with students changes me." The teacher role in the generative field resembles McWilliams *meddler in the middle.*

The opposite teacher role is 'sage on the stage', where the students: "spent time guessing what the teacher wants to know like a quiz." 'Quizzing'. We interpret this as 'listening downloading' or 'projective listening', (Scharmer, 2007, pp. 275–276) and being in the position of the 'I-in-me' where the teacher only hears what students say insofar as it fits into the mental models that already exist in his or her own mind. The rest of what students say is more or less ignored.

A MATRIX

Looking at modes of attention AND intention in the context of teaching is highly relevant, as is the emphasis on communication. Taking steps towards understanding how co-creating knowledge is related to communication as well as roles and intention could then be done by combining the teacher typology outlined by McWilliam with the set of social fields described by Scharmer. The point of so doing would be to develop a hypothesis on how teacher position and communication are related, when it comes to identifying prerequisites for co-creation to take place in teaching. In a simple matrix we place communication and mode of attention on the y-axis and teacher roles on the x-axis, generating a model looking like this:

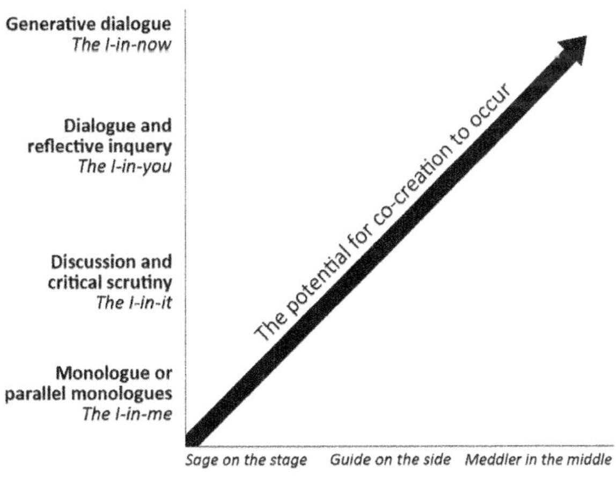

Figure 2.1. The co-creation matrix (Iversen & Stavnskær, 2016)

Drawing on both Scharmer and McWilliam and comparing their writings to the experiences of the teachers interviewed, it would be our hypothesis that the potential for co-creation to occur in teaching can be described as an outcome of communication and teacher position. Moving from the lower left corner to the upper right the potential increases. As *sage on the stage,* the teacher is not inclined to include the students in knowledge production. Communication will tend to be monological, since the teacher is regarded as the knowledge bearer. For the most part, the teacher lectures and the students listen. As the *guide on the side,* the teacher may join the students in a discussion or a critical scrutiny of the state of the world. Or (s)he could be the empathic listener and dialogue partner. As *meddler in the middle*, the description of teachers and students as co-directors and co-editors of their social world (McWilliam, 2008, p. 263) matches the coming-to-be of a collective field of emergence expressed as the I-in-now mode of attention. And generative dialogue, then, is the type of communication that represents the highest potential when it comes to co-creation in teaching. Generative dialogue – with teachers and students as co-directors and co-editors – calls for a change in the way knowledge production takes place in teaching, and in the design and framing of learning processes. Below we suggest a possible approach to reframing teaching and operating from basic co-creation principles.

FRAMING AND DESIGNING CO-CREATIVE LEARNING PROCESSES

Through years of personal experimenting with different types of participatory approaches in teaching, a progression or design-model emerged. It describes phases in a co-creation process customised to a teaching-learning environment. Its origin is higher education but it most likely has a broader relevance due to its relatively simple composition.

The design progression comprises five phases. Through all phases, teachers and students co-operate through generative dialogue with a shared goal of developing and carrying out curricular activities. Not as an extraordinary or extra-curricular activity, but as a basic methodological approach to designing and performing education. The five phases are as follows:

1. Framing/contextualising; defining the intention and understanding the field – which journey are we embarking on? The where and the why
2. Finding the question(s); what are the challenges of the field we are entering? The what
3. Co-designing micro-prototypes (of knowledge production); in which ways will we try to engage with the challenges? The how
4. Co-operative performance
5. Evaluating

Given a visual expression, the design progression will come out like this:

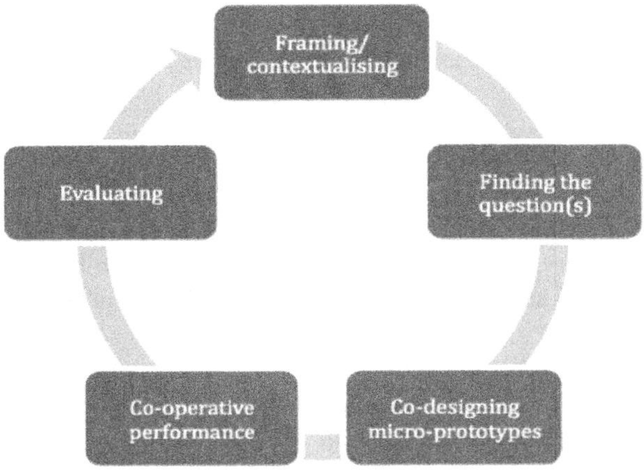

Figure 2.2. The co-creative learning process wheel

FRAMING/CONTEXTUALISING

Framing and contextualising is about clarifying both the where and the why. In what specific context are teachers and students situated? Which course, class, lecture or training session and so forth is the objective of the teaching situation? And what are the formal requirements, the learning goals and academic demands of the forthcoming process? All of these are potential subjects of discussion and shared reflection among teachers and students. A shared awareness of these basic conditions constitutes a platform from which direction can be taken for the design process. Also, goals and objectives of a more informal character can be integrated during this phase. For instance, both students and teachers may have personal aspirations and ambitions related to the process.

FINDING THE QUESTIONS

The next phase is focused on finding the question(s) and looking at the challenges of the field we are entering. In other words, defining the 'what' of the teaching.

Part of designing a learning process that facilitates co-creation is finding the questions or challenges that the students strive to solve. A challenge and questions where there are no pre-given or self-evident solutions or answers are more likely to facilitate co-creation and co-creative dialogue than *sage on the stage*-type processes.

These challenges and questions could be real-life projects. This means that in the preparation phase, either students or teachers, as part of preparing a specific project, investigate who it would be relevant to work with, contact them, and agree on what the project's character and goals are. This is to say that, for the teacher, there is a didactical balancing act between academic demands and a real-life challenge. The point is that students, like the teacher, have to learn to balance the academic demands of their disciplines with the challenges.

Or it could be simply by challenging or questioning knowledge domains.

CO-DESIGNING MICRO-PROTOTYPES

The expression "prototype" – or "micro-prototype" – is used regarding the different potential solutions to the challenges established in phase one. In practice, these kinds of prototypes can vary, from suggestions, to solving actual problems formulated by external stakeholders and partners, to teaching design. The prototypes spring from non-linear, open space, improvisatory processes involving students and teachers as co-designers. Co-designing involves collective creativity and socio-epistemic practice. Students and teachers are co-developers of whatever designs and solutions emerge. There are no pre-defined answers.

There are points of similarity between this learning design and some of the factors identified by Teresa Amabile as encouraging creativity. Amabile concludes, among other things, that individuals must be offered a degree of autonomy if one hopes to encourage the development of intrinsic motivation: "Autonomy around process fosters creativity because giving people freedom in how they approach their work heightens their intrinsic motivation and sense of ownership" (Amabile, 2002, p. 82).

One of the teachers interviewed describes the transformation occurring in students when they encounter co-creative teaching design:

> We see students with a long history of discouraging experiences with education systems. They appear withdrawn and frustrated when they come to us, but we see that they gradually and quietly discover that they actually have a pool of competencies inside themselves. We see them straighten up, pull the hair back from their faces, see light come back into their eyes. What a transformation! It's one of the most meaningful things we experience as teachers, and it happens fairly often when you work in this way.

All in all, the interviews with teachers could indicate that the intention of dynamic flow in the design of the co-creative learning process between (1) learning goals and (2) challenges – between theory and practice – in some way has a potential for creating new solutions and new knowledge. Brown and Isaac's discussion of learning in the following passage could lend support to the potential of this co-creative way of designing the teaching:

> It's never enough just to tell people about some new insight. Rather, you have to get them to experience it in a way that evokes its power and possibility. Instead of pouring knowledge into people's heads, you need to help them grind a new set of sunglasses so they can see the world in a new way. (Brown & Isaacs, 2005, p.12)

This is not a new insight, as Ib Ravn points out: "For teaching to be effective and learning to take place, educators must realize that students are actively engaged in constructing their worlds [...] They learn from engaging" (Ravn, 2007, p. 215). Ravn continues his point with reference to older learning theories by Dewey, Piaget and Vygotsky, which also emphasise that teachers often ignore the importance of context and engagement, and instead teach in a way that pacifies students. And, we could add, Carl Rogers in his groundbreaking book, *Freedom To Learn*, first published in 1969, introduces significant learning with a set of characteristics similar to the points made by Brown & Isaacs, and Ravn. Significant learning is self-initiated, has a quality of personal involvement, and is driven by a sense of meaning to the learner (Rogers, 1983, p. 20).

CO-OPERATIVE PERFORMANCE

The name of the fourth phase indicates that this is the phase of enacting the prototypes developed in phase three, be they teaching designs or prototypes related to challenges put by external partners Or a combination of both. Types of action can vary from carrying out courses, workshops, training programmes and so forth to presenting and/or carrying out prototypes in co-operation with external partners. The performance is co-operative in the sense that it progresses as a co-operative action driven by shared knowledge production. Steps are taken on a basis of generative dialogue and shared reflexion.

Integrating co-operative performance in teaching design facilitates action. Consequently it stimulates both teachers' and students' capacity for action. And at the same time – and more importantly – it stimulates the capacity for actually creating sustainable proto-types. They are, so to speak, tested by action.

The action perspective is identified by researcher Anne Kirketerp as initiative-taking didactics. (Kirketerp, 2010). Kirketerp explores different teaching designs that support entrepreneurial initiative, and develops the SKUB (English: PUSH) method, a method of integrative learning, which leads to changes in patterns of both thinking and acting in students:

> With regards to teaching entrepreneurship, it should be the norm that the greater part of teaching must be action-oriented. The methods that encourage initiative specially belong to the didactics of entrepreneurship. If one of the goals is to stimulate innovation competence generally, one of the means to that end is to push the students out into action. (Kirketerp, 2010, p. 258)

Teaching in this sense always involves practice alongside elements of reflexion and analysis. The students and teachers are, in other words, pushed to act. Kirketerp's point is supported by Brown and Duguid (1991). They argue that there is a huge difference between espoused practice and actual practice and that acquiring abstract knowledge about, for instance, co-creation will have little or no effect on the capacity of co-creating. Consequently, teaching design aiming at developing co-creation skills in students must include co-creation practice.

EVALUATION

The last phase is evaluation. It consists of two parts. One part is the evaluation, done by the external partners, of practical real life proto-types. Criteria for this are the quality and the practical applicability of the proto-types in the context for which the prototypes are designed. The second part of the evaluation is an internal one with teachers and other students. In this part, both the quality of the teaching design and the correspondence between learning goals, academic demands and the final outcome of the entire process are evaluated.

From a teacher's perspective, there are specific challenges that arise with designing evaluation methods that can measure co-creative competencies. Co-creative knowledge production, in some ways, constitutes an opposition to strict academic norms. Standards for exams and evaluations for the most part stem from the latter. Evaluation, then, to some extent will risk reproducing academic standards far from the methodology in co-creative knowledge production. This remains a challenge to be taken into consideration in a future perspective.

CO-CREATIVE KNOWLEDGE PRODUCTION AND ITS FUTURE POTENTIAL

One of the aims of this chapter was to give some pointers towards preparing students for becoming 21st century knowledge workers, and preparing them for an unknown future. Another aim was to answer the question of what it takes to re-invent higher education and for teachers to become 21st century educators and designers of education characterised by a high degree of relevance to both society, and culture and the to the coming generations of students.

The answer suggested in this chapter is building significant parts of knowledge production and knowledge exchange *on co-creative generative dialogue*. The purpose of this would be to develop new types of knowledge and subsequently potential answers to the questions of our time. It would require breaking habits and changing modes of communication. Building education round the emerging future is no easy task. It is, however, a task to be taken on – and why not involve the students?

REFERENCES

Adler, N. J., & Hansen, H. (2012). Daring to care: Scholarship that supports of our convictions. *Journal of Management Inquiry, 21*(2), 128–139.

Amabile, T. (2002). How to kill creativity. *The Harvard Business Review, 76*(5), 76–87. Harvard Business School Publishing.

Bason, C. (2010). *Leading public sector innovation: Co-creating for a better society.* Bristol: Policy Press.

Bateson, G. (1972). *Steps to an ecology of mind.* Northvale, NJ: Chandler Publications.

Belling, L. (2010). *Fortællinger fra U'et: Dansk psykologisk Forlag.*

Bens, I. (2006). *Facilitating to lead!: Leadership strategies for a networked world.* San Francisco, CA: Jossey-Bass.

Besselink, T. (2014). Learning choreography. In J. W. Moravec (Ed.), *Knowmad society.* San Bernardino, CA: Education Futures.

Brown, J. S., & Duguid, P. (1991). Organizational learning and communities- of- practice: Toward a unified view of working, learning and innovation. *Organization Science, 2*(1), 40–57.

Brown, J., & Isaacs, D. (2005). *The world cafe: Shaping our futures through conversations that matter.* San Francisco, CA: Berrett-Koehler Publishers.

Darsø, L. (2004). *Artful creation: Learning-tales of arts-in business.* Frederiksberg: Samfundslitteratur.

Darsø, L. (2011). *Innovationspædagogik: Kunsten at fremelske innovationskompetence.* Frederiksberg: Samfundslitteratur.

Degnegaard, R. (2014). Co-creation, prevailing streams and future design trajectories. *CoDesign, 10*(2), 96–111.

Drucker, P. (1999). Managing oneself. *Harvard Business Review*, March-April, 1–60.

Ghais, S. (2005). *Extreme facilitation: Guiding groups through controversy and complexity.* San Francisco, CA: Jossey-Bass.

Hassan, Z. (2014). *The social labs revolution: A new approach to solving our most complex challenges.* San Francisco, CA: Berrett-Koehler Publishers.

Iversen, A., Stavnskær, A., Krogh, L., & Aarup Jensen, A. (2015). Learning, leading and letting go of control: Learner-led approaches in education. *Sage Open, 5*(4), 1–11.

Kahane, A. (2012). *Transformative scenario planning: Working together to change the future.* San Francisco, CA. Berrett-Koehler Publishers.

Madsen, J. (2016, May 6). *Jeg lærte mere af en måned på højskole end to år på universitetet.* Politiken. Retrieved from: http://politiken.dk/debat/art5637856/Jeg-l%C3%A6rte-mere-af-en-m%C3%A5ned-p%C3%A5-h%C3%B8jskole-end-af-to-%C3%A5r-p%C3%A5-universitetet

McWilliam, E. (2008). Unlearning how to teach. *Innovations in Education and Teaching International, 45*(3), 263–269.

Mezirow, J. (1997). Transformative learning: Theory to practice. *New Directions for Adult and continuing Education, 74*, 5–12.

Moravec, J. W. (2008). *Towards society 3.0: A new paradigm for 21st century education.* Minneapolis, MN: University of Minnesota.

Moravec, J. W. (Ed.). (2014). *Knowmad society.* San Bernardino, CA: Education Futures.

Mowles, C., Stacey, R., & Griffin, D. (2008). What contribution can insights from the complexity sciences make to the theory and practice of development management? *Journal of International Development, 20*(6), 804–820

Ravn, I. (2007). The learning conferences. *Journal of European Industrial Training, 31*(3), 212–222.

Rogers, C. (1983) *Freedom to learn.* Oledo: Bell & Howell Company.

Sanders, E. B., & Stappers, P. J. (2008). Co-creation and the new landscapes of design. *CoDesign, 4*(1), 5–18.

Scharmer, O. C. (2007). *Theory U: Leading from the future as it emerges: The social technology of presencing.* Published for SOL (The Society for Organizational Learning), San Francisco,CA & London: Berrett-Koehler McGraw-Hill distributor.

Scharmer, O. C., & Käufer, K. (2000). *Universities as the birthplace for the entrepreneuring human beings: MIT sloan school of management.* Retrieved from http://www.ottoscharmer.com/sites/default/files/2000_Uni21us.pdf

Scharmer, O. C., & Kaüfer, K. (2013). *Leading from the emerging future: From ego-system to eco-system economies.* San Francisco, CA: Berrett-Koehler Publishers.

Shaw, P. (2002). *Changing conversations in organizations: A complexity approach to change.* London: Routledge.

Shaw, P. (2005). Conversational inquiry as an approach to organisation development. *Journal of Innovative Management,* 19–22. Retrieved from http://www.dacapo.as/wp-content/uploads/2015/06/Pshaw_Conversational_Inquiry_as_an_Approach_to_Organisation_Development21.pdf

Stacey, R. D. (2003). Learning as an activity of interdependent people. *The learning organization, 10*(6), 325–331.

Stacey, R. D. (2007). *Strategic management and organisational dynamics: The challenge of complexity to ways of thinking about organisations*. London: Pearson Education.

Stavnskær, A. (2014). *Human* (Unpublished Master's Thesis). Laics Master, CBS (Copenhagen Business School), Copenhagen, Denmark.

Thompson, T. A., & Purdy, J. M. (2009). When a good idea isn't enough: Curricular innovation as a political process. *Academy of Management Learning & Education, 8*(2), 188–207.

Ann-Merete Iversen
University College Nordjylland

Anni Stavnskær Pedersen
University College Nordjylland

CHUNFANG ZHOU, OLE RAVN AND XIANGYUN DU

3. FACILITATING REFLECTIVE LEARNING AND CO-CREATIVE TEACHING BY PORTFOLIOS IN PROBLEM-BASED LEARNING (PBL)

INTRODUCTION

Propelled by advances in global communication and information technologies, the nature of interactions among individuals and their environments has been changing rapidly, driving an ongoing metamorphosis of value creation in business, economy, and society. Individuals are attempting to push through previously impervious institutional boundaries to express their various demands and expectations and they are active stakeholders, who want to be more intensively engaged in value creation than ever before. In short, all stakeholding individuals have been described as co-creators (Ramaswamy & Ozcan, 2014).

The co-creation-based view has had great influence in higher education. Within the literature (Bovill, 2014), there are growing arguments highlighting the roles of active student participation in a range of student engagement, student-centred learning and enquiry-based learning initiatives – for example, Problem-Based Learning (PBL). In this learning environment (Bovill, 2014), students are not submissive, silent individuals in the learning environment, but rather they are viewed as motivated partners in a collaborative enquiry based on dialogue, experimentation and mutual learning for teachers and students. In practice, the models of co-creating curricula design can be found in diverse educational areas such as language teaching, environmental justice and teacher education. In these models, teaching staff and students are partners in learning processes and become co-producers of knowledge.

In teacher education, reflection and self-assessment have been regarded as key principles of building a co-creation educational model to enable teachers to examine the relationships between their cognitions and instructional practice (Artze et al., 2007). In a PBL environment, even though the teachers' role in mediating learner experience can take many different forms, all with different roles in the simplification and facilitation process, teachers can be thought of as "learning experts" among students. It is essential for teaching staff to reflect on their own teaching experiences in order to make sense of learning how to teach better. This reflective phase is likely to uncover difficulties or problems, which if the teacher does not address them, may impede progress towards self-improvement in teaching (Artze et al., 2007). Using informal and formal formative and summative assessment strategies can help teachers engage in accurate, reflective decision-making. For example, a

T. Chemi & L. Krogh (Eds.), Co-Creation in Higher Education, 31–47.

teaching portfolio can help to collect and select evidence of learning processes and attainments that are linked and put together in a variety of formats (Pitts, 2010), thereby providing the conditions for exerting reflective capability.

Our chapter will focus on the following question:

> How does the development of a teaching portfolio enable new teaching staff to improve reflective learning ability and to develop co-creation teaching value in a PBL environment?

From a theoretical perspective, we examine co-creation as the nature of the teaching culture in a PBL learning environment, based on a discussion of social theories of learning. Empirically, the teaching portfolio of one of the authors of this chapter contributes to a specific case analysis of how reflective experiences were developed through her participation in a staff development programme at Aalborg University (AAU), Denmark – a learning environment with a long tradition of PBL in higher education. The discussion of the findings leads to deeper understanding of the benefits and challenges of using teaching portfolios in a PBL set-up.

A Social Perspective to Learning and Reflection

When something is social, it is automatically interconnected with and referred to other people. Weber (1922) defined "social acting" in a way that the sense of the action is related to others' behaviour. Social acting is an essential part of our everyday life that also occurs in the workplace and its sequence is always oriented to others. According to Wenger (1998), a social theory of learning integrates the components necessary to characterise social participation as a process of learning and knowing. These components include (1) meaning, (2) practice, (3) community, and (4) identity. They are deeply interconnected and mutually influence learning experiences. This is similar to what Illeris (2007) has described as the three dimensions involved in all learning: namely the content and the incentive dimension, which have to do with the individual acquisition process; the emotional or psychodynamic dimension, which encompasses mental energy, feelings and motivation; and the social and societal dimension, to do with the interaction processes between the individual and the environment. These three dimensions form a learning circle, indicating that learning always takes place within the frames of an outer societal context. On the general level, this is decisive for learning possibilities. Furthermore, theories on communities of practice (1998) indicate that learning is the interplay between social competence and personal experience, which is a dynamic, two-way relationship between people and the social learning systems in which they participate. In other words, learning combines personal transformation with the evolution of social structures.

So a social perspective of learning suggests that it cannot be separated from practice. According to Wenger (1998), in a community of practice, "practice" can be regarded as the learners' shared historical and social resources, frameworks, and perspectives that sustain their mutual engagement in action within a certain community. Skilled practice uses experience, knowledge and enquiry processes to increase the capability to intervene, interpret, and act positively on successes, problems, issues, and significant questions. So practice is therefore associated with learners' reflection. Reflective practice helps us to understand the links between feeling, thinking and doing and the links between what we do and how we might improve our effectiveness by developing new insights (Ghaye, 2010). In other words, reflective practice is concerned with learning how to account for ourselves. This means learning how to describe, explain and justify our teaching. This is important in the context where both individual and collective teacher strengths and weakness are observed, and where practice is questioned. Thus, reflective teachers are also critical thinkers. This critical reflection is essentially where education acquires a language, a set of arguments, the skill and the power to transform the existing order of things, so as to improve the quality of learners' educational experiences (Ghaye, 2010).

Reflectivity as a Key Principle of Co-Creation Curriculum

From a viewpoint of organisational studies, Pamaswamy and Ozcan (2014) outlined a definition of 'co-creation': it is a joint creation and evaluation of value with stakeholding individuals, intensified and enacted through platforms of engagements, virtualised and emergent from ecosystems of capabilities, and actualised and embodied in domains of experiences, expanding wealth-welfare-wellbeing. In order to facilitate an enterprise's transformation towards the co-creation paradigm, reflectivity is a key principle in building up engagement platforms. It is the movement that enables the transformation of outcomes of value, and reflections on these outcomes, so it becomes at of the assemblage system and the value it generates. This involves tools, information, insights, recommendations, meanings, lived experiences, and valuable creations of others.

By introducing the configuration of co-creation in organisational studies to higher education, co-created curriculum design highlights at least the following elements: (1) students' active and reflective participation, (2) changes of teachers' role towards becoming facilitators of learning, (3) a dynamic and interactive process of teaching and learning, (4) multiple channels of resources of teaching and learning, and (5) increased levels of individual and collective students' responsibility for their learning (Bovill, 2014). These elements indicate that we can regard a co-created curriculum as a basis for developing a community of practice, where all learners and teachers are reflective partners who contribute to mutual engagement, a joint enterprise and a shared repertoire (Wenger, 1998). This also takes the belief that professional learning stems from continuous action and reflection on everyday problems, often involving tacit knowledge that is difficult to identify and analyse. So when professionals reflect on an experience, they develop their own theoretical system. Besides learning from one's own primary events, it is also important to consider, and value, learning from secondary experiences of others, communicated in writing or verbally, by individuals or within groups (Pitts, 2010).

Portfolio as a Tool for Promoting Reflective Capability

It is no longer unusual to read about "portfolios" in many areas of education. Portfolio-based learning has become an approach that has the critical intellectual task of moving from description of an experience to identification of the learning derived from that experience and ultimately deciding what further education is required to fill in gaps revealed by the analysis of the described experience (Pitts, 2010). In effect, the portfolio has become a distinctive model of performance assessment, serving as a meaningful alternative to conventional papers and standardised testing (Michelson & Mandell, 2004). Although there may be many differences in purpose, structure and assessment requirements, certain key aspects are usually highlighted (Michelson & Mandell, 2004):

- The experience – what has happened, what has been done, seen, written, made etc.
- The learning – the discovery that what has been recalled has significance for doing or changing things in the future
- The evidence – a demonstration of how the learning is being applied in a particular context
- Learning needs – an identification of where it would be appropriate to go next
- Learning opportunities – an educational action plan identifying ways in which learning needs might be met.

The three most important steps of the portfolio building process are "collect", "select", and "reflect" and each requires a reflective capability (Ng, 2010). Although, in reality, portfolios from different individuals vary in their depth of reflection, it is suggested that promoting reflection is the greatest value of portfolios as this enables the authors to become reflective learners (Gordon, 2003) who engage in constant self-reflection in any activity, whether learning or in the workplace (Lonka et al., 2001). The portfolio also provides a clear picture that highlights the degree of suitability of different career paths, so this becomes a tool for authors to map their career pathways (Weddle et al., 2002).

Problem-Based Learning (PBL) as a Model of Co-Creation

Recently, PBL has been argued as a co-creation curriculum model that helps students to reach learning objectives effectively and reflectively (Hmelo-Silver, 2004). Although it functions in a diversity of models in different universities and cultural settings, the core principle of PBL is "student-centred learning". In practice, students' learning focuses on complex problems that do not have a single answer, or on solving real-life projects. Students work in collaborative groups to identify what they need to learn in order to solve problems. The teacher acts to facilitate the learning process rather than to provide knowledge (Dolmans et al., 2001). Poikela, Vuoskoski, and Kärnä (2009) provide a model of PBL learning cycle that has been cited by Zhou, Otrel-Cass, and Børsen (2015) (Figure 3.1).

In this cycle, the PBL process begins with students looking for a problem and working towards a shared understanding of the problem presented to them. They then brainstorm ideas about the content area related to the problem using their existing knowledge and prior experiences. Similar types of ideas are grouped into named categories. The most important problem areas among the named categories are determined. The first tutorial session is then held to decide on the learning tasks to be undertaken and the goals to be achieved. Following the tutorial, students engage in information search and self-study, working both individually and in pairs or in small groups, depending on the learning tasks and goals as well as on the strategy deemed most appropriate for seeking information. The second tutorial is the time for applying the new knowledge acquired, to tackle the learning tasks and to reconstruct the problem in a new way. New and in-depth knowledge is synthesised and integrated to provide a basis for deeper learning. Participants clarify and reflect on the whole problem-solving process in the light of the new knowledge. Assessment is part of every single phase of the process. It is necessary to emphasise the tutorial roles with feedback about students' own learning, their information-seeking behaviour, their problem-solving skills and the group processes, so that improvements can be made (Poikela, Vuoskoski, & Kärnä, 2009). Such a cycle develops a type of learning environment that enables students to be qualified persons who are self-confident in their social roles within a group, ready to take risks in the public social arena of the classroom, willingly collaborating with others to interpret and develop meaning from challenging problems (Porath & Jordan, 2009).

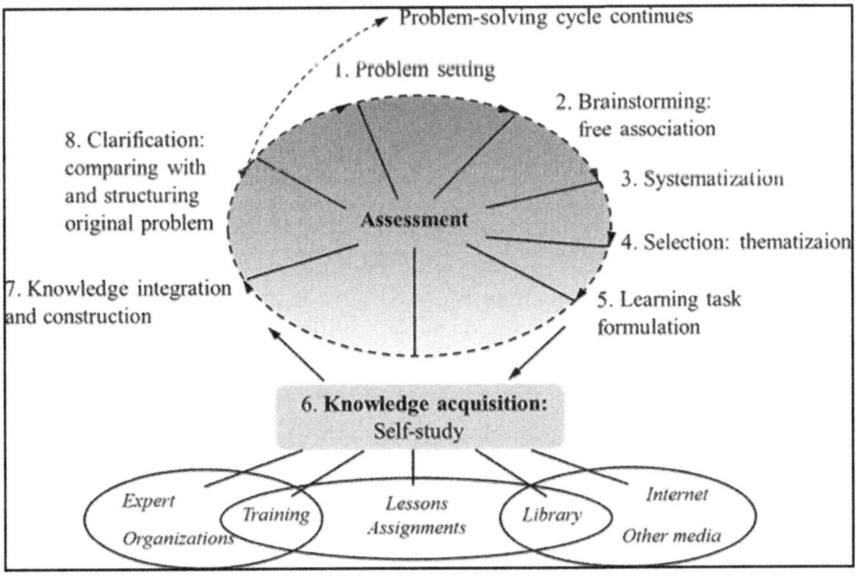

Figure 3.1. Problem-based learning cycle

The tutors coach the group by monitoring the group process and helping the students to identify the knowledge that is needed to resolve the problem (Poikela, Vuoskoski, & Kärnä, 2009). So the tutors play the roles of learning experts, able to model good strategies for learning and thinking, rather than experts in the content itself. They are responsible both for moving the students through the various stages of PBL and for monitoring the group process. This monitoring ensures that all students are involved and encourages them to externalise their own thinking and to comment on each other's thinking (Hmelo-Silver, 2004). This means educators need to engage in meaningful enquiry and form general theories. They must be aware of the conceptual landscape of their classes, crafting the form of instruction in consideration of students' knowledge and group dynamic (Porath & Jordan, 2009). They must also have a general theory of how learning environment and pedagogy can support deep understanding of the curriculum and nurture professional responsibility in their students (Zhou, Otrel-Cass, & Børsen, 2015). These aspects of teaching – representing the art and the craft of education – are also the challenges usually met by new teaching staff in PBL.

Briefly, the PBL environment can be seen as a model of a co-created curriculum, as we have seen that its learning cycle involves a dynamic and interactive process of teaching and learning, and multiple channels of resources of teaching and learning. A co-created curriculum also involves other elements, such as students' active and reflective participation, changes of teachers' role towards facilitation and increased levels of individual and collective students' responsibility for their learning (Bovill, 2014). In other words, PBL locates all learners in a community of practice where there is an aggregation of people who, through joint engagement in some enterprise, come to develop and share ways of doing things, ways of talking, beliefs, values – in short, practice. Therefore, it requires a wide range of capabilities – knowing facts, concepts, and principles; understanding social relations and norms of interaction; knowing how to communicate and how to interpret documents and other information sources. Learning these practices and perspectives is crucial for a newcomer who wishes to participate in, and contribute to, a community of practice (Wenger, 2006).

This indicates that new teaching staff in PBL should have effective tools, in order to develop co-creation teaching value in a PBL environment. Among those tools, this chapter addresses the importance of reflective learning abilities and regards developing teaching portfolio as a good method, as the following case illustrates.

A CASE OF DEVELOPING TEACHING PORTFOLIO

Background

As mentioned above, this chapter draws its selected empirical resource from one of the authors' teaching portfolio that was developed through her experiences of participation in the university pedagogy programme during 2013–2014, at Aalborg University (AAU), Denmark – a university with a long tradition of PBL education since the 1970s.

Every academic year, AAU organises a university pedagogy programme that lasts two semesters. All participants in this programme are new members of the teaching staff, most of whom are supposed to have little knowledge or teaching experience regarding PBL. So the overall aim of the programme is to help new teaching staff to manage their teaching challenges in order to better integrate themselves into the PBL community. A series of activities are organised, such as workshops, observation of teaching by senior staff, and developing teaching portfolios. More specifically, the following are parts of the learning goals of all new teaching staff:

- Further insight into and an understanding of teaching and learning theories, related to personal practice;
- Become better in developing, planning, carrying out suitable teaching and learning activities in relation to general and specific teaching objectives, the subject(s), the context and students' background;
- Become more familiar with learning theories and learn to better identify students' learning needs and to initiate learning processes among a variety of students, both individually and in groups;
- Strengthen insight into problem-based project work and the role of the supervisor, in order to realise the potential of PBL in initiating and supporting the students' group and learning processes.

So one of the learning goals is the development of teaching portfolios, in which new teaching staff are required to record their reflective teaching experience in a process of self-assessment. Meanwhile, each participant has two teaching supervisors who are usually senior staff with a wealth of teaching experience at AAU. The responsibilities of supervisors are mainly to facilitate new staff members' participation in their teaching activities and evaluation, so they observe their teaching context, propose problems related to the teaching observed, share teaching experience, and complete an evaluation report. The new staff members' teaching portfolio is a part of the final evaluation when the pedagogy programme is finished.

The author of the portfolio in our case study is an international staff member from China. She had an interdisciplinary educational background: bachelor degree in Engineering, master degree in Philosophy of Science and Technology, and PhD degree in Engineering Education. Since 2013, she has been employed as an assistant professor and her main teaching subjects relate to techno-anthropology and organisational learning. Her two supervisors are senior staff (one is an associate professor, the other is a professor) who are – among other things – teaching her same subjects.

The Main Structure of the Portfolio

The structure of the portfolio, in the university pedagogy programme, comprises 5 sections. Each section is guided by a "task" for the new teacher to carry out. These tasks are designed based on diverse activities in the programme and help to develop the teaching portfolio. The 5 tasks are to:

1. Develop a teaching CV,
2. Identify teaching problems or challenges,
3. Make plans for solving these problems and further teaching development in general,
4. Reflect on learning experiences from workshops and meetings with supervisors, and
5. Sum up with reflections on previous problems defined or new problems to be solved.

In order to finish each task, the new staff members are advised to start by working with and reflecting on "questions" or "sub-tasks" that they find easily accessible.

Table 3.1. A part of structure of teaching portfolio

Task 1	*Please construct a development-oriented teaching CV by following questions.*
Questions/ Sub-tasks	1. Describe your teacher role model(s), if you have actually experienced a role model, which led to you attaining the relevant knowledge/skills within the subject area in question. 2. Describe what the person(s) did during the teaching/supervision, which had great impact on your learning. 3. How do you normally succeed? a. In relation to the lecture situation b. In relation to the supervision situation c. By using other teaching forms 4. What are the largest challenges for you as a teacher/supervisor? a. In relation to the lecture situation b. In relation to the supervision situation c. By using other teaching forms 5. Please make a description of your typical students (age, cultural/social background, etc.), and furthermore what these aspects offer you as challenges related to your teaching and supervision 6. Try to put down a few words about the traditional and knowledge approaches within your subject(s) – and which consequences they have for the teaching approaches that are expected from your teaching environments 7. Sum up: your experiences with role models, your teaching and supervision, your students and your subject(s) and teaching areas in question – where do you especially wish to qualify yourself during your participation in university pedagogy programme? a. In relation to the lecture situation b. In relation to the project supervision c. By using other teaching forms d. In relation to other situations regarding teaching, project supervision, planning/designing of teaching/supervision 8. Now finally try to transform your reflections under the above mentioned points in summing up to a problem formation, which you will work on solving in the first semester in pedagogy programme as a part of your personal qualification processes.

Based on their learning experiences from reading literature, workshops, and meeting with supervisors and peers, new teaching members are encouraged to analyse their teaching issues, and then go back the "question" again, and supplement with more reflections. For example, Table 3.1 shows Task 1 and its questions and sub-tasks.

Experiences and Learning Outcomes Recorded by Portfolio

The author of the portfolio developed her teaching portfolio according to the content structure. The development process also included her collective experiences when she had finished all the learning tasks in the process of participating in teaching activities. These experiences provided resources and conditions for reflecting on the author's teaching problems and making an action plan for working on the problems during the programme. Some experiences also indicated learning outcomes, for example, to propose the explicit teaching problems. Details are shown in Table 3.2.

Table 3.2. Collective experiences and learning outcomes

Activity	*Experiences and learning outcomes*
Developing Teaching CV	A development-oriented teaching CV has been completed, listing all teaching experiences gained from diverse contexts (both in traditional teaching in China and innovative PBL model in Denmark), in educational institutions and companies and with different levels of learners (ranging from primary school to higher education).
Formulating Teaching Problems	1. As a foreign teacher, how can I improve teaching ability in order to tackle the challenges of teaching international students? 2. Furthermore, how can I fill in the ability gaps created by the differences of educational systems between different countries around the world?
Action Plans to Solve Problems	1. To learn more Danish culture and Danish educational culture, to be better acquainted with Danish educational system that indicates the needs of more collaboration and communication with local colleagues. 2. To share teaching experiences with other international staff who may meet similar challenges in the international classrooms. To learn more skills and experiences of dealing with the challenges met in the teaching. 3. To apply an evidence-based teaching approach to international students. This means to design the questionnaire survey on the needs of the teaching and background of the students before the course is started, or to have formal or informal talks with students before the course. 4. To learn from senior staff and share teaching experiences and discuss more with other colleagues regarding possibilities of collaborative teaching or initiation of new teaching tasks. 5. To develop international network involving potential collaboration with local colleagues and partners outside Denmark.

(Continued)

Table 3.2. (Continued)

Activity	*Experiences and learning outcomes*
Workshops	A total of 8 workshops were followed during spring, 2014: 1. Introduction to university pedagogy programme 2. How to benefit best from the university pedagogy programme and to get the best out of the feedback from supervisors and from colleagues 3. Teaching and learning: from planning a teaching activity to planning the assessment 4. Introduction to PBL model at AAU 5. Lecturing in English 6. PBL beyond Project at AAU 7. Supervision 8. PowerPoint is necessarily boring Benefits gained by the author from participation in workshops: 1. A more comprehensive and a more overall picture about what PBL is, including its diverse learning theories, models, development, and teaching principles. This laid the theoretical basis for me to hold onto the philosophy of PBL – such as "student-centred learning" – in future teaching practice. 2. A deeper understanding of AAU PBL model including the historical background and development of AAU, the Danish learning culture and educational system, the characteristics of AAU PBL model, and diverse methods of applying PBL at AAU, which was helpful to understand differences of teaching and learning cultures between China and Denmark. 3. A series of teaching techniques related to PBL contexts that can be used in different teaching situations. These techniques can be understood from aspects such as designing teaching activities, assessment, educational technologies, and supervision. These techniques are pathways both to students' meaningful learning process and to successful teaching experiences. 4. A diversity of perceptions about teaching issues in PBL from peer participants through sharing experience and group discussions in workshops, indicating that challenges of teaching in PBL is both personal-general and personal-specific.
Supervisor Observation	Two supervisors observed 4 times the author's student project supervision contexts. Short meetings and discussions with supervisors took place before and after the observations. The discussions involved the supervisors' oral and written comments, suggestions, experience sharing and the author's immediate reflection and response to the comments.

Table 3.2. (Continued)

Activity	*Experiences and learning outcomes*
	Benefits from supervisor observation: The author learned 1. To rethink the general principle of supervision in PBL environment and individual specific roles of acting as a supervisor in dealing with issues of diversity. 2. A lot of specific supervision techniques in the communication with students. These techniques can be employed in situations such as asking questions, analysing problems, making plans, and giving suggestions, etc. 3. Some more practical issues to be dealt with in the future. The issues mainly derived from two aspects: one regarded the shift of professional identity from "a researcher in PBL" to "a staff member in PBL" involving more efforts in filling in the gaps between theoretical understanding of PBL and practical teaching experiences in PBL. The other was concerned with how to break the barriers created by previous learning and teaching experience in China when teaching in PBL environment. 4. Self-reflection is a tool for improving oneself by asking for supervisors' comments and reflecting on oneself.
New Problems Reflected	1. As a student project supervisor, how to enact the role of facilitation instead of direct teaching? 2. How to improve communication skills in order to construct a more meaningful discussion by leaving more spaces for students?

DISCUSSION

As our research question indicates, the discussion will mainly focus on how the teaching portfolio helps a new teaching staff member to improve reflective learning ability and develop co-creation teaching value in a PBL environment. Based on the evidence shown in the previous section and some quotes from the teaching portfolio, the discussion will pursue the following themes: (1) self-enhancement by reflective teaching experience and (2) developing co-creation value by conversations with self.

Self-Enhancement by Reflective Teaching

The case study in this chapter shows that, unlike traditional assessments such as multiple choice questions which measure factual knowledge and decontextualized issues, the portfolio aims to gauge complex intellectual capabilities (Ng, 2010) and, in particular, to achieve an individual assessment by highlighting contextual issues. A portfolio captures evidence of an individual's experiences in different forms, as a record that documents development. Completing the portfolio over time allows for multiple attempts and opportunities, revision and reflection, making it possible to address multiple tasks and use many forms of data entry. So the portfolio offers the opportunity to continue further professional development and to develop a career log (Pitts, 2010). The author explicitly recognised this after participating in the first workshop when the portfolio method was introduced:

> As introduced in the workshop, by working with a teaching portfolio I will attain skills to describe, assess, and reflect on issues of teaching and student project supervision. The portfolio represents a way of documenting growing teaching practice and allows for reflection on theory learned from the lectures and workshops in the university pedagogy programme. The portfolio process also involves the support of two supervisors in attaining the expected competencies.

Experience plays a central role in learning through reflection, as Table 3.2 shows, and the author benefited greatly from the experience of participating in workshops and of supervisor observation. By "experience" we mean something that is lived, felt, reconstructed, reinterpreted, and understood. To look into the process of development, the teaching portfolio in this case provides opportunities for a self-directed learning process. As Ghaye (2010) described, the practice of reflection is an exploratory, purposeful, creative pursuit for better knowledge and understanding. Once achieved, we then have to make a decision about how to put this new knowledge and understanding to good use. Reflective behaviour involves the practitioner investigating the seeking of insights into her practice. It accepts the subjectivity of data and interpretations, and focuses on individual insights and development. It allows individuals to define who and where they are, and to take stock of their professional positions (Pitts, 2010). It drives the self-motivation that is a force causing a person to act in order to achieve a goal, and then to sustain that action until successful (Ghaye, 2010).

Self-Enhancement by Reflective Teaching

"Problem setting", encouraging the practitioner to identify her own strengths and weaknesses in her professional practice, often stimulates motivation (Splid & Qvist, 2013). It requires the positivity that is linked with self-regard and job satisfaction (Ghaye, 2010). In other words, the individual's growth is a process of self-understanding in her context. For example, in Table 3.2, in order to formulate the practical teaching issues at AAU, the author was first asked to develop a teaching CV, based on which she could figure out the capability gaps, as stated in the following lines:

> The main challenge is the gaps in knowledge and experiences between the Chinese and the Danish educational systems. Therefore, the challenge is a barrier to effectively preparing knowledge for the lecture and to the problems or questions proposed in the lecture. In some cases, it is also a barrier to engaging in teaching contexts, such as open group discussions.

Then, based on the above challenges, the author made an action plan responding to how to overcome cross-cultural issues in her teaching practice, as shown in Table 3.2. So the guided reflection is a process of self-enquiry to enable the practitioner to achieve desirable and effective practice within a reflective spiral of being and becoming (Ghaye, 2010). This is also a process of shaping one's identity. As Wenger (1998) described, identity is about how learning changes who we are and creates personal histories of becoming in the context of our communities; it is a trajectory in time that incorporates both past and future into the meaning of the present. This also involves "identification" which means an individual need to provide experiences and material for building identity through an investment of the self in relations of association and differentiation. This, too. may be seen in Table 3.2: the author reflected on the shift of her professional identity from "a researcher in PBL" to "a staff member in PBL" involving more efforts in filling in the gaps between theoretical understanding about PBL and practical teaching experiences in PBL. For the author, learning, therefore, is the process of transforming experience into knowledge, skills, attitudes and values, and as such has been described as cycles by Kolb and Fry (1975). Concrete experience, observations and reflections, formulation of abstract concepts and generalisations, and the testing of implications in new situations are the stations around the cycle (Kolb & Fry, 1975). The following lines underpin such a cycle, when the author described how she learned a tool for collaborating with supervisors by reflection:

> The flow of collaboration with supervisors should be: (invitation before) observation for comments – discussion of problems (found in observation) – reflection of problem solving – improvement in practice – observation for new comments – discussion of new problems – reflection of problem solving – improvement in practice.

This also indicates that the process of writing a teaching portfolio represents a form of "conversation with self" that is similar to a discussion with another person and enhances reflective capability (Pitts, 2010); it is also a process of building dialogues with oneself as well as with others, from which process the meaning of learning is co-created. As Ghaye (2010) argued, reflective practice needs to be understood as a discourse. A discourse can be understood as a set of meanings, statements, stories, and so on, which produce a particular version of events. The reflective discourse, or conversation, is at the heart of the improvement process. It demonstrates *par excellence* the process of continuing professional development and provides a means of displaying this to another person, while the use of qualitative assessment approaches that are open and capable of being validated allows judgments to be made about the writer (Pitts, 2010). As Kleowski (2004) suggested, teaching portfolios might engender individual reflection and improve practice, however, their value in promoting teaching effectiveness is more likely to dramatically increase when they serve as the focal point for conversations with colleagues about teaching. So teaching portfolios may be important as a professional development activity through peer review. Teachers reflect on the evaluation of their own teaching practice and they are also able to engage in dialogue with others, which helps to highlight the complexity and diversity of those teaching and learning practices, as the author described in the following passage:

> This supervisor meeting gave me very good comments that indicated I made progress after the first teaching observation. I was also given detailed suggestions for improving my communication skills with students. The suggestions were about ways of questioning, commenting, and asking for feedback from students. This led to my further reflection: how to give students more help to analyse their problems in seeking for answers by themselves, rather than only provide supervision suggestions directly? I should be more aware of asking open questions by learning more linguistic techniques. I can also learn from the experiences of other senior teachers.

As Pamaswamy and Ozcan (2014) suggested, "dialogue" is a principle of enabling co-creation experience. It is about the shared communication and learning among equals. It entails empathic understanding built around experiencing and recognising the emotional, social, and cultural background of experiences. It calls for a deep understanding of individual experience perspective, which cannot be achieved without active conversation and sharing views about what is meaningful to individuals. Nurturing active dialogue is about engaging individuals on their terms and learning along with them as everyone evolves in their needs and experiences of value. This can also be interpreted by the concept of "shared repertoire" described by Wenger (1998), which means a community of practice including routines, words, tools, ways of doing things, stories, gestures, symbols, genres, actions, or concepts that the community has produced or adopted in the course of its experience, and which have become part of its practice. Furthermore, the repertoire combines both reificative and participative aspects. It includes the discourse by which members create meaningful statements about the world, as well as the styles by which they express their forms of membership and their identities as members. In professional development, and particularly in the context of becoming a qualified teacher, as Ghaye (2010) suggested, reflective conversations, seen as an act of collaborative meaning-making, are important educational activities. They should be forward-looking, and be conversations of both possibility and hope, which means they contain not only what was thought and done, but also what might be or "that which is not yet". However, the particular context of becoming reflective teachers should be emphasised, as the following comments were given after one supervisor observation of the author:

> This student is in a "frustration phase" of the project, which is not uncommon (in project supervision at AAU). Generally in this situation (in the PBL environment at AAU), there are a few tasks facing the supervisor: (1) How to help students solve the problem and move on with the project? (2) How to maximise student learning in this situation by helping them figure out things on their own? These are the tasks and challenges for a supervisor. It is important and comparatively easy to reach the first goal (finding a way to move on). Reaching the second goal is not always easy. Very often the supervisor can see things more clearly and with more structure than the student, and it can be tempting to tell them straight out how the supervisor sees it, while not always does the student see that clearly. This can be challenging for the communication setting.

It should be noticed that at AAU, the PBL model is an umbrella covering both Problem-based and Project-organised learning approaches. The projects are initiated through contextualised problem areas – situations, potentials, values or problematic instances – wherein lies the basis for posing and identifying (documenting) delimited, yet still complex, problems to be solved or explained. Therefore, to face the uncertainty of project work together with students is one of biggest of challenges for project supervisors, when a supervisor serves as a methodological resource and as an external validator of the learning objectives (Moon, 2004). By developing the teaching portfolio, collaboration with at least one other person will enhance development and provide feedback through assisted reflection and discussion. Similarly, when an external judgement becomes necessary, discussions with and between the assessors are opportunities for explanation, clarification and context setting (Pitts, 2010). Through the communication, exploration, challenge and justification of the teacher's "lived experience", shifts in perspective, attitude and values may arise in the context of co-created curriculum models (Ghaye, 2010).

To summarise the above discussion of our case study, we observe at least two ways in which the author benefited from her experience of developing the teaching portfolio: (1) a teaching portfolio can be regarded as a means of self-enhancement through guided reflection on teaching experiences, which is helpful in shaping one's professional identity as a reflective teacher in a PBL environment; and (2) a teaching portfolio can also be a way of building dialogues, in order to develop co-creation as a core value in PBL learning environments, that involves reflective conversations of a teacher with himself/herself, between teacher and students, and between teacher and colleagues.

CONCLUSION

Learning is always affected by its context, by the manner in which understandings have been constructed in past social situations and by how learning is expressed (e.g., in speech/written conventions/in action, etc. there are social conventions governing these) (Moon, 2004). Meanwhile, education is value-laden practice. Values help those involved in teaching and learning to make decisions on how to proceed. Evidence helps educators to make wise and principled decisions. Confident and competent teaching requires one to reflect systematically and rigorously on evidence derived from practice. Reflective teaching and learning, then, is evidence-based (Ghaye, 2010). In this sense, the development of teaching portfolios particularly links teaching, evidence and reflection, and it is about a tool of developing the engagement platform in a co-created curriculum model, such as PBL. The portfolio itself is an evidence of self-improvement that can be seen to be a meaning-making process, as it is linked to the idea of interpretation of reality. In other words, it is about the process of developing self-knowledge, the ability to "see" through teaching and learning situations and understand the meaning of what is happening in particular PBL contexts. For the new teaching member in PBL, engaging in such a process helps to establish the improvement agenda for integrating herself into the PBL community. This is also a co-creative process between senior and new staff that involves joint creation of the values of the learning and teaching of PBL. Through becoming reflective teachers, new staff members can try to determine, individually and collectively, what has been learnt from the enquiry process, the consequences of the intervention, and the need to re-formulate the necessary teaching concerns. However, teaching is always a complex, multifaceted activity. As the new teacher's challenges of communication issues with PBL students discussed in the case show, the design of the teaching portfolios should focus more on how to accurately portray the complexity, depth and scope of teaching and learning in PBL. This is undoubtedly a challenge for researchers working on staff development and professional learning programmes in PBL, which is also a valuable topic to be explored further in the future.

REFERENCES

Artze, A. F., Armour-Thomas, E., Curcio, F. R., & Gurl, T. J. (2007). *Becoming a reflective mathematics teacher: A guide for observations and self-assessment.* London: Routledge.

Bovill, C. (2014). An investigation of co-created curricula within higher education in the UK, Ireland and the USA. *Innovations in Education and Teaching International, 51*(1), 15–25.

Dolmans, D. H. J. M., Wolfhagen, I. H. A. P., van der Vleuten, C. P. M., & Wijnen, W. H. F. W. (2001). Solving problems with group work in problem-based learning: Hold on to the philosophy. *Medical Education, 35*, 884–889.

Ghaye, T. (2010). *Teaching and learning through reflective practice: A practical guide for positive action.* London: Routledge.

Gordon, J. (2003). Assessing students' personal and professional development using portfolios and interviews. *Medical Education, 37*, 335–340.

Hmelo-Silver, C. E. (2004). Problem-based learning: What and how do students learn? *Educational Psychology Review, 16*(3), 235–266.

Illeris, K. (2007). *How we learn: Learning and non-learning in school and beyond.* London: Routledge.

Klwnowski, V. (2004). *Developing portfolios for learning and assessment: Processes and principles.* London: Routledge.

Kolb, D., & Fry, R. (1975). Towards an applied theory of experiential learning. In C. Cooper (Ed.), *Theories of group practices.* London: John Wiley and Sons.

Lonka, K., Slotte, V., Halttunen, M., Kurki, T., Tiitinen, A., Vaara, L., & Paavonen, J. (2001). Portfolios as a learning tool in obstetrics and gynaecology undergraduate training. *Medical Education, 35*, 1125–1130.
Michelson, E., & Mandell, A. (2004). *Portfolio development and the assessment of prior learning: Perspectives, models, and practices.* Virginia, VA: Sterling.
Moon, J. A. (2004) *A handbook of reflective and experiential learning: Theory and practice.* London: Routledge.
Ng, C. K. C. (2010). Portfolios: An affordable and effective means to pursue lifelong learning. In P. C. Margaret (Ed.), *Handbook of lifelong learning developments* (pp. 347–360). USA: Nova Science Publishers, Inc.
Pitts, J. (2010). Portfolios, personal development and reflective practice. In T. Swanwick (Ed.), *Understanding medical education: Evidence, theory and practice* (pp. 99–110). London: Willey-Blackwell.
Poikela, S., Vuoskoski, P., & Kärnä, M. (2009). Developing creative learning environments. In O. S. Tan (Ed.), *Problem-based learning and creativity* (pp. 67–85). Singapore: Cengage Learning Asia Pvt Ltd.
Porath, M., & Jordan, E. (2009). Problem-based learning communities: Using the social environment to support creativity. In O. S. Tan (Ed.), *Problem-based learning and creativity* (pp. 51–66). Singapore: Cengage Learning Asia Pvt Ltd.
Ramaswamy, V., & Ozcan, K. (2014). *The co-creation paradigm.* Stanford, CA: Stanford University Press.
Splid, C. M., & Qvist, P. (2013). The aalborg model and management by objectives and resources: A theoretical frame. In L. Krogh & A. A. Jensen (Eds.), *Visions, challenges, and strategies: PBL principles and methodologies in a danish and global perspectives* (pp. 87–102). Aalborg: Aalborg University Press.
Weber, M. (1922). Die protestantische Ethik und der Geist des Kapitalismus. In. M. Weber (Ed.), *Gesammelte Aufsätze zur Religionssoziologie* (Vol. 1, pp. 17–206). Tübingen: Mohr Siebeck.
Weddle, D. O., Himburg, S. P., Collins, N., & Lewis, R. (2002). The professional development portfolio process: Setting goals for credentialing. *Journal of the American Dietetic Association, 102*(10), 1439–1444.
Wenger, E. (1998). *Communities of practice: Learning, meaning, and identity.* Cambridge: Cambridge University Press.
Zhou, C., Otrel-Cass, K., & Børsen, T. (2015). Integrating ethics into engineering education. In S. S. Sethy (Ed.), *Contemporary ethical issues in engineering* (pp. 159–173). USA: IGI global.

Chunfang Zhou
Department of Learning and Philosophy, and
Department of Planning
Aalborg University

Ole Ravn
Department of Learning and Philosophy
Aalborg University

Xiangyun Du
Department of Learning and Philosophy
Aalborg University

CLAUS SPRINGBORG

4. TEACHING CO-CREATION IN HIGHER EDUCATION THROUGH DANCE EXERCISES

INTRODUCTION

Higher education today needs to teach skills relevant to the world of today. In recent years, the ability to co-create has been seen as increasingly important due to the growing complexity of our interconnected and quickly changing world (Leclercq, Hammedi, & Poncin, 2016; Nahi, 2016; Prahalad & Ramaswamy, 2004). Whereas co-creation skills, thus, may be valuable to teach at any level of education, they seem indispensable at the level of higher education.

In this chapter, I argue that exercises from improvised couples dance (exemplified by tango exercises) (Biehl-Missal & Springborg, 2015; Springborg & Sutherland, 2014, 2015) are useful to give students a concrete, embodied ground from which they can develop general co-creation skills applicable in many different contexts.

THE CHALLENGES OF TEACHING CO-CREATION SKILLS IN HIGHER EDUCATION INSTITUTIONS

General co-creation skills are not easy to teach. To better understand the challenges related to teaching co-creation skills in higher education (and elsewhere), I will first look at teaching co-creation skills from two related perspectives: deutero-learning (Bateson, 1972a) and embodied cognitive metaphors (Lakoff, 2012; Springborg, 2015). After defining some important challenges in teaching co-creation skills, I will suggest that these challenges can be met by using exercises from improvised couples dance. I illustrate this by showing how such exercises can be used to teach four concrete co-creation skills (voicing, listening, respecting, and suspending) described by Isaac Williams (Isaacs, 1999).

From the perspective of deutero-learning, teaching co-creation can be seen as a matter of teaching specific ways of organising experience – or as Bateson formulates it: "habits of punctuating the stream of experience" (Bateson, 1972b, p. 129). According to Bateson, such habits are created when individuals develop more general ways of organising their experience, which support the responses fitting for the learning context. In this sense, the habits developed reflect the structure of the learning contexts to which the individual is exposed. For example, if the learning context is one where a teacher asks questions and the students have to come up with

T. Chemi & L. Krogh (Eds.), Co-Creation in Higher Education, 49–65.

the right answers, the students will not only learn those answers but will also learn the habit of categorising claims in terms of right or wrong – instead of, for example, in terms of usefulness or reflexive depth. I will unfold this perspective in the next section.

From the perspective of embodied cognition, our abstract cognition is fundamentally body-based. Therefore, an important element of teaching co-creation skills is providing concrete, sensory experiences, which can work as the body-based ground from which students can develop such co-creation skills. Based on this perspective, I will argue for the importance of considering which sensory-motor experiences students have within the learning context. I will discuss this perspective in the second section below.

Co-creation refers to a broad range of practices practiced in a broad range of contexts. The co-creators may include employees from different departments within an organisation, people from other organisations, customers, suppliers, public organisations, competitors and other social groups who are affected by the activities of the organisation (Leclercq et al., 2016; Prahalad & Ramaswamy, 2004). Similarly, the purpose of engaging in co-creation can vary from organisations wishing to gain legitimacy in and access to social groups, wishing to create cost-effective products and/or new business models, seeking to create social and environmental value, or seeking to empower marginalised social groups (Nahi, 2016, p. 9).

This raises the question of whether it makes sense to talk about co-creation skills independent of the context in which such skills are practiced. We can, for example, imagine a person who is skilled at co-creating with the customers of his company to create more cost-effective products or services. We can then ask, whether the co-creation skills this person has developed in the context of co-creation with the customers will also make him good at co-creating with politicians and minorities in society with the purpose of empowering such minorities. In this example, we may argue that some skills probably are specific to the context. For instance, the ability to relate customers' wishes to production costs may be useful in the first context but not the second. However, the skill of suspending one's own worldview in order to understand other peoples' worldviews may be equally useful in both contexts. Thus, in this chapter, I will work from the assumption that it makes sense to talk about certain *general* co-creation skills, which can be applied in a broad range of contexts.

Co-creation can be defined as "interaction that integrates different partners' knowledge and capabilities" (Nahi, 2016, p. 2). Thus general co-creation skills are skills that enable such creative interaction and integration of knowledge and capabilities of diverse groups of people. Different authors have proposed different lists of co-creation skills, which these authors claim are useful or even necessary to cultivate for the co-creation efforts to succeed. In this chapter, I will focus on William Isaacs' four skills: voicing, listening, respecting, and suspending, which Isaacs sees as fundamental in learning "the art of thinking together" (Isaacs, 1999), i.e. in co-creating ideas. I will describe these four skills in detail in the third section below. In that section, I will also illustrate how the use of dance exercises can provide concrete, embodied, sensory experiences, which are a particularly suitable body-based ground for developing these general co-creation skills.

I now turn to look at what the perspectives of deutero-learning and Embodied Cognitive Metaphor theory may tell us about the challenges of teaching general co-creation skills.

CO-CREATION SKILLS AS THE ORGANISATION OF EXPERIENCE

According to Bateson it is important to distinguish between different levels of learning. When a rat, through a number of experiments, learns that it will find food behind the red door and not the blue door, it also learns that whether or not it finds food depends on its own action. In contrast, a rat that is consistently punished regardless of its actions learns that its actions do not matter – a phenomenon often referred to as "learned helplessness" (Seligman, 1975). In other words, an important part of learning consists of individuals adopting more general ways of organising their experience, which support the responses fitting for the learning context.

When looking at the challenge of teaching co-creation in higher education from this perspective, one may ask whether the structure of the learning context (e.g. the way people interact and the structure of the class) generates habits of punctuating experience, which are supportive of the aim of teaching co-creation skills. In the last section, I will suggest how the use of dance exercises can provide a structure to the learning context, which is useful for the purpose of teaching co-creation skills.

To unpack this more fully, I will first describe Bateson's work on deutero-learning in some detail.

Bateson introduced the concept deutero-learning. He sometimes referred to it as "learning 2" or "learning to learn". This concept has been very influential. It is, for example, the foundation for Argyris and Schön's popular concept of double-loop learning.

Bateson developed a framework of "The Logical Categories of Learning and Communication" (Bateson, 1972b, pp. 205–224) by applying Bertrand Russell's theory of logical types to the phenomenon of learning. The basic notion of Russell's theory is that to avoid paradox one needs to distinguish between classes and members of such classes. Applied to learning, this means that there are a number of levels of learning, which must be clearly distinguished between in order to avoid paradoxes. Bateson distinguishes between 5 levels of learning. Deutero-learning is the third of these. To better understand deutero-learning, it is useful to have a quick overview of the different levels of learning.

First, there is a kind of learning where an organism acts in response to a stimulus – without ever changing this response. This kind of learning occurs when an organism has already learned to react in a particular way to a particular stimulus and will keep doing so without fail. One may learn what time it is from looking at a watch and you will always learn the same time from the same position of the hands. Similarly, once you have learned to do maths correctly, you will always respond with the same answer to the same arithmetic problem. This form of learning is so basic, that one may not even think about it as a form of learning.

Bateson defines the next level of learning, learning 1, as "changes in learning 0". These are cases, where an organism responds differently when exposed to the same stimulus repeatedly. This could, for example, be the classical trial and error learning, where an organism tries to improve the way it responds to a particular stimulus. If the first response to a stimulus does not produce a desired result the organism may try different responses from its repertoire of responses until a satisfactory outcome is achieved. One might think of a dolphin in a show, which tries to get fish when it sees the caretaker (stimulus) by performing all the jumps and flips it knows (different responses). Other examples of learning 1 include situations where the organism's response to a particular stimulus changes because (1) this stimulus becomes associated with another stimulus, which causes physiological response (classical conditioning). For example, dogs begin to salivate at the sound of a bell, because the sound of the bell becomes associated with food; (2) the response changes because the stimulus becomes a sign of possible reward or punishment (operant conditioning). For example, a dog jumps at the sound of a buzzer, because this sound becomes associated with the floor becoming electrified; (3) the stimulus is repeated so often that the organism stops responding to it at all (habituation). For example, a person may react to a loud sound, but if the loud sound is repeated often enough, the person may even stop noticing it at all. Learning 1, thus, contains many of the phenomena we normally think of as learning.

Just as Bateson defines learning 1 as "changes in learning 0", he defines learning 2 (deutero-learning) as "changes in learning 1", or changes in the organism's approach to trial and error. It could, for example, be a change in the organism's repertoire of responses. It could also be a change in the way the organism decides on how to change its response in order to achieve a more satisfactory outcome. For example, an organism could initially simply try all responses in its repertoire one by one. An example of deutero-learning would be if this organism changed its approach to selecting responses to the approach of analysing the result of one response and basing the choice of the next response on this analysis, or to the approach of repeatedly trying the same response with increased intensity. Bateson relates a story of a dolphin, which performed various tricks in shows in order to get fish. One day, the dolphin realised that the trainer was interested not merely in the tricks this dolphin already knew, but in new tricks. It then changed its strategy from trying out different tricks to the strategy of creating new types of tricks. In one show, it produced an outstanding number of new tricks – including a number of moves never before seen in dolphins.

Learning 3 is a change in learning 2. Bateson sees this as extremely rare. And learning 4 (a change in learning 3) he believes never occurs in any living organism on the planet.

Bateson developed the concept of deutero-learning to explain a phenomenon that had been observed in learning experiments like rote learning. In these experiments the participants had to memorise series of nonsense words and it was observed that participants who repeatedly engaged in these experiments began to learn these series faster and faster even when there were no repeated words. The participants simply acquired the general skill of learning series of nonsense words.

Based on this fact, Bateson suggested that whenever an individual learns, not only does he learn some specific content, such as a string of nonsense words, but he also learns to organise his experience in ways that support the kind of actions, which help him deal with this particular kind of learning context.

An interesting consequence of this is that individuals will often approach new learning situations as if they were similar to the ones previously encountered. However, sometimes the ways of organising our experience, which were useful in the learning contexts previously encountered, will not support us in dealing with the new learning contexts.

As a simple illustration of this, you can imagine a dog growing up in a psychological laboratory where they work with conditioned response experiments. Certain stimuli will signal the arrival of food and the dog will learn to distinguish between many different stimuli, learning which of these are irrelevant and which mean that it should get ready to eat. After a few years the dog is transferred to another laboratory where they work with shaping behaviour through patterns of reinforcement. Here the dog has to learn which behaviours it has to perform in order to get food. But the dog has learned to look for signs telling it that food is on its way and if it keeps holding on to this way of organising its experience, it may accidentally perform the actions which are reinforced with food, but every time this happens, it will try to understand what the stimuli was that signalled the arrival of food – not noticing that it had to do with its own actions.

As another example, one could mention the commonly known phenomenon that, as managers rise through an organisation, they must several times profoundly change their ideas about managing. Moving from team leader or frontline managing to higher management positions, they need to be able to stop trying to solve problems and start concerning themselves with selecting which problems should be solved when. As they move to even higher levels of management, they need to stop looking for the right thing to do and learn to navigate in situations where they longer have (even approximately) clear-cut answers. Thus, failing to transform their habits of punctuating experience can mean failing to hold higher managerial positions.

In short, whenever we learn to *do* something, we also learn to organise our experience in particular ways, which support us in dealing with the context in which this learning takes place. We learn what parts of our experience are important and what parts are not important. We learn to select sequences of experience from that vast flood of experience we are exposed to every moment. Over time these ways of organising experience become habits operating seamlessly in the background, and it can be difficult to notice them or to imagine that we could organise our experience differently.

If we, as previously suggested, understand co-creation as interactions, which integrate different partners' knowledge and capabilities, it is fair to say that co-creation is a learning context. The above then suggests that co-creation skills can be supported by certain ways of organising experience, which one can develop through repeated exposure to this particular kind of learning context, where diverse partners are brought together with the aim of integrating their knowledge and capabilities. It also suggests that when teaching co-creation, we must think carefully about the structure of the learning context in which we teach co-creation.

In today's higher education, we often find learning contexts consisting of lectures, tests, predefined intended learning objectives (ILOs), grades, and certificates. It is worth considering how well the ways of organising experience that students acquire through dealing with such learning contexts will support the student in dealing with the learning context of co-creation. On this basis, one could argue for a thorough restructuring of the learning contexts provided by higher education. However, the goal of this chapter is to show how less drastic measures may also be useful – in this case the inclusion of dance exercises.

EMBODYING CO-CREATION

Several new theories in the area of embodied cognition hold that cognition is fundamentally grounded in sensory-motor experiences. In other words, our understanding of abstract concepts, such as legitimacy or access to social groups or social and environmental value or empowerment and marginalisation, are grounded in concrete, body-based experiences. Thus, if two people ground their understanding of the concept of value in two different body-based experiences, they are in effect talking about two different concepts and, as a consequence, their thinking about value and their approaches to working with value creation may differ radically.

This suggests that that it is important to consider which bodily experiences students are introduced to as part of teaching them co-creation in higher education. In the last section, I will illustrate how dance exercises can be used to give students a number of bodily sensory-motor experiences, which provide a useful ground for learning about more abstract co-creation skills.

To unpack this perspective, I will go over some relevant research within the field of embodied cognition.

Embodied Cognition

From the early 90's researchers have increasingly proposed various claims about the embodied nature of cognition. It is possible to distinguish between six such claims "(1) cognition is situated; (2) cognition is time-pressured; (3) we off-load cognitive work onto the environment; (4) the environment is part of the cognitive system; (5) cognition is for action; (6) off-line cognition is body-based" (Wilson, 2002, p. 625). The most far-reaching and the best documented of these claims is the last one (Wilson, 2002, p. 625). This claim is also particularly relevant when it comes to understanding how and why co-creation skills can be taught through the bodily experiences of improvised couples dance.

To understand how off-line cognition can be body-based, one can think of learning to count and do simple arithmetic using one's fingers. In the beginning one may hold out the number of fingers corresponding to different numbers. However, with practice such movements may become smaller and smaller until they are reduced to a mere priming of the motoric systems responsible for moving fingers. Thus, the physical aspect becomes completely invisible to an outside observer. The claim that off-line cognition is body-based simply means that many of the cognitive processes we would normally think of as abstract are, in fact, based on the body, in a similar fashion as counting on the fingers without actually moving them. The neurological systems originally developed to serve the function of moving fingers get appropriated for the use of counting and arithmetic. This brings a new view of cognition where the neurological systems developed for perception and movement (the sensory-motor systems) in general can be decoupled from the input and output organs and used for abstract thinking. Empirical evidence for this claim has been mounting in several fields of study over at least the last 25 years. For reviews see Wilson (2002), Rohrer (2007), Niedenthal et al. (2005), and Barsalou (2008).

Cognitive Metaphor Theory

One field in which the body-based nature of abstract concepts has been explored is Cognitive Metaphor Theory. In 1980, Lakoff and Johnson used evidence from the field of linguistics to propose that our understanding is metaphorical in nature (Lakoff & Johnson, 1980). They showed how commonly-used metaphorical expressions form clusters, which can be seen to indicate that we understand one domain of experience (a target domain) in terms of another domain (a source domain). For example, there are a number of commonly-used expressions, which draw on terminology from warfare to describe argumentation. Such expressions include: to shoot down someone else's arguments, to defend one's claims, to win or lose arguments, to deliver a critique that is right on target, etc. Thus, one target domain (here argumentation) is understood in terms of a source domain (here warfare) creating the conceptual metaphor: argumentation is war.

The use of cognitive metaphors is one of the ways in which we organise experience. One effect of this is that the use of different conceptual source domains for the same conceptual target domain will highlight different aspects of this target domain, whilst hiding other aspects. Thus, using different conceptual source domains will organise our experience of the conceptual target domain in different ways. For example, argumentation could also be seen as a collaborative search for truth as in the Socratic cooperative argumentative dialogue. However, when one sees argumentation as warfare, the collaborative aspect of argumentation is hidden.

That conceptual metaphors highlight certain aspects of the target domain and hide other aspects opens the possibility of using several different conceptual metaphors for one particular target domain to get a fuller view of this target domain. Each cognitive metaphor works as a different vantage point from which we can look at a particular phenomenon. For example, in his famous book *Images of Organizations* (Morgan, 2006), Gareth Morgan shows how organisations (the target domain of interest) have been understood through a number of conceptual metaphors, such as, organisations are machines, organisations are organisms, organisations are brains, organisations are cultures, etc. Each conceptual metaphor highlights certain important aspects of the phenomenon under investigations, namely organisations. Looking at organisations as if they were machines highlights goals, objectives, plans, and control in organisations. Looking at organisations as if they were organisms highlights the relationship between an organisation and its environment, the survival needs of organisations, and how organisations can be classified as different species. The brain metaphor highlights how organisations can learn, innovate, and be governed by principles of self-organising as opposed to principles of control. The culture metaphor highlights the symbolic significance of actions and artefacts, creation of shared meaning, and social construction of meaning.

If our understanding of any phenomenon is metaphorical in nature, and different conceptual metaphors through which we understand a phenomenon will highlight/ hide different aspects of this phenomenon, then it becomes interesting to select good cognitive metaphors through which we can understand co-creation. Improvised couples dance would be one of many possible source domains we could use for this purpose. And the relevance of using this source domain would be determined by whether or not it reveals important aspects of co-creation in a way which enhances co-creation skills.

Cognitive Metaphor Theory has evolved since the eighties and has increasingly explored the body-based roots of cognitive metaphors. And this provides a stronger argument for the use of dance as a source domain through which we may understand the target domain of co-creation.

Body-Based Cognitive Metaphors

If one domain is understood in terms of another and this other domain is understood in terms of a third, then where would the chain of cognitive metaphors end? Lakoff and Johnson (1980) propose that our metaphorically organised understanding is grounded in structures arising from physical experiences of being a body in a three-dimensional space, such as, centre–periphery, up–down, front–back, etc. To support this claim they refer to the existence of common conceptual metaphors, such as, happy is up, sad is down, importance is central, importance is big, etc.

In 1997, Joseph Grady proposed a distinction between primary and complex cognitive metaphors. This distinction was quickly picked up by Lakoff and Johnson in their book *Philosophy in the Flesh* (Lakoff & Johnson, 1999). Primary cognitive metaphors are cognitive metaphors that are found in different languages throughout the world, across cultures. They are grounded in sensory-motor, body-based experience and, according to Grady, they are formed early in life through universal correlations in human experience.

For example, friendly/hostile attitudes are understood in terms of warmth/cold. Time is understood (with a few exceptions) in terms of either moving forward through a landscape or standing still and having the landscape pass by you from front to back so that the future is in front of us and the past is behind us. Other primary metaphors include: knowing is seeing, understanding is grasping, causes are physical forces, categories are containers, happy is up, and difficulties are burdens.

The existence of primary conceptual metaphors supports the strong claim in embodied cognition, that even our most abstract concepts are grounded in body-based, sensory-motor experiences. Cognitive Metaphor Theory also provides insight into how Bateson's habits of organising experience may be formed, namely by using the sensory experience of the learning context as source domain for understanding the phenomenon of learning.

Sensory Templates

From 2010–2014, I conducted research on different approaches to facilitating managers' learning around organisational problems, which they experienced as both very important and unsolvable (Springborg, 2015). My goal was to explore the effects of identifying and changing the body-based experiences used to understand a particular task. I chose to work with tasks that at the beginning of the research seemed unsolvable to the individual participants, because if the participants at the end of the research could see any kind of solution, this would be a strong argument that something had shifted in the way they saw the problematic situation.

The most important finding from this research was that a work situation can appear as an unsolvable problem when the manager understands it through *one* conceptual metaphor, but as a simple matter that is easily dealt with when the manager understands the situation through *another* conceptual metaphor – in particular, when the source domain of the new cognitive metaphor is grounded in a different body-based experience.

For example, one manager in the research – we can call her Sue – was part of a management team. The team would meet and make decisions together. However, Sue experienced that the other managers would agree on certain decisions when they met, but would do something completely different back in their own departments. Sue found this very frustrating. She had tried for many years to change this state of affairs without success. The situation appeared unsolvable to her. At the start of the research, Sue described the problem as one of making all the managers commit to follow up on the common decisions they had made. She spoke about this as making the managers head in the same direction and pursue the same goals. Listening to her language, it was clear that she structured her experience of the situation in terms of trying to achieve coordinated movement. I gave Sue a camera and asked her to take pictures to illustrate the problem. She took pictures of trains heading in opposite directions, further confirming that her understanding was grounded in primary metaphors such as: goals are physical destinations, purpose is movement through space, woven into the overall conceptual metaphor of this situation is a matter of making people move in a coordinated way towards the same physical destination.

However, during a workshop I facilitated as part of the research, Sue changed the sensory experience she used to structure her understanding of the problematic work situation. Instead of seeing people who did not move in a coordinated way towards the same physical destination, she saw people who had no physical connection. The experience of touching vs. not touching became the sensory experience in which she grounded her understanding of the situation. Once this happened, she changed from seeing the problem as a problem of making people commit to the decisions they made in the team, to seeing it as a problem of how to make the team members form relationships to each other. Seeing this was a great relief to her, because she knew how to do this. She had many methods of making her own employees form relationships, but had just never thought about applying these methods to the management team. The metaphor she had used to structure her understanding of the problem before the research workshop had simply hidden this possibility from her. When I interviewed her one month after the workshop, she had already had some success in achieving better collaboration by focusing on creating relationships, rather than on creating commitment.

This example shows that using one of these sensory experiences (objects moving in coordinated fashion toward the same point in space) as a basic template for the abstract understanding of the situation made the situation appear as an unsolvable problem of creating increased commitment, whereas using another sensory experience (objects touching or not touching) made the situation appear as a – for Sue – much simpler matter of creating relationships between the members of the management team.

The example also shows that sensory experiences can function as fundamental structures or templates upon which abstract understanding of a situation can be organised. In the example, Sue changed from the fundamental organising principle of entities moving through space towards either the same physical destination or different physical destinations, to the fundamental organising principle of objects either touching or not touching. These experiences are the kind of body-based, sensory-motor experiences in which Lakoff and Johnson proposed that all our understanding is fundamentally grounded. Changing the sensory experiences we use as a fundamental structural template upon which we model our abstract understanding of a situation can, thus, be seen as a means of changing the way we punctuate the continuous stream of experience.

In the example above, both conceptual metaphors were grounded in fairly common sensory experiences. However, there is nothing to prevent one from using sensory experiences that are less common, as sensory templates upon which one may build one's understanding of a situation. Such sensory experiences could, for example, be experiences developed through various forms of physical practice, for example, improvised couples dance. In the next section, I will describe what kind of sensory experiences one can get through practicing improvised couples dance and suggest that these sensory experiences are particularly suitable as sensory templates for developing four general co-creation skills.

USING IMPROVISED COUPLES DANCE TO LEARN CO-CREATION SKILLS

Above, I have used the perspectives of deutero-learning and Embodied Cognition to define some important challenges one should consider when teaching general co-creation skills in higher education.

The perspective of deutero-learning reveals the importance of considering whether the structure of the learning context generates habits of punctuating experience, which are supportive of the aim of teaching co-creation skills.

The perspective of Embodied Cognition highlights the importance of considering whether students are introduced to bodily experiences, which form a useful body-based ground for developing general co-creation skills.

In this section, I suggest that engaging in dance exercises can provide a structure to the learning context and a number of bodily sensory-motor experiences, which provide a useful ground for developing general co-creation skills. I illustrate this by looking at the general co-creation skills described by William Isaacs in his book *Dialogue – the art of thinking together* (Isaacs, 1999).

Dialogue

William Isaacs works with facilitating what he calls generative dialogue. Generative dialogue is an example of co-creation, in that the participants co-create new ideas, insights and common understandings through conversation, which in turn form the basis of common action. Isaacs and his colleagues at MIT have worked with facilitating generative dialogue all over the world between groups of people with radically different perspectives and even mutual hostility. They have, for example, led dialogue with management, employees, and union representatives in the UK coalmining industry and with different social groups in post-apartheid South Africa. Thus, Isaacs' work is very much about interaction that integrates different partners' knowledge and capabilities, i.e. co-creation.

In generative dialogue the new ideas, insights and common understandings do not come from any individual participant, but rather emerge from the group. In this way, generative dialogue is different from most everyday conversations. What makes generative dialogue possible is the development of a number of skills in the participants. In generative dialogue everyone listens to others in a respectful way and holds their own views lightly, with a willingness to let them change at any given moment. And from this position, they give voice to what they perceive.

Isaacs distinguishes between four general co-creation skills: listening, suspending, voicing, and respecting. Below, I will briefly describe these four general co-creation skills and look at how each one can be grounded in bodily experiences of participating in improvised couples dance. In particular, I will use tango as an example. In the examples, I will refer to the leader as male and follower as female for the sake of clarity in the description. But obviously woman can lead and men can follow in life, as well as in dance, and when using dance exercises in teaching situations, it is important that the leader and follower roles are not related to any specific gender.

Voicing

Every human being has a unique blend of past experience and personality, giving them a unique vantage point from which they look at the world. Voicing is the ability to give voice to what you can see from your particular vantage point. It is letting other people know what seems true and important to you at any given moment. There can be many reasons for not doing this, from self-doubt and fear of being attacked or humiliated, to worry about hurting others or being seen as too pushy or forceful. Both people who hold back their own voice and people who seem very assertive when speaking their mind may be influenced by such patterns. Voicing is about speaking what is true for you in a direct, clear and simple way – and that is not always simple to do.

In tango we can experience this in a physical form both in the role of the leader and of the follower. Imagine the following basic exercise often used in tango introduction classes. The couple is standing still in a dance embrace. The leader shifts weight from one foot to the other and the follower notices and follows these weight shifts. At some point the leader stops with all his weight on one foot and the follower does the same. When the leader senses that the follower has all her weight on one foot, he has three options. He can take a step forward, backward or to the side of the free leg. When he does this he keeps the embrace firm (but not tense) and pushes the floor with the standing leg to produce a clear direction. When the follower feels the direction, she takes a step that matches the step proposed by the leader.

When taking the step, the leader has to be clear and make the decision about the direction purely out of his own inner feeling. There is no negotiation. The clearer he is, the easier it will be to follow him. Thus, taking the step is a physical equivalent of making a clear personal statement. Similarly, when the follower feels the direction, she will take a step to match what she feels. Thus, the step of the follower is also a clear personal statement about what she perceived. Once the follower takes her step, the leader may need to adjust so that his own step matches the follower's. This is easier to do if the follower is clear when taking her step.

In this way, taking steps is a physical form of making clear statements in both roles. And the clearer the statements are, the easier it is to dance. If these physical statements are not clear, the other partner has nothing clear to relate to and respond to.

In the same way, in co-creation it is good to make clear statements. Even if the statements are later rejected or proven to be false or silly, they still fulfil the function of giving others something clear to respond to – for example by building on it, modifying it, or opposing it.

Thus, the physical experience of taking clear steps together is a good bodily experience from which one may develop one's skill of voicing.

Isaacs writes that, to practice voicing, we can ask: what needs to be said? When we take clear steps in tango, we practice making statements about what we, at the present moment, believe would be a good next step. If we try to decide what step to propose by referring to someone outside ourselves, for example, guessing what our partner would like or what people looking at you would think is impressive, we often become unclear in our statement.

Listening

Listening is often much harder than voicing. Krishnamurti, a teacher who's teaching has had profound influenced on the dialogue method, makes the difficulty of listening clear when he writes:

> If we try to listen we find it extraordinarily difficult, because we are always projecting our opinions and ideas, our prejudices, our background, our inclinations, our impulses; when they dominate, we hardly listen at all to what is being said. In that state there is no value at all. One listens and therefore learns, only in a state of attention, a state of silence, in which this whole background is in abeyance, is quiet; then, it seems to me, it is possible to communicate. (Isaacs, 1999, p. 84)

It may seem natural that part of listening is making sense of what we hear by relating it to our own experience and recognising it as something we already know. But in doing so, we are very active and we easily misconstrue what we hear. If someone arrives late to a meeting and says: "Sorry I'm late", we could hear this sentence as an apology or a disarming act or even as a complaint about excessive punctuality. When we categorise the sentence as a specific kind of act, we project everything we know about such acts onto the sentence and then we are no longer listening. Another example could be when someone proposes an idea, which is similar to another idea we have tried earlier which did not work well. We feel we recognise the idea and then go straight to explaining why this idea won't work without listening to why this particular person came up with the idea at this given moment. It is possible that the one who proposed the idea was in the process of formulating something beyond the idea we previously tried out. John Dewey talks about how we use sensing for recognition and that once we've recognised something, we stop sensing more details – we stop listening (Dewey, 1934).

In the basic tango exercise described above, there is the moment before the step, when both parties are standing on one leg. When one has a stable balance on one leg, the loose leg is free to go anywhere. As long as all the body weight is placed on one leg, the follower does not need to have any fixed ideas about where to go next. In the same way, the leader will often have the full body weight on one leg and if the follower takes a step that is different from what he had in mind (and tried to lead) he has the possibility to simply change the plan. However, the moment weight is shifted to the free leg, this openness is lost.

Paying attention to what the openness in the free leg feels like in the moment before any step is taken provides a bodily experience from which one may develop one's skill of listening. When we listen, we are like the free leg without any weight on it. The moment we hear what we hear as something particular, i.e. we interpret what we hear, we place weight on the free leg and this limits our ability to listen.

In co-creation, we need to give time for people to speak without trying to draw any conclusions. We are like a free leg hovering in suspension, willingly waiting to understand what the other is trying to convey. In co-creation we may even listen to the silence or the gap where nobody knows in this way.

Isaacs writes that to practice listening, we can ask: how does this feel? Standing on one leg, we practice feeling the direction. The moment we try to predict the direction with the mind, we usually go wrong.

Respecting

Respecting refers to the skill of seeing the integrity and coherence of another's position (in particular when you do not agree) and the skill of knowing that you can never fully understand this position (Isaacs, 1999, p. 419). For example, in conversations, it is easy to get the feeling that someone else is saying what they say because they do not understand what you understand and if only the other knew what you know they would come to the same conclusions as you. As another example, think of how leaders often feel that what seems like irrational behaviour from their employees is due to their employees lacking the organisational overview of the leader. They do what they do, because they don't see the big picture. However, employees generally have the advantage of knowing the details of everyday work much more intimately than the leader. Thus, the leader and the employee have two different vantage points and they can, therefore, see different things. Both parties draw conclusions, which have integrity based on their particular vantage point, both parties reach for something truly valuable, even if this is not immediately visible to the other part, and neither party can fully understand the position of the other because they do not have the fullness of the other party's experience. Thus, each party needs to listen to the other.

In tango both leader and follower dance to the same music. However, they may have very different ways of listening to and interpreting this music. Similarly, the movement repertoire of tango is very broad. The different types of movements used in tango have names, such as *barridas, ganchos, colgadas, sacadas, giros*, etc. Not every dancer is equally skilled or comfortable in regard to all possible types of movements. Furthermore, different bodies move differently. Some may be very light and quick. Some like to bring connection by offering resistance in the movements. Some are tall and some are short. Some are expressive and playful and some prefer to move in simple patterns with a lot of intensity.

When dancing with a new partner, one must respect the partner's musicality, movement preferences, dancing style, and body type. Once a dancer told me that she did not mind dancing with partners with very stiff bodies. Instead of seeing this as an obstacle to the dance, she saw it as something she could rely on and as something that opened possibilities not present with other partners.

Isaacs writes that we can practice respecting by asking the question: "How does this fit?" Thus, dancing with different partners and searching for that physical fit provides a sensory experience from which one may develop one's skill of respecting.

Suspending

Suspending is the skill of setting aside the urge to argue particular points of view, regardless of how right they appear, or the urge to pursue particular actions, regardless of how necessary they seem. It is about suspending opinions, preferences, convictions, and certainty. In short, it is the ability to suspend what we think we know and hang out in our ignorance – the empty void where our certainty used to be. This can at first feel scary and/or vulnerable. We may feel defenceless and worry that others may take charge and that our voice will not be heard and what is important to us will not be taken into account. However, suspending is not in contradiction with voicing. When you suspend your knowledge, you do not take away validity of the truth you speak. You do not invite others to overrule you. It simply puts your voice into the right perspective: it is *your* voice. It is what you see to be true from your particular vantage point. Suspending brings openness and through this openness can come immense creative energy.

Because tango is an improvised dance, both leader and follower must constantly be willing to give up any prediction of where the dance is heading and convictions about where the dance should be heading. When doing this, one leaves room for a dance to emerge, which is decided neither by the one nor the other. It is the dance, which emerges in the meeting between two dancers and the music and the broader context like the movements of the other dancers on the floor, the atmosphere in the room, etc. When the improvisation goes well, no single individual is the author – everyone is simply participating and the dance arises from this mutual participation.

The question Isaacs proposes for training suspending is: how does this work? This question encourages us to look at a fuller picture. Simultaneously bringing our bit to the table and relinquishing control of the process of creation. Trusting that the outcome will supersede anything any individual could have imagined by him/herself. Having the experience of dance unfolding on its own, once again, provides a sensory experience from which one may develop one's skill of suspending.

DISCUSSION

Above, I have argued that when teaching co-creation skills in higher education, we need to take into account that part of what students learn in higher education is dealing with the structures of the context in which learning takes place. Thus, we need to consider whether the skills students develop to deal with the learning environment are the kind of skill we wish to teach.

Furthermore, I have argued that when teaching co-creation skills in higher education, we should also take into account which bodily experiences the students are exposed to the teaching context and whether these bodily experiences provide a useful bodily grounding for the various abstract concepts taught.

I have then illustrated how letting the students engage in simple dance exercises can provide a learning context suitable for teaching certain general co-creation skills, namely, voicing, listening, respecting, and suspending.

Of course, this is not the only way to teach these skills and the skills mentioned are obviously not the only important skills needed to become good at co-creating. This chapter can be read both as inspiration for educators and as a more general illustration of a growing conflict between the learning contexts often found in higher education and the kind of subjects institutions of higher education at present need to teach to produce students who are prepared for a society where co-creation skills are needed to thrive.

Questions naturally arise concerning teaching students about co-creation in a learning environment where the majority of bodily experience consists of sitting, speaking and writing and where students ultimately need to convince the teachers to give them grades good enough for them to get a certificate. To deal with such an environment, students may not develop the skill of voicing. Considerations of whether what they say will help them get good grades can easily overrule considerations of what seems true from the students' current vantage point. Similarly, students may not necessarily develop a habit of respecting, when immersed in a setting where the teacher's perspective is ultimately the right one. Suspending would mean to set aside any agenda – including the agenda of doing what needs to be done to pass the course. And listening from the openness created by suspending would also not be encouraged in a learning environment, which emphasises testing.

Of course it is no simple matter to envision new forms of higher education and to question institutionalised practices, which have been useful for decades. However, we need to take a serious look at how such practices may be in conflict with what we wish to teach in higher education. In this chapter, I have proposed that by suspending our beliefs about what higher education should look like and integrating knowledge and capabilities from other domains, such as dance, we may co-create better forms of higher education.

REFERENCES

Barsalou, L. W. (2008). Grounded cognition. *Annual Review of Psychology*, *59*, 617–645.

Bateson, G. (1972a). Social planning and the concept of deutero-learning. In *Steps to an ecology of mind: Collected essays in anthropology, psychiatry, evolution and epistemology* (pp. 127–137). New York, NY: Chandler.

Bateson, G. (1972b). *Steps to an echology of mind*. San Francisco, CA: Chandler Pub. Co.

Biehl-missal, B., & Springborg, C. (2015). Dance, organization, and leadership. *Organizational Aesthetics*, *5*(1), 1–10.

Dewey, J. (1934). *Art as experience*. New York, NY: Capricorn.

Isaacs, W. (1999). *Dialogue and the art of thinking together*. New York, NY: Currency.

Lakoff, G. (2012). Explaining embodied cognition results. *Topics in Cognitive Science*, *4*(4), 773–785.

Lakoff, G., & Johnson, M. (1980). *Metaphors we live by*. Chicago, IL: University of Chicago Press.

Lakoff, G., & Johnson, M. (1999). *Philosophy in the flesh: The embodied mind and its challenge to western thought*. New York, NY: Basic Books.
Leclercq, T., Hammedi, W., & Poncin, I. (2016). Ten years of value co-creation: An integrative review. *Recherche et Applications En Marketing*, *31*(3), 26–60.
Morgan, G. (2006). *Images of organizations*. Thousand Oaks, CA: SAGE Publications Inc.
Nahi, T. (2016). Cocreation at the base of the pyramid: Reviewing and organizing the diverse conceptualizations. *Organization & Environment*, *29*(4).
Niedenthal, P. M., Barsalou, L. W., Winkielman, P., Krauth-Gruber, S., & Ric, F. (2005). Embodiment in attitudes, social perception, and emotion. *Personality and Social Psychology Review*, *9*(3), 184–211.
Prahalad, C. K., & Ramaswamy, V. (2004). Co-creation experiences: The next practice in value creation. *Journal of Interactive Marketing*, *18*(3), 5–14.
Rohrer, T. (2007). The body in space: Embodiment, experientialism and linguistic conceptualization. In T. Ziemke, J. Zlatev, & R. M. Frank (Eds.), *Body, language and mind volume 1: Embodiment* (pp. 339–378). Berlin, NY: Mouton de Gruyter.
Sandberg, J. (2000). Understanding human competence at work: An interpretative approach. *Academy of Management Journal*, *43*(1), 9–25.
Seligman, M. E. P. (1975). *Helplessness: Depression, development and death*. New York, NY: W H Freeman.
Springborg, C. (2015). *Art-based methods in management education*. Cranfield University.
Springborg, C., & Sutherland, I. (2014). Flying blind? In S. S. Taylor & D. Ladkin (Eds.), *The physicality of leadership: Gesture, entanglement, taboo, possibilities*. Bingley, UK: Emerald Books.
Springborg, C., & Sutherland, I. (2015). Teaching MBAs aesthetic agency through dance. *Organizational Aesthetics*, *5*(1), 94–113.
Wilson, M. (2002). Six views of embodied cognition. *Psychonomic Bulletin & Review*, *9*(4), 625–636.

Claus Springborg
CoCreation
Denmark

OLE RAVN

5. CO-CREATION IN PBL PROJECT WORK

When searching among research papers using the terms "co-creation" and "higher education" you are very likely to stumble upon insights about the marketisation of education (see for example Fagerstrøm & Ghinea, 2013) or the "value co-creation" generated by integrating students' assessment feedback on teaching in order to develop better teaching approaches (see for example Díaz-Méndez et al., 2012). These marketing and assessment connotations fill the concept of co-creation with debates about the aim of drawing on students' experiences in higher education teaching and sometimes in the sense of treating students as a special type of customer.

The concept of co-creation is about how students and teachers can co-create and produce value together in different ways. But assessment and marketing – however important they may be – are not the only places where educators can co-create with students. Co-creation between students and teachers for learning and knowledge production goes on all the time as a part of the many types of learning settings in higher education.

Here, the idea is to relate the notion of co-creation to the particular situation in higher education teaching and learning where teaching takes the form of supervision of a group of students, who produce a project report over a fairly long period of time. In this scenario, the teaching process by the supervisor and the learning processes of the students are closely entangled in a co-creative process.

It is characteristic of this type of teaching scenario that the content of the teaching is developed continuously during meetings with the students and as a function of the specific problematics students bring into the teaching and learning situation. And the scenario for the students, at the same time, entails that the students' learning processes and knowledge production are shaped and formed in a co-creative process fuelled by their own and the supervisor's contributions.

Such processes can be imagined to occur under many different types of supervision circumstances but in this chapter the setting is limited to the Problem Based Learning (PBL) model where the teacher takes on the role of a supervisor for a small group of students who have the task of writing a problem-oriented project report together.

In the PBL model a project report is the common end product and the processes undertaken in developing this report as a final outcome have many dimensions. For example, one dimension is the complex cooperation and collaboration among students in the project group and the many aspects of planning, negotiation of ideas etc. As indicated above, we shall limit our focus to the meeting points between the group of students and the supervisor.

T. Chemi & L. Krogh (Eds.), Co-Creation in Higher Education, 67–82.

CO-CREATION IN PBL SUPERVISION

The type of learning activity that goes on in a PBL setting is usually referred to as active learning, collaborative learning, peer learning and so on. The PBL model is a rich and complicated model, which has many aspects and includes many different learning spaces. Here the idea is that co-creation of knowledge between teacher and students is a fairly unexplored area related to the PBL environment but that it is in fact one of the most central to understand and explore for a full conceptualisation of the model.

As a first step towards a conceptualisation it should be highlighted that any productive co-creation between supervisor and students entails the active construction by the supervisor of the necessary learning space. The construction of a co-creative space for students and supervisor is very much a task for the supervisor to accomplish. Even the most motivated, skilled, progressive group of PBL students, fully engaged with their project, cannot establish a co-creative space for learning that includes the supervisor and therefore it becomes highly relevant to look at how a supervisor can nurture this type of learning space.

Based on the above reflections, this chapter takes as its problem formulation: how can a supervisor establish a space for a co-creative process with a group of students working on their PBL project?

The answer to the problem will be the development of a vocabulary about a co-creative learning space. The approach to reach this vocabulary will have four steps. To start working on the interaction between the supervisor and the project group, our first step is to elaborate on the concept of PBL as it is used here and the role of the supervisor in this framework. Secondly, a connection is built between the space for co-creative processes and a theoretical framework related to dialogical processes in education. Thirdly, we take a closer look at a typology of supervisor approaches and discuss how they can be related to the notion of a co-creative space. Finally, the goal is to establish a vocabulary about a co-creative space in four dimensions and see how supervisors can address these dimensions for constructing a fruitful co-creative space with their students.

In the second part, we shall discuss the framework developed by Alrø and Skovsmose in their study of dialogical processes in education. They develop a vocabulary about how we can interpret dialogic learning as a space where certain characteristics of the dialogue between teacher and student are highlighted as the most important. Their work builds, among other things, on the ideas of Paulo Freire's dialogical pedagogy and the language theoretical ideas of speech acts. By choosing this perspective we gain an insight into the type of dialogue needed for dialogic-based learning to build upon in establishing a vocabulary about supervision in a PBL setting.

In the third part, development of different types of supervisor roles is discussed. This will produce another set of highly focused PBL supervision concepts to later build upon. This part will be inspired by Olsen and Pedersen (2015) and their profiles of archetypical supervisors and supervisor approaches in a PBL setting.

Finally, these theoretical inputs will be used to develop a vocabulary on how supervisors can be successful in producing co-creative processes with students in the PBL setting.

PBL – Problem Based Learning

The PBL framework in higher education is a well-established practice in many universities around the world but it comes in all shapes and sizes. The version of the PBL model discussed here will be inspired by the Danish tradition, as it has been practised in the universities in Aalborg and Roskilde since their start-up in the early 1970s.

In this model, some key elements can be considered the basic principles – the projects are student-driven, students work in teams, projects are ideally interdisciplinary in character, project periods are several months long and often a full semester.

For a deeper insight into these principles I will refer to the work of Illeris (1974) and for some discussions on the model today, to Andersen and Heilesen (2015) and Kolmos et al. (2007). See also the official PBL principles of Aalborg University (2015) as an example of an institutional PBL setup or the explanation of the model in the specific disciplinary setting of mathematics in Vital et al. (1995).

Here, to set the scene, let me just give some short interpretations of some of the above principles. Students work in teams of anything from 2 to 8 participants depending on the field of study but the average group has 3 to 5 members in it. Students usually have a lot of course activities at the beginning of the semester and then a "free" schedule for working intensively on their PBL project for the final few months of the semester.

Students working in the PBL model are in control of the project, in the sense that they themselves choose the topic to work on and in principle they have the final say in any matter concerning the direction of the project. The supervisor has the role of supporting the project groups' working and learning processes towards a fully developed project report.

The project report's central elements are (1) the development of a problem formulation within a chosen theme which the group finds interesting to explore, (2) the development of an approach to work scientifically with this clearly formulated problem, and (3) the work on the problem through the developed approach to establish an answer to the problem formulation. Together, these elements typically end up in written form to comprise the project report, which could be anything from 30–100 pages long, depending on the number of students in the group and the requirements of the study programme.

However, the project report is only the end product of a complex process where students and supervisor have normally had many, many discussions about the theme, the problem formulation, the scientific approach and methods, the conclusions, the use of theory and the way to handle empirical data and so on.

In the PBL model considered here, the interest is in these processes and how a framework can be built that optimises and furthers a co-creative process between the group of students and the supervisor.

Supervision in PBL

In the framework of this chapter the educational programme's coordinators choose a supervisor for a specific group of students. Supervisors might supervise many groups in each semester and their possible workload for one particular group of students might be something like 5 well-prepared meetings over a period of a few months.

At first this might not seem to be a lot of contact between group and supervisor, but in practice these meetings are highly condensed and normally well-prepared, often with a clear focus and points of discussion related to working papers and issues the students can see they need to address as the next problematic things. Frequently, the supervisor has read many pages of materials and part of the meeting time with the group will comprise discussions about these materials and how to develop them or go beyond them and make a change of direction.

The meetings often take an hour, or one and a half hours, of intense discussion and debate and this is really the stage for the main co-creative processes going on in PBL supervision. The supervisor can take on different types of roles in these encounters, as we shall explore later, but here it will suffice to say that the different stages of the project process and the different types of content of the focus in the meetings obviously greatly influence which type of role the supervisor will adopt in the co-operation with the group.

Above, we divided the process of constructing the project into three elements – developing a problem, developing a scientific approach and the work with this approach. These different elements call for slightly different supervision approaches. The formulation of the problem can be a troublesome affair with many proposals and questions in the melting pot and is often accompanied by quite a lot of frustration from students who just like to get on with a clear-cut task. However, the idea, in a PBL setting, is precisely that this type of difficult and frustrating period is a rich source for learning processes and the supervisor will need to know this and act accordingly. This period calls for patience in the co-operation and the supervisor can focus on helping out with suggestions for improving provisional problem formulations or explaining procedures for researching deeper into the broader theme to find the right problem to work on.

In the later phases of the project, the working papers discussed in meetings could be about techniques of doing interviews or experiments, or about the presentation of a specific theoretical framework and so on, where the supervisor has a completely different role as an expert in the field or an expert in how to work scientifically in this or that respect.

This way, the type of content of the discussions and the stage in the project process clearly influences the character of the meetings between supervisor and group. We can begin to think of several types of co-creative spaces between students and supervisor.

DIALOGUE IN THE CO-CREATIVE SPACE

In the following pages, we set out to develop some ideas on the importance of dialogue for constructing a co-creative space in a PBL supervision setting. As indicated, we will discuss the work of Helle Alrø and Ole Skovsmose and their concept of dialogic learning in collaborative investigation. Their approach is among other things inspired by Paulo Freire's dialogical pedagogy and the project of challenging the "banking" model of learning with processes of dialogue in learning.

Alrø and Skovsmose presented the idea of dialogue and learning in the field of mathematics education. In their book *Dialogue and learning in mathematics education: intention, reflection, critique* (2002) they outlined their "inquiry co-operation model" which was developed on the basis of theoretical perspectives about dialogue and empirical work with mathematics pupils in a dialogue-based classroom setting. Below, we consider their later reflections on the key issues at stake in conceptualising dialogic learning.

Dialogue as a pedagogical approach is presented as resting on three key elements. First of all, it is an inquiry process; secondly it entails taking risks, and thirdly, equality must be maintained in the dialogue. Let us address these three points and relate them to the higher education PBL setting.

Dialogue as a process of inquiry emphasises that the learning process is about acquiring knowledge in a new terrain and building on the existing resources that can be related to the particular problem formulation of the project and the sub tasks at hand.

> We understand dialogue as part of an *inquiry process*, its aim being to obtain new insights. During this process, those involved act towards each other and the subject matter with curiosity, wonder and reflective pondering. Dialogue in this sense is different from instruction, order, and persuasion. Dialogue implies a willingness to question one's understandings and pre-understandings and to examine what is new and different but also what is considered knowledge already acquired. Entering into a dialogue means taking ownership of the process of investigation. (Alrø & Skovsmose, 2004, pp. 40–41)

This focus on the inquiry process in dialogic learning resonates well with the ideas of PBL where students need to develop their own research problem to work on. This in itself demands curiosity and the willingness from both students and supervisor to seek out new knowledge and new understandings using what might be a new approach or perspective on the specific topic worked on.

And for the supervisor entering the dialogue, it means taking ownership in the process of investigation. The students clearly maintain the ownership of the project and whatever outcome the process will lead to but, by entering the dialogue, the supervisor connects to the investigation process and thereby engages in the project, taking on a shared responsibility for the project process to become a success.

Going into a dialogical process with a group of students is, however, for supervisors by no means an easy task. It entails supervisors putting themselves at risk by going into explorations of knowledge in areas where they are not the obvious expert. And, on the other side, it can be quite challenging for students, too, as entering into dialogue is also about a loss of control.

> A dialogue *includes risk-taking* in terms of unpredictability. When entering a dialogue you may touch issues that are delicate or unforeseen; there is a risk of losing control or steering into a dead end. But at the same time, it is possible to address one's tacit knowledge or to come to see things in new and different ways. It is possible to learn! (Alrø & Skovsmose, 2004, p. 41)

The unpredictable nature of the course of a PBL project is a well-known feature of PBL settings in the literature (Olsen & Pedersen, 2015). It is actually a prerequisite for establishing the kind of learning environment that is truly problem-oriented and where the driver of learning is the focused endeavour towards an answer to the problem formulation, even though this might lead into different kinds of fields of science, demand the development of a new situated knowledge that has not been discussed directly in research literature and so on. This way, dialogic learning is unpredictable and in the PBL setting it can lead to a lack of control for supervisors in the sense that the project drifts away from the areas of their specialisation or specific expertise. In the case of interdisciplinary projects the content may even be far beyond the point where the supervisor has a privileged position, for example, as being the "knower" about the ups and downs in a specific type of experiment or in the use of a certain type of statistics.

It could be tempting to propose that the supervisor should or could just regain authority and demand the project go in directions that steer clear of the uncontrollable, interdisciplinary and risky parts of tackling the problem in the project report. This, however, goes against the idea of dialogic learning as described above, where the main idea is to enter into an open inquiry, with the risks this entails. Under these less controllable conditions, the authority of the supervisor will shift from the expert in a specific theory or approach, towards a generalised expert role in doing science. The most important role for supervisors is then their skills as researchers and their experience in how to do research.

The final dimension in the notion of dialogic learning relates to the connected point about establishing equality in the dialogue.

> A dialogue *maintains equality* including a respect for diversity. This does not mean that a dialogue presupposes similarity or symmetry. We are speaking of

> interpersonal equality and human respect. In a dialogue there should be no use of power or force, no persuasion of the other, and no winning. The purpose of a dialogue should not be defined or decided by an authority. To be productive, a dialogue develops as a dynamic process between equal communicating partners. (Alrø & Skovsmose, 2004, p. 41)

Equality in the higher education PBL scenario can quite easily fall apart if violated by either students or supervisor. On the supervisor side, the obvious mistake is becoming too strong an authority in the dialogue and show unnecessary power in dialogue about the project choices to be taken or the way to proceed. On the other hand, the group of students can be highly dependant on the authority of the supervisor if they are insecure about what to do, how to go on etc. They can even reach levels of frustration where they demand a straightforward answer about what the right way to proceed looks like. Of course, the authority of the supervisor as a research expert is a constant presence in the relation between supervisor and students, and so it should be. But the supervisor's insights into the importance of maintaining equality in the dialogue and attempts to create the best possible learning space, tone and playing rules of the dialogue will make a huge difference in shifting from situations of authority back to an equal participation in the dialogical inquiry.

From these dimensions of dialogical learning Alrø and Skovsmose build a deeper insight into the different types of dialogical speech acts that dominate in dialogic learning. Speech acts are part of the 20th century language philosophy movement called "the linguistic turn". It can be summarised as a growing interest in the importance of language philosophy for other areas of philosophy or for our understanding of, for example, science or education. Speech act theory was developed by, among others, Searle and Austin and an important source of inspiration behind this development was Wittgenstein's later emphasis on the performative role of language inherent in his concept of language games (see e.g. Searle, 1969; Austin, 1975; Wittgenstein, 1997).

Alrø and Skovsmose identify the following series of dialogic acts as central to dialogic learning: getting in contact, locating, identifying, advocating, thinking aloud, reformulating, challenging and evaluating. (Alrø & Skovsmose, 2004, pp. 47–48). These speech acts are referred to as dialogic acts, that is, speech acts with the qualities of making an inquiry, running a risk and maintaining equality. Other types of speech acts are less imbued with these qualities as, for example, persuading someone, ordering, instructing, correcting etc. (Alrø & Skovsmose, 2004, p. 47). These types of speech acts can also be found in many educational settings but they work against the idea of establishing dialogic learning, which is defined as the learning that takes place where the use of dialogical speech acts are predominant.

We will not go deeper into the reflections on dialogical speech acts here, but just reiterate that overall they relate very well to the general ideas of teaching within a PBL framework – advocating for ideas, thinking aloud in a space of inquiry, reformulating ideas based on evaluation of previous thoughts, challenging these from new perspectives and so on.

In this way, dialogic learning is a powerful framework for building a vocabulary about co-creation in PBL supervision and we will return to this construction later on and reframe the ideas of dialogic learning in this specific scenario.

SUPERVISING IN THE CO-CREATIVE SPACE

We have discussed how a focus on dialogic learning can be a platform for establishing a co-creative space between students and supervisor. Next we will look into the different types of roles presented in literature for the archetypical PBL supervisor. This will provide us with detailed vocabulary about the roles in play in PBL supervision. Building on these and the ideas of dialogic learning we shall then construct a vocabulary for a supervisor to build a co-creative space with his/her students.

In the Danish PBL tradition one important typology of supervisor roles is presented by Olsen and Pedersen (2015). Below we will follow their vocabulary of supervision and discuss it in the context of establishing a co-creative space between supervisor and students.

Olsen and Pedersen (2015) first outline two different supervision approaches related to the *content* of the supervision (1) problem-oriented supervision and (2) disciplinary supervision. These are in practice closely interrelated but it is possible analytically to make an important distinction between them. Let us first take a closer look at problem-oriented supervision by highlighting three dimensions.

Problem-oriented supervision is focused on the methodological perspectives in the PBL project – that is, being able to make distinctions between the theme of the project, the problem formulation, the design of the project and the methodological approach in the project, the empirical work, the analysis, the conclusion and so on. This part of the problem-oriented supervision relates to developing a strong idea in students about what these elements in a project process and project report mean.

Another dimension relates to the supervisor's efforts to develop the students' work with the methodological perspective in the project by keeping the emphasis on how and why the group would like to proceed in this and that way, theoretically and empirically. This dimension connects to a third dimension presented by Olsen and Pedersen (2015), that the problem-oriented supervisor makes group project work become highly reflexive. The students should understand that what they choose to do eliminates other options and choices and in this way the supervisor strengthens the students' reflections on what knowledge they are about to produce.

In contrast to problem-oriented supervision, disciplinary supervision emphasises the project's connection to the knowledge and approaches in the scientific domain in question. This type of supervision is about helping students to find the important theories in the particular field, guiding students regarding the central position in the scientific debates for the relevant topics of the project. Disciplinary supervision also relates to the way in which theories are developed in a project and to how empirical work is conducted and corroborated. It deals with the detailed scientific investigations of the problem formulation and all the project's sub-tasks in arriving at a conclusion that is well founded in the scientific theories and methods chosen.

The difference between these two supervision approaches is interesting in relation to this chapter's efforts to develop a vocabulary for co-creation in supervision. Even though the disciplinary supervision approach seems necessary and very important for the students to complete their project report, it none the less has the potential to disrupt a co-creative space of collaboration. The disciplinary supervision approach strongly positions the supervisor as the expert and thereby makes it easy to slide into a "supervisor knows best" supervision where the group of students asks questions about the proper approach, about technique in every detail, about which theory to choose etc. In actual fact, the supervisor in almost all cases does know best but acting as an "answering oracle" might not be the best teaching strategy in supervision of PBL projects and especially not when the emphasis is on building a co-creative space for collaboration.

In contrast, the problem-oriented supervision approach has some advantages in relation to building a co-creative space. Its aim is not explicitly to socialise students into a specific scientific tradition or paradigm – as one might interpret the disciplinary approach – but rather to produce in students a high level of reflexion upon the scientific choices made in the project, to produce transparency in the communication to readers about the scientific choices of the project and so on. In this way, the problem-oriented supervision approach is a more promising line to pursue in building a co-creative space, as it can open the scientific debate with challenging questions like "Why do you want to do it like this?" or "What does this choice entail for your analysis?" There is a difference between focusing on a supervision content about the reproduction of disciplinary tradition and scientific paradigm, and on a content that challenges the students' reflections on the reasons for their choices in, for example, empirical methods, problem formulation or theoretical grounding. This difference is an important building block in constructing a vocabulary about co-creation in supervision.

In addition to these two different approaches to the content of supervision, Olsen and Pedersen also present four types of supervision styles that each reflect a certain attitude or role taken in the *form* of supervising a PBL group. The four styles are called (1) product supervision, (2) process supervision, (3) laissez-faire supervision and (4) control supervision. This typology is inspired by Tofteskov (1996) but here we follow Olsen and Pedersen's outline (2015).

Product supervision is a style where the supervisor is focused on students gaining solid input from the supervision session, for example, clear input regarding their project report's structure or learn about a specific theory. In this type of supervision, the supervisor is very active in developing ideas and suggestions for the project report, to solve the problems of the group. One aspect of this supervision style is also a thorough and continued focus on details and on the norms for producing the final written report.

Product supervision does not hold much promise for producing a co-creative space with students. The supervisor is far too aggressive in producing the right content in the right way and the co-creation process will be unfruitful, in the sense that it is not driving the students' learning process. Instead it is driving the project report forwards, but this is not necessarily the most important task for the supervisor and it is certainly not the main issue for creating a co-creative learning space.

Process supervision represents a focus on the student group's learning processes. This type of supervision, instead of focusing on the final product, will be focused on the insights the group develops during the process of writing the project. The process supervisor will not produce a lot of ready-to-use suggestions but instead ask the group questions for reflection and focus on nurturing the learning and knowledge processes going on in the group. This style of supervision also includes a focus on supervising the group's internal working processes in order to maximise the development of process skills.

Process supervision is a promising approach in the context of supervision for co-creation. The supervisor's agenda is here to increase the students' insights and their working processes as a group. This means that focus is mainly on how to develop the skills of the group towards effective group processes and the ability to reflect about how to proceed.

Laissez-faire supervision comes in two forms – one where the supervisor thinks that students are best not met with too much problematising of their work. Ample amounts of positive feedback are best to help maintain positive motivation in the group, which is considered the most important element in producing the final result.

The other version of the laissez-faire approach involves the supervisor who lacks engagement in the student group's project. Only general suggestions or rules of thumb are given, with a clear distance from any details of the project. This supervision style is presented by Olsen and Pedersen as the supervisor who just wants to get on with his/her own research.

Finally, *control supervision* is the style of PBL supervision that focuses on testing the knowledge of the group of students. Taken to its extreme, the meetings between supervisor and group of students can be a sort of extension of the final examination situation to the entire period of writing the project. Another version of the control supervision style is about a search for the "capacity" of the group for the purpose of finding the right level of abstraction, theory, empirical challenge that the group can muster.

Control supervision might be thought of as detrimental to constructing a co-creative learning space – it emphasises clear boundaries between students and teacher and focuses directly on the exam through tests, thereby developing a clear hierarchy and a closing of open inquiries. Laissez-faire supervision closes any approach to opening a co-creative space of inquiry, either by overuse of appraisal or by non-engagement in the project. Positive feedback is, of course, not detrimental to a co-creative process but it does not necessarily include the required engagement and investment in the project from the supervisor.

The two-times-four categories of supervision outlined above are based on analytical distinctions and there are naturally many overlaps between them in a situated supervision setting. A supervisor might even use several of them during just one supervision meeting. Here, however, they will suffice for reflecting upon the type of supervisor role and approach that is needed to establish a co-creative space of learning and knowledge production.

CONSTRUCTING A CO-CREATIVE SPACE FOR SUPERVISION

This section will be aimed at constructing a vocabulary for establishing a co-creative learning space in PBL supervision. Drawing on the above perspectives and discussions, four dimensions will be suggested as essential elements in a supervisor's vocabulary for constructing a co-creative space with students.

For supervision in the PBL model, many other dimensions than these four are needed, depending on the focus of the supervision. One could think of five essential dimensions for a supervisor vocabulary on developing problem formulations, or four elements for keeping students on a productive timeline. Here our focus is only to construct central dimensions in building a co-creative learning space, as in our original intentions.

It should be noted that co-creation will always occur in the interaction between supervisor and students, no matter which type of supervision is used. The idea here is to produce a vocabulary that will increase the quality of the co-creative learning space by providing some dimensions that can be used to think and reflect about the situated construction of a specific co-creative space.

It should also be noted that all supervision settings are unique. They depend, for example, on the element of the project in focus (see the division into three project phases mentioned above). They are dependent on the module learning goals described in the curriculum. Also, some supervisors have a great deal of experience and some have just started. In addition, and most importantly, no student groups are alike and the dynamics of a supervisor meeting are very much entangled in the persons present, their backgrounds and foregrounds and the mutual understanding of the situation. Given all these complexities, the aim below is to highlight general dimensions for constructing a co-creative learning space.

The four dimensions in combination will define the meaning of a co-creative learning space in PBL supervision as an answer to the chapter's problem formulation and the elements will be called (1) the *atmosphere* of the space, (2) the *approach* of the supervisor in the space, (3) the *involvement* of the supervisor in the space and (4) the *topology* of the space.

Atmosphere – Constructing an Inclusive Dialogue

The atmosphere of the co-creative space relates to the supervisor's active efforts to construct a learning space with the students. The metaphor of *atmosphere* is chosen in order to highlight that an important dimension in a co-creative space is the ability to work with the feeling and sensation of the space.

Inspired by the concept of dialogic learning, we can borrow some of its key elements for building the right kind of dialogue for joint exploration or inquiry. A first feature relates to the issue of maintaining equality in a co-creative space. This means that unnecessary use of authority by the supervisor should be avoided and instead emphasis should be given to equal participation in the inquiry of all persons involved in the project. An equal communication between all participants rests on the supervisor's ability to create a learning space of interpersonal equality and human respect, with minimum use of power or force by either students or supervisor. This will often demand a quite active role from the supervisor in inviting all students into the discussions, or in holding back one's own good ideas for preserving an equal dialogue to obtain a rich learning space for the students.

PBL projects end with exams, where the supervisor role will change to that of an examiner and this makes it a complicated relationship of power between the supervisor and the group of students. There is no way of escaping the influence of these circumstances and they have to be addressed directly to secure a safe atmosphere by discussing openly what will be the yardstick for the final assessment of the project. However, this need not be in opposition to constructing a co-creative space in the project process, as long as the issue is addressed and the equal and non-authoritarian space is restored with this knowledge.

The construction of an atmosphere promoting imagination and creativity is an important dimension of the co-creative space as defined here and the supervisor will have to work actively for the initial confidence of the students and a relaxed environment to achieve this. Stupid questions must be welcomed and the inclusion of all participants in the dialogue is an important element in forming a positive and safe atmosphere during the supervision meeting.

Approach – Focusing on a Problem-Oriented Supervision Style

The approach of the supervisor in the co-creative space concerns the different roles it is possible to take in PBL supervision. The metaphor of *approach* has been chosen to highlight that an important dimension relates to the way supervisors address and possibly plan the content and form of their supervision.

From the above discussion of the PBL supervisor roles it has already been argued how an emphasis in the supervision towards a problem-oriented, as opposed to a disciplinary approach is preferable. Acknowledging the importance of both approaches, the co-creative space benefits from a supervisor who approaches the subject of the project with an open agenda and in this way does not overly explicate "how things are done around here". A co-creative space for imagination, open inquiry and a joint exploration of the problem worked upon will benefit from the emphasis on constant reflections about the choices made, the phases of the project, the many possible ways to proceed empirically etc.

The supervisor role presented above as process supervision has a connection to this problem-oriented emphasis in the supervision. The process-oriented supervisor is mostly interested in producing strong process skills in the group of students to strengthen their own ability to explore the problem formulation of the project. Process supervision is less occupied with the production of ready-to-use solutions for the group or the final look of the project report and in this way supports an emphasis on building a strong dialogue especially between the members of the group. This will be productive for a co-creative space by focusing on an inclusive dialogue about how to proceed with the project, as opposed to a more supervisor-driven approach like control supervision or product supervision.

However, it also raises the question about the very position of the supervisor in the co-creative space and this leads us to the third dimension.

Involvement – Engaging in a Risky Inquiry

Supervisors' level of involvement in the co-creative space relates to the extent to which they take ownership of the project process.

In the vocabulary presented above on supervision roles and styles, the involvement of the supervisor is not explicitly portrayed from a positive point of view. In product supervision or control supervision, there is a strong involvement in the project, but for specific reasons that do not directly relate to the positive potential for co-creation in the supervisor's engagement. At the same time, several of the archetypical supervision roles are clearly detached from the project processes, trying to avoid too much interaction with the group or the project.

However, there seems to be a space for a productive role of involvement when we are to define a co-creative space in PBL supervision. If we refer back to the key elements of dialogic learning, the argument is raised that unequivocal involvement and engagement in the dialogue is absolutely necessary. Engaging oneself in the project means to enter the unknown together with the group of students. It portrays the entering into the dialogic learning space as engaging in a risky exploration, as opposed to staying detached or being in control of the process of supervision.

Building on this idea, it seems important for a supervisor to be aware of the level of involvement in the explorations and open inquiries of the project. It is obviously a fertile setting for the construction of a co-creative space to throw oneself into the discussions and learning process on equal terms with the students. Hence, on a scale from "being totally detached from the project" to "total involvement in the project", taking a step towards active participation in the inquiries seems to be an important aspect in constructing a co-creative space.

Here, several points require careful thought, as some will suggest the project process is the students' and no one else's. In the exam situation, the supervisor will be examining the final product and thereby potentially has to dramatically shift position during the project period from involvement to detachment. Even though these arguments may have some weight, I would argue that the involvement should be quite thorough, in the sense that the supervisor should be an active thinker in relation to the project in general and to many of the decisions and choices made. This will serve as the best possible condition for a co-creative space – which is our main concern here – but also for producing the right kind of atmosphere for an open and equal inquiry in the learning space, while directly showing how a trained researcher thinks in this or that open situation or problem scenario.

Having argued in favour of the necessary level of involvement in the project, let us turn to the fourth dimension in the definition of the co-creative space.

Topology – Representing the Complexity of Science

The topology of the co-creative space relates to the character and breadth of the space of inquiry. The metaphor of *topology* has been chosen to highlight the dimension of the co-creative space that relates to the scientific landscape, which will be available for the group of students to explore.

Depending on the supervisor's imagination and concerns about this issue the co-creative space can end up in very different frameworks. Having argued above for the importance of engaging in the project process, a consequence is the risky landscape of science one enters into as a supervisor. No matter how well prepared or senior one may be, there is no chance of one knowing all the possible theories or journal articles or subdomain knowledge that might enter into the thinking about the project if one engages in an open investigation with a project group. The role of expert will – as argued above – be lost. And as the students, too, have time to study new-found theories or case studies or a statistical method unknown to the supervisor, the knowledge gap may even grow during the project period in favour of the students. For strong PBL groups this can be a positive and rewarding outcome of an open co-creative space, but it challenges the supervisor by being risky and going beyond one's professional expert landscape.

The challenge of the supervisor is how to tackle this. The dimension of topology is here meant to underline that the co-creative space between supervisor and students is highly dependent upon the supervisor's attitude to the boundaries of the scientific landscape allowed in the project process.

The space can be thought of as dependent upon the supervisor's level of allegiance with a specific scientific paradigm and her ability to let go of this allegiance if the co-creative process, or the group itself, challenge this or want to enter new and different paths.

Arguing for a productive co-creative space in PBL, there is no question that a too narrow scientific paradigm on how to explore a certain type of question or the handful of few well-known canonical theories will put a brake on the open inquiry that has been argued as a key element of co-creative space. In this line of reasoning the supervisor should be representing the complexity of science – not its canons.

CONCLUSIONS

Above we have defined four dimensions of a co-creative space for supervision in PBL. They relate to the atmosphere of this space, the supervisor's approach in the space, as well as the supervisor's involvement in the project process going on in the space. Finally, the topological dimension highlights how a supervisor directly or indirectly has a big role to play in the breadth and character of the scientific space available for the supervision dialogue.

It was concluded that the active construction of this space by the supervisor will further a co-creative learning process, if the atmosphere of the learning space is constructed as an inclusive dialogue of inquiry between equal participants. The supervision approach should be aimed at strengthening a problem-oriented approach and the level of involvement in the project should be high. Finally, it was argued that the topology of the co-creative space should be constructed to represent the complexity of science, as opposed to specific paradigms of knowledge.

Let me end by underlining that the everyday situated supervision meeting has many parameters for the supervisor to navigate among, as we have touched upon above. In that sense, the arguments for the most open, equal, non-authoritarian, predominantly problem-oriented and process-oriented, engaging, dialogic and non-paradigmatic inquiry construction by the supervisor may meet other challenges that become more important in the specific moment of supervision. However, it could still be important as a supervisor in general to try and reflect upon the best possible co-creative space with each group of students and hopefully make some use of the discussions and vocabulary presented above.

REFERENCES

AAU PBL Principles. (2015). *Principles of problem and project based learning – the aalborg PBL model*, edition 2.0 – Briefly describes nine principles of PBL at Aalborg University. It can be downloaded from this address. Retrieved from http://www.en.aau.dk/about-aau/aalborg-model-problem-based-learning

Alrø, H., & Skovsmose, O. (2002). *Dialogue and learning in mathematics education: Intention, reflection, critique*. Dordrecht, the netherlands: Kluwer.

Alrø, H., & Skovsmose, O. (2004) Dialogic learning in collaborative investigation. In *Nordisk matematikkdidaktikk (Nordic Studies in Mathematics Education)*, *9*(2), 39–62.

Andersen, A. S., & Heilesen, S. B. (Eds.). (2015). *The roskilde model: Problem-oriented learning and project work*. Dordrecht, the netherlands: Springer.

Austin, J. L. (1975). *How to do things with words* (2nd edition). Massachusetts, MA: Harvard University Press.

Barrett, T., & Moore, S. (Eds.). (2011). *New approaches to problem-based learning – Revitalising your practice in higher education*. Routledge.

Díaz-Méndez, M., & Gummesson, E. (2012). Value co-creation and university teaching quality: Consequences for the European Higher Education Area (EHEA). *Journal of Service Management*, *23*(4), 571–592.

Fagerstrøm, A., & Ghinea, G. (2013). Co-creation of value in higher education: Using social network marketing in the recruitment of students. *Journal of Higher Education Policy and Management*, *35*(1), 45–53.

Freire, P. (1972). *Pedagogy of the oppressed.* Harmondsworth: Penguin.

Freire, P. (1993). *Pedagogy of the city.* New York, NY: Continuum.

Hernández, C. H., Ravn, O., Valero, P. (2015). The aalborg university PO-PBL model from a socio-cultural learning perspective. *Journal of Problem Based Learning in Higher Education, 2015,* 16–36.

Illeris, K. (1974). *Problemorientering og deltagerstyring: Oplæg til en alternativ didaktik.* Copenhagen: Munksgaard.

Kolmos, A., Fink, F. K., & Krogh, L. (Eds.). (2007). *The aalborg PBL model – Progress, diversity and challenges.* Aalborg: Aalborg University Press.

Olsen, P. B., & Pedersen, K. (2015). *Problemorienteret projektarbejde – en værktøjsbog.* Copenhagen: Samfundslitteratur.

Rule, P. (2004). Dialogic spaces: Adult education projects and social engagement. *International Journal of Lifelong Education, 23*(4), 319–334.

Searle, J. (1969). *Speech acts – An essay in the philosophy of language.* Cambridge: Cambridge University Press.

Skovsmose, O. (2014). Dialogical teaching and learning in mathematics education. In S. Lerman (Ed.), *Encyclopedia of mathematics education.* Dordrecht: Springer Netherlands.

Tofteskov, J. (1996). *Projektvejledning.* Frederiksberg: Forlaget Samfundslitteratur.

Vital, R., Christiansen, I., & Skovsmose, O. (1995). Project work in university mathematics education – A Danish experience: Aalborg University. *Educational Studies in Mathematics, 29*(2), 199–223.

Wittgenstein, L. (1997). *Philosophical investigations* (First published 1953.). Oxford: Blackwell Publishers.

Ole Ravn
Department of Learning and Philosophy
Aalborg University

HENRIK FIND FLADKJÆR AND KATHRIN OTREL-CASS

6. A COGENERATIVE DIALOGUE

Reflecting on Education for Co-Creation

INTRODUCTION

This chapter is presented as a reflection that has been produced by the two authors after they implemented a pedagogical intervention in a problem-based first year university course.

We were considering the following educational challenge: university education ought to lead to higher order learning outcomes, including "thinking, problem-solving, constructing, transforming, investigating, creating, analyzing, making choices, organizing, deciding, explaining, talking and communicating, sharing, representing, predicting, interpreting, assessing, reflecting, taking responsibility, exploring, asking, answering, recording, gaining new knowledge, and applying that knowledge to new situations" (Cameron, Tate, Macnaughton, & Politano, 1998, p. 6). This means that students should develop the competencies to think independently and work in a self-directed, way but for that they need to include reflection and assessment in their learning process to make it complete (Davies & Le Mahieu, 2003). Problem based learning (PBL), the teaching philosophy applied at this particular university, is a direct response to traditional teaching and learning approaches and aims to create the conditions for higher order thinking. PBL has been credited with leading to the acquisition of flexible knowledge, effective problem-solving skills, self-directed learning skills, effective collaboration, and intrinsic motivation (Hmelo-Silver, 2004). However, for the individual student this may be difficult to grasp. This holistic learning approach presents some unique challenges for individual students to identify solutions to complex problems, since PBL project work is typically done as a team (Major & Palmer, 2001). This means that specific approaches are needed that allow students to learn how to critically assess their learning products. In our case, we experimented with an educational intervention that aimed at increasing students' ability to think more critically.

The chapter is presented as a cogenerative dialogue (Roth & Tobin, 2001). The notion of cogenerative dialogue emerged, as Wolff-Michael Roth and Ken Tobin explain, from experiencing pedagogical approaches of co-teaching that led them to consider "the collective and generative nature of theorizing praxis together" (paragraph 3). Cogenerative dialogue can be used as an evaluative tool for the co-construction of an analysis through what is referred to as metaloguing (Roth &

T. Chemi & L. Krogh (Eds.), Co-Creation in Higher Education, 83–98.

Tobin, 2004). Metaloguing is the act of theorising over practice, based on practice and this allows connections to be made back to policy, and again back to practice and theory. Taken this way, it represents an iterative process between different concerns to do with practice.

We use this approach of thinking together to discuss our experience of students engaging in an educational intervention aimed at the co-creation of critical and reflective problem-based group work. The cogenerative dialogue approach provides us with the room for accommodating our insights and imaginings on what it means to improve problem-based learning programmes for university students. By utilising a cogenerative dialogue format, our different voices can be positioned more prominently, not to share our anecdotal discernments but to showcase how we catalysed our own thinking of a shared educational experience. Catherine Milne, Susan Kirch, Sreyashi Jhumki Basu, Mary Leou and Pamela Fraser-Abder, who used this approach, explain that metaloguing is "collective remembering" (p. 418).

Overall, however, this chapter is focused on an educational intervention that was based on the concepts of peer learning. From the numerous definitions of peer learning, we utilise here the explanation of David Boud, Ruth Cohen and Jane Sampson (1999) who refer to iterative learning, meaning that peer learning should be two-way and reciprocal, and be to the benefit of all involved when they are sharing their knowledge, ideas and experiences. The authors point out that this kind of learning leads to interdependence of the participants through the co-construction of understanding.

The next section will explain the background – the exposition – of the learning activity, expanding notions of expert and novice knowledge and learning in group settings. We will then follow this up with the cogenerative dialogue between the two authors of this chapter reflecting on this educational intervention.

EXPOSITION: THE EDUCATIONAL BATTLE – A PROBLEM-BASED LEARNING INNOVATION

This intervention was implemented in a degree programme in business studies. Students entering the Danish bachelor programme are typically admitted to university from two different high-school programmes: a regular high-school programme or a business high-school programme. In addition, a number of students enter this programme from so-called university colleges, tertiary providers who offer bachelor degrees with a more practice-focused angle. Students from university colleges have studied business economics, but not to the extent necessary to correspond to a full bachelor programme. On the basis of a detailed course analysis, these students can receive between 1 and 1.5 years of credit, which means that they need to spend another 1.5 to 2 years on completing their bachelor degree at the university level.

The different educational backgrounds, but also the different extra-curricular interests that occupy students' lives, are of importance in a PBL environment, since

PBL builds on the benefits that can be gained from the diversity of people when they come together and solve problems. It is therefore important that this diversity is actively recognised by the teacher and invited into the classroom. The underpinning ideas behind the teaching intervention included to work with the differences that exist between individual students, to foreground how those differences benefit the learning process. PBL builds on the practice of thinking in groups where each individual needs to learn how to think critically. In this respect, knowledge and skills must be made available to all students so that they can utilise and develop those competencies. Elder (2005) presents a set of components that should support development of "critical thinking". It includes the ability to "create activities and opportunities that foster critical thinking throughout the year" (Elder, 2005 p. 42), and the need for teaching strategies to "keep the focus on a substantive concept of critical thinking" (p. 43).

This teaching intervention was coined the *Educational Battle,* since it involved that second semester bachelor students confronted each other one-on-one to explore their ideas. A particularly important element was, to partner each group up with a second semester master student (i.e. in their fourth year of study). The master students had several roles and needed a certain set of prerequisites: firstly, they had to possess the academic skills required to serve as facilitators for the learning of the bachelor students; secondly, they needed the competencies to act professionally. For that reason, the master students were employed to take on the role of professional "process consultants" and asked to consider themselves as such in their interaction with the bachelor students. A hoped-for benefit from this approach was that the first-year bachelor students would be able to see the master students as role models and form an idea and impression of the skills and competencies they themselves would acquire in the following three years. Since the coming together and applying of knowledge and skills is at times difficult to explain to students, we hoped the power of example from a more senior peer would have more impact. We also hoped that the master students' knowledge and experience of solving similar issues would enable them to enter into a different type of discussion with the bachelor students than their supervisor would. It was hoped that the master students would re-voice and perhaps translate information they had received from their teachers to the bachelor students, to bridge the novice–expert difference in problem solving. This was a particular focus since expert knowledge is typified by being able to integrate structural, behavioural and functional elements of dynamic systems, while novices tend to focus on static components (Hmelo-Silver & Pfeffer, 2004). Also, experts tend to spend more time on problem solving compared to novices, they organise the information they retrieve in order to prepare the presentation of their analysis and most importantly, unlike novices, they tend to pay attention to the formulation of the problem (Brand-Gruwel, Wopereis, & Vermetten, 2005). What we anticipated was to create the conditions for another type of discussion, perhaps even peer discussions that would invoke emotional responses (Watanabe, 2008) where the expert can engage from an insider's perspective. The master students all possessed a high level of academic skills and had long-term experience of working with the processes involved. As a spin-off, we found that being a "process consultant" turned out to be a highly attractive student job.

During their second semester, bachelor students of Economics and Business Administration must apply information they acquire in three 5-ECTS courses (ECTS=European credit transfer and accumulation system) and in one 5-ECTS project, giving a total of 20 ECTS. Typically, the project is based on an independently selected case. The three courses students have to attend at the same time are: Fundamental Business Economics, Scientific Methods and Information Management and Information Systems. As far as possible, the bachelor students are encouraged to include relevant aspects of all three courses in their project. If this is not possible, their proficiency within the missing course will be tested in the examination at the end of the semester. The method of instruction is relatively traditional; the three courses are taught lecture style, with 250+ students, while the project work is carried out concurrently in groups of up to 5 or 6 students and supported by a supervisor.

Despite the group work approach, students' knowledge often remains latent and may only become available to their group members. This may also mean that students feel comfortable talking to each other but perhaps less so with outsiders to their project. The idea behind the *Educational Battle* was to create the conditions to make this knowledge accessible to more students and introduce students to the practice of discussing and justifying their ideas. While other students were presenting and discussing things as groups in traditional fashion we asked a single member of a group to share and discuss his knowledge with another individual from another group. On return to their groups the individuals could then share what they had learned with their own group. The idea was that this should give all individuals the opportunity to discuss their ideas one-on-one with a dialogue partner, ensuring that those students who tend to be more introvert would also get an opportunity to practise critical thinking.

Usually, study activities include a mid-term seminar during which each group presents their project to another group, who then give the other group critical feedback. However, first year students, especially, tend to adopt a strategy of safety, assigning specific roles/topics to each member to defend, but without necessarily responding or utilising comments and solutions. Also, students typically treat one another very carefully, i.e. they avoid asking any curly or too difficult questions. They would also not necessarily question the issues that had been raised in order to avoid being challenged by the other group.

In traditional lectures, the individual student often focuses on understanding the content of the curriculum presented. However, if students are also to be inspired to apply this understanding, teachers need to support this in specific ways. If we accept that one educational aim is to teach students to become critical thinkers, we need to give students the opportunity to learn how to form a judgement and how to do so independently (see also Siegel, 2013). Adopting such a position shifts the focus from learning the contents of a curriculum to students becoming autonomous and asking questions independently. The argument here is that this will support students' ability to adopt different perspectives and apply knowledge in numerous contexts.

The knowledge and skills that are initially introduced in the context of a particular curriculum can then be applied by the students to generate new knowledge and new ideas. Developing such competencies has also been ascribed to life-long learning approaches since they involve the ability to think and operate in a flexible and adaptable way (Pithers & Soden, 2000).

Group work is helpful in this process, since this is where the diversity of insights can become visible when students depart from having received the same amount of information input. To make sense of and deal with a problem scenario, students in a group setting need to have dialogue with each other and to explain ideas in relation to the problem. It has been argued elsewhere that this can broaden the dimensions of the new knowledge the students generate (Tiwari, Lai, So, & Yuen, 2006).

This type of aggregation of knowledge is supported by the *Educational Battle*. The *Battle* entails a process that is guided throughout by an academic advisor.

The first step in this process is that two groups of students exchange documents describing their project's problem formulations, theories and any models they want to use, including their ideas on how to go about their project. On the basis of these documents, the individual groups attempt to identify one question for each member of the group so that they can discuss these questions with their opponent group. At this step, each group is supported by a more experienced peer from a higher semester, the so-called catalyst student. Thereafter, individuals of the two groups meet one-on-one. First, one person presents the problem he or she has been assigned. The individual from the other group listens and takes notes. After a certain period of time (determined by an advisor), the presentation is brought to an end, and the receiving individual is given a few minutes to reflect on the issue and its implications for the project. Then the two group members work together to identify a possible solution or ways forward.

When the process comes to an end for one individual, the two participants switch roles and the person from the other group presents the problem he or she has been assigned. When both have made their presentations, taken notes and completed the relevant discussions, the individuals return to their respective groups, where all members should now have received new inspirations for their project. The knowledge gained by each individual group member is presented to the other members. The group, led by the catalyst student, then spends time weighing the various options and/or further developing solutions. Then the group prepares a joint decision or action plan. When all group members have presented their issues and the decisions/action plans are noted, the relevant tasks are divided among the group members.

Following the implementation of the *Educational Battle* we observed two groups challenging each other. We recorded those interactions on video and combined this data with interviews with the students when we asked them to reflect on the activity in focus groups. However, before we reflect on what we experienced and our analysis, we discuss next the idea of cogenerating findings.

PREPARING A CHAPTER AS A COGENERATIVE DIALOGUE

Kathrin: I like the idea of using a cogenerative dialogue format for writing this chapter because it allows us to show and retain our different voices (spelling of cogenerative dialogue by Roth & Tobin, 2001, 2004). Otherwise I thought writing a chapter for a book about co-creation in university teaching would underplay the role of our different expertise in shaping and generating information. I like the text by Roth and Tobin because it shows a historical way of jointly remembering, reconstructing and collectively theorising (2001, 2004). They talk about this historical reconstruction of praxis. For us it was the praxis of conducting this research project together and the reflective forces of making sense from our different points of view. Also, we have expertise in different fields. My area is educational research while your field is business studies, an area I am unfamiliar with. This meant that I had to listen to you carefully and find out what was important to you, to achieve the aim of implementing new learning activities.

Henrik: I have been teaching for 25 years, maybe 30, so I know something about learning in practice, but I am also aware that I'm not an expert in learning. I am of course an expert in my field of discipline and have been for long time. I have also been very interested in teaching, from teaching in an auditorium to doing group supervision. My interest is in trying to develop my own skills and to teach students in a better way. In my first-year classes I have up to 300 students sitting in an auditorium and when I look at them I see immense collective knowledge in these classes. In my teaching I am really interested in working with this collective wisdom that you can find in crowds. James Surowiecki (2005) explains that "diversity contributes not just by adding different perspectives to the group but also by making it easier for individuals to say what they really think"- and this is something that has driven my way of rethinking the supervision of groups of students. I was really interested in the article by Roth and Tobin (2004), also because they talk about collective remembering through communicative action. This means getting all the students together and working in a way where you can bring diverse perspectives and experiences into the learning.

Kathrin: In our reconstructive dialogue we will prompt each other's reflections also through the imagery we captured during our video observations and the interviews we conducted with the students.

Henrik: When you take a look at Figure 6.1 you can see how the three individuals have come together, each representing different insights – the two individuals sitting opposite each other from the two different groups and the catalyst student.

Kathrin: Let's continue discussing the process of thinking and working in PBL project groups and the aims in this project student project group work dynamics.

Figure 6.1. Dialogue between students together with a "catalyst student"

Henrik: One of the traditional ways of groups sharing their projects and getting feedback is to organise seminars, where one group is the opponent to another group who have to examine and question the proposal put forward by the other group. But I have seen many times that this exercise turns into a game, where only one half of the group asks questions and one half of the other group answers them. So, only half of the students are visibly active and perhaps only half of them learn something. They are typically very polite to each other and perhaps they think that if they don't say anything critical the opponent from the other group won't criticise their own project. So, it was very important to me to try and change this dynamic, to perhaps break up old practices and not make it into a safe game. My idea was to ask older students to act as kind of a catalyst, so that students in the 2nd semester could see and learn. Perhaps they might be impressed by the senior students who were just a few years older and this could help them to see themselves and how they might be in a few years. They might think to themselves: this could be me. Also, it is very rare that we have any dialogue between different year groups or semester groups. Dialogue typically occurs only within a group.

Kathrin: I was very intrigued by this idea. Research tells us that one of the problems between the expert knowledge holder and the novice is that sometimes it is difficult for the expert to remember what the novice does not know (Hmelo-Silver & Pfeffer, 2004). The language that the expert uses can at times create a real obstacle for the novice learner. And even if the novice understands the language, with its special disciplinary vocabulary it takes time to acquire the skills in applying this language. When I use the term *language* I mean it metaphorically in so far as it also comprises practices. But more concretely, when we want our students to be more critical, for example, when they examine each other's problem formulations, it means that they have to be able to utilise this language in quite a sophisticated way. This is what I found particularly interesting in this project because the older student is closer to the expert but also closer to the novice learner. In a sense, they re-voice this disciplinary vocabulary for the novice learner. So, they translate the language.

Henrik: Yes, they remember how they learned this new vocabulary and translate it. When we look at this next scene in Figure 6.2, the students of one group are sitting together and individually take notes as they examine the other group's project description.

Figure 6.2. Student group carefully examining the problem formulation of a project

Kathrin: They were prompted by the additional questions the catalyst student raised. The catalyst students played another important role: they were role models for the other students but also reflected through this exercise on their own identity.

Learning and Finding an Identity

Kathrin: This is very important since students need to find an identity in their studies. Students are under a lot of pressure these days to be successful, and pass exams within certain time limits. They compete and need to identify a possible professional pathway for themselves (Jensen & Jetten, 2015).

Henrik: I think that's a very interesting point. Students are very focused on the future and finding a job and they are very competitive. However, when I observed them in this project, where they had to face each other one-on-one from each group to discuss their projects together, they were very polite, thoughtful and constructive in their feedback, despite being competitive. In fact, I tried to build this into the teaching model so they were also constructively and collaboratively thinking of a solution together but are constructively and collaboratively think of a solution together. I thought, too, that some students who in a group setting perhaps would be a bit shy seemed to overcome their fear because they were working together. So the key here was that they were talking to another student they could relate to. I could see that they really helped each other.

Kathrin: So the aim of this activity was learning together to become critical but also to co-construct knowledge. In this next scene (Figure 6.3) we captured a moment where the students took turns presenting their reflections while the others listened, then building on and extending the points that were made.

Kathrin: It takes time to develop an identity and you only slowly break into the culture of a new group. What is really required are possibilities for practice, where students get meaningful opportunities to apply and use new knowledge and skills in an environment that is both safe and challenging. The approach in this teaching activity was providing exactly such an opportunity. After receiving instructions students could work in a safe environment within their own group, but also with students from a different group, as well as with students from another year. In a normal teaching situation where the students face the teacher, students have to be very brave and confident to raise their hand and participate actively in the learning. This activity allowed them to practise without fear of making mistakes, listening to other students, getting reassurance and also co-constructing ideas together to find solutions to problems that they had identified. For me, the question arises: what does it mean to think together, what does it mean to co-construct things together, in particular in the group formation, where you find different individuals with different strengths and weaknesses who have come together?

Henrik: This is also a difficult competency to develop: to trust when you're collaborating with others, that you're not going to miss out or that the others might steal your ideas, and that you gain from the diversity within the group. And it may

Figure 6.3. Making an argument and listening carefully

take some time for you to develop that relationship and trust each other. So, the learning environment I would like to create is one where students discuss their ideas, they share them, they learn about each other's expertise and they get enthusiastic about exchanging their proposals for working through a problem scenario. This is also a competency that I believe is necessary for the citizens of a small country like ours to succeed.

Kathrin: Let's take a closer look at the nature of how the students co-constructed their understanding.

A Co-Construction at Three Levels

Henrik: Yes, the co-construction between the students happened on three levels: there was the co-construction between the two peers from each group who were discussing and working on a specific problem. Following that, there was a co-construction within the group when the individuals returned and shared the solutions they had come up with from talking to their peers. The groups also worked with the catalyst students who helped them to critically evaluate each other's contribution. At a third level, the groups had to co-construct their revisions with their supervisor to negotiate and clarify how they should proceed with the project from here on. This was also challenging for the supervisors because it meant that they had to realign their own thinking and accommodate new ideas in the research process of the students' work and at times adjust ideas the students suggested that were perhaps too ambitious.

Kathrin: Yes, this is also about developing competencies, knowledge and skills in a field. Typically, in the early years of university, study is focused on developing structure and acquiring small mechanical competencies, such as, how to prepare a reference list. Critical competencies may only be developed much later. To achieve this they need opportunities to reflect (Davies & Le Mahieu, 2003).

Figure 6.4. Co-construction through careful documenting of developing ideas

Henrik: True, opportunities for reflections are necessary and sometimes university teachers are too focused on the curriculum and don't give the students enough opportunities to think and reflect. There is too much focus on exams and consequently students are so concentrated on passing individual exams and work their way through their studies from one exam to the next. This is interesting, also because we do not harness the diversity of expertise students bring with them. So, giving students opportunities and tools to reflect is important. You can see in this scene (Figure 6.4) that they were annotating the text and kept additional sticky notes, so this was quite a structured way of thinking individually together. It was also a creative way of thinking together.

Creative Thinking through Co-Construction

Kathrin: Constructive and creative thinking is only possible if you invite diversity and learn to work with it. Jeffrey and Craft (2006) describe what they call "possibility thinking", a teaching method that supports the development of an exploratory attitude, speculation and creativity. This requires an environment that encourages and cultivates developing new and original ideas. It is important to set the conditions for students to develop constructive, collaborative and critical ways to engage with each other. This is what I found very powerful in this learning activity where the students engaged with each other to critically examine someone else's proposal. The catalyst students modelled that critical thinking should be constructive and they demonstrated to the students what it means to critically examine and unpack ideas and how to work with them. The students learned how to co-think with the students from the opposite group and then co-construct with the own group members to propose new solutions. Such competencies need to become transferable skills that students take away and apply to new projects and learning challenges, but this requires a systemic infusion of such teaching approaches so that they can be sustainable.

Henrik: I think this is something that the students need to do, not only when they are with their supervisor, but they need to spend real time with each other where they get into the habit of exchanging and testing their ideas. This is also so they can listen to their own arguments and find out what qualities are required for good arguments.

Kathrin: I agree but this is also a competency that needs to be developed over time. This becomes apparent when you talk to students from different levels. You notice a difference between bachelor students and master level students, where the master level students have developed stronger skills in critically examining ideas and working with them. Perhaps you see that students at the bachelor level work more cooperatively and later on more collaboratively with each other. The difference is that in a cooperative modus students will divide tasks up, while in a collaborative mode they tend to co-construct their ideas and findings. In order to achieve this they need practice. Schoor, Narciss and Körndle (2015) explain that in either case the participants not only need to self-regulate but also have to manage the regulation of the group process. When we look at the scene in Figure 6.5, where the students from the two groups discuss their ideas and come up with solutions, they keep notes from their discussion that they take back to their groups. They brought their notes and the specific questions they had written on the sticky notes, collected their new solutions and this framed the process for discussing these ideas back in the group.

Figure 6.5. Working jointly to find a solution

Kathrin: This way or learning allows them to develop skills to become future innovators.

Future Innovators

Henrik: Yes, I think it is important to teach students how to think collaboratively and be innovative. A key is to learn how to think creatively and learn how to discuss ideas with others. Let's take for example the developers of Skype (https://www.skype.com), Janus Friis and Niklas Zennström. Janus Friis started with an idea and had conversations about how to get people together using the Internet about 12 years ago. He spent hours and hours talking with others about these ideas, building on his out-of-the-box thinking. In order to be successful, you have to learn how to listen to others and pick up on ideas and suggestions – sometimes also to criticism – to make your ideas better. The traditional way of teaching where students have to study and sit an exam at the end of semester is not the kind of competency that will support such a development.

Kathrin: Moving forward in education means going beyond a compartmentalised way of teaching and moving towards teaching models that prepare students for what is needed in the real world.

Henrik: This kind of thinking does not need to result in a new Google product each time, but if you have learned to transform normal thinking into working on creative solutions you have gained a lot. In a sense, we are already halfway there through the problem-based learning environment, where students have to work in groups tasked with solving real challenges.

Kathrin: University education still lacks some of the fundamental pedagogical principles of establishing what exactly students need to know and be able to do that can be transferred to a new situation, in addition to new information that they are being introduced to. This also includes learning how to construct together in a new situation.

Henrik: And of course students are facing the fact that companies or future employers may not be interested in the detailed study focus the students are bringing with them, so they need to be able to identify and point out those transferable competencies that include how to negotiate and co-construct with others to create the best conditions for a good dialogue.

Kathrin: This may also be an opportunity for students to disrupt conventional thinking, and come up with real innovative solutions. When we talked to the students after this learning activity, they told us how motivated they were about how individual thinking contributed to the construction of knowledge.

CODA

In conclusion, we find that the process of sharing our impressions of the learning activity, the *Educational Battle*, visualised the meta-process of thinking together. In some way, this was similar to that of the students, where they visualised their individual ideas through their notes (see Figure 6.6), which resulted in a co-generated and jointly negotiated product.

In their 2004 article, paragraph 33, Roth & Tobin reflect that, to them, cogenerative dialoguing and metaloguing are "not only …methods and genres but …norms to live what we are doing." To us, this reflects in many ways the intentions of this educational intervention, our joint work in this research project and the aims of this book. We have tried to capture our diverse ideas and insights as researchers and, by capturing them as unique contributions, to show how they have also led us to an appreciation of the different insights, memories, and trajectories.

What we were able to identify as key points from the *Educational Battle* activity was an expansion on our nested research expertise. Presenting this through a cogenerative dialogue made this process visible. The dialogue that we captured shows our joint thinking process and the peer learning process that occurred between us authors, through the iterations of our experiences and reflections (Boud, Cohen, & Sampson, 1999).

Together, we have come to the conclusion that, while working as a group in a PBL environment has the advantage of diversity and collaboration, this learning approach can present challenges for the individual student (Major & Palmer, 2001). The specific approach utilised in the *Educational Battle* was a contextualised response to specific challenges presented in this setting, aimed at improving individual

Figure 6.6. Innovative idea creation through co-construction

students' ability to critically assess their own and others' learning products through co-construction processes.

REFERENCES

Boud, D., Cohen, R., & Sampson, J. (1999). Peer learning and assessment. *Assessment & Evaluation in Higher Education, 24*(4), 413–426.

Brand-Gruwel, S., Wopereis, I., & Vermetten, Y (2005). Information problem solving by experts and novices: Analysis of a complex cognitive skill. *Computers in Human Behavior, 21*(3), 487–508.

Cameron, C., Tate, B., Macnaughton, D., & Politano, C. (1998). *Recognition without rewards.* Winnipeg, MB: Peguis Publishers.

Davies, A., & LeMahieu, P. (2003). Assessment for learning: Reconsidering portfolios and research evidence. In *Optimising new modes of assessment: In search of qualities and standards* (pp. 141–169). Springer. Retrieved from http://link.springer.com/chapter/10.1007/0-306-48125-1_7

Elder, L. (2005). Critical thinking as the key to the learning college: A professional development model. *New Directions for Community Colleges, 2005*(130), 48.

Hmelo-Silver, C. E. (2004). Problem-based learning: What and how do students learn? *Educational Psychology Review, 16*(3), 235–266.

Hmelo-Silver, C. E., & Pfeffer, M. G. (2004). Comparing expert and novice understanding of a complex system from the perspective of structures, behaviors, and functions. *Cognitive Science, 28*(1), 127–138. Retrieved from http://doi.org/10.1016/S0364-0213(03)00065-X

Jeffrey, B., & Craft, A. (2006). *Creative learning and possibility thinking. Creative Learning Practices: European Experiences,* BERA 2003 Paper-D2, 73–91. Retrieved from https://www.researchgate.net/profile/Anna_Craft/publication/42792429_Creative_learning_and_possibility_thinking/links/0deec53988464c4d99000000.pdf

Jensen, D. H., & Jetten, J. (2015). Bridging and bonding interactions in higher education: Social capital and students' academic and professional identity formation. *Frontiers in Psychology, 6*. Retrieved from https://doi.org/10.3389/fpsyg.2015.00126

Major, C. H., & Palmer, B. (2001). Assessing the effectiveness of problem-based learning in higher education: Lessons from the literature. *Academic Exchange Quarterly, 5*(1), 4–9.

Pithers, R. T., & Soden, R. (2000). Critical thinking in education: A review. *Educational Research, 42*(3), 237–249. Retrieved from https://doi.org/10.1080/001318800440579

Roth, W.-M., & Tobin, K. (2001). The implications of coteaching/cogenerative dialogue for teacher evaluation: Learning from multiple perspectives of everyday practice. *Journal of Personnel Evaluation in Education, 15*(1), 7–29.

Roth, W.-M., & Tobin, K. (2004). Cogenerative dialoguing and metaloguing: Reflexivity of processes and genres [35 paragraphs]. *Forum Qualitative Sozialforschung / Forum: Qualitative Social Research, 5*(3), Art. 7. Retrieved from http://nbn-resolving.de/urn:nbn:de:0114-fqs040370

Schoor, C., Narciss, S., & Körndle, H. (2015). Regulation during cooperative and collaborative learning: A theory-based review of terms and concepts. *Educational Psychologist, 50*(2), 97–119. Retrieved from http://doi.org/10.1080/00461520.2015.1038540

Siegel, H. (2013). *Educating reason*. Routledge.

Surowiecki, J. (2005). *The wisdom of crowds*. New York, NY: Anchor Books.

Tiwari, A., Lai, P., So, M., & Yuen, K. (2006). A comparison of the effects of problem-based learning and lecturing on the development of students' critical thinking. *Medical Education, 40*(6), 547–554. Retrieved from https://doi.org/10.1111/j.1365-2929.2006.02481.x

Watanabe, Y. (2008). Peer-peer interaction between L2 learners of different proficiency levels: Their interactions and reflections. *Canadian Modern Language Review, 64*(4), 605–635.

Henrik Find Fladkjær
Department of Business and Management
Aalborg University

Kathrin Otrel-Cass
Department of Learning and Philosophy
Aalborg University

TATIANA CHEMI AND PIERANGELO POMPA

7. THEATRE AS CO-CREATIVE SPACE AND AS INSPIRATION FOR HIGHER EDUCATION

The director stands up on the left corner of the stage, facing the audience that is sitting in a semi-circle. The actors sit on chairs facing the audience, still sweating and catching their breath after a physically demanding performance. They are having a conversation with a group of scholars. Together we are trying to enquire into the concept of co-creation. The director, Pierangelo Pompa, could not be more explicit – he is saying to the audience: "Of course we [in the ensemble] are co-creating: we are physically present in the same space and the same time. Whatever each of us does, or doesn't do, has an objective impact on the work situation and on each of the partners. We need to adapt ourselves all the time to the way others behave". Co-creation in theatre is a truism: a self-evident phenomenon. In any kind of theatre and performing art, creators are never left alone. Performative creations are always collaborative, based on relationships and responses to others. In this chapter, a scholar and a theatre director will dialogically address the co-creative ontology of theatre, looking at contemporary performative traditions and with a special focus on acting and directing.

ACTORS WITHOUT SHOES

A newcomer enters the main door at Odin Teatret Nordisk Teaterlaboratorium in Holstebro, Denmark. The building is a former farm, now decorated with cultural artefacts from all over the world. Pierangelo works here in residency with his international group, Altamira Studio Teater.

The newcomer has a vague idea of what he is going to experience – Odin Teatret is known for its anthropological and experimental approach. Guests are heading towards one of the theatre halls in order to watch a work demonstration, where the actors will talk about their creative processes in a performance-like format. The work demonstration will describe how some scenes of the performance *The River*, by Altamira Studio Teater, have been created. The hall is an empty space with wooden floors and high ceiling. Before entering the door, the actors take their shoes off and leave them outside the hall. The newcomer is puzzled. Is this a religious ritual or perhaps just a way of keeping the hall clean? Why does it seem that all the actors have a clear agreement on this procedure?

T. Chemi & L. Krogh (Eds.), Co-Creation in Higher Education, 99–116.

The present article is about to explain to this newcomer how relational codes of conduct structure the professional, artistic and organisational work of actors and how this establishes the core of theatrical co-creation. As a consequence, this newcomer may find similarities to learning processes in higher education, especially to group and project work in the problem-based learning (PBL) tradition. These connections will not be the main focus of the present contribution, but they will be suggested and hinted at. Our conclusions will not serve as ready-made solutions, but rather as perspectives for further studies. In this way, the authors aim to challenge the myth of theatre ensembles as open and liberating experiences of creation, outlining instead the structured rule-setting, requiring both implicit and explicit codes of conduct. We will draw from contemporary theatre practices and theories, with special attention to theatre laboratories, group theatre, third theatre and theatre anthropology (Barba, 1995).

We will confine our attention to the co-creative processes that happen internally in the ensemble and not to external co-creation involving the spectator, which is indeed fundamental to the performative arts, but would lead us too far from our main focus. The topic of actor-audience relationships has been researched in reception studies (Radbourne, Glow, & Johanson, 2014) and the co-creative element has been emphasised in most constructivist and post-modern theories (Hickman, 2007). Even though we fully acknowledge the fundamental role of the spectator and its continuous presence, even in virtual forms or *in absentia* during the process of creation, we have chosen to look exclusively at the processes of co-creation within the ensemble. The risk here is to leave out of our story the central ghost of the performance, the *arbiter*, the balancing force of any performative or dramaturgical process. The spectator is in fact the "reality principle", a concept that Pierangelo uses – in a partially metaphorical way – in his work with actors and that he takes from Freud's 1920 essay *Beyond the Pleasure Principle* (see Freud, 2003). This reality principle preserves theatre processes from self-referentiality and implosion, both on the aesthetical and the relational level. The existence of the spectator means that any relational process among the artists will remain within the concrete dimension of the construction of a form and that any social or psychological dynamic will find its development in objective artistic actions. The word *process* is another of the vital myths of so-called alternative theatre and, like any myth, it is surrounded by a generic *aura*, which was powered by specific cultural tendencies during the Sixties and the Seventies (Gosse & Moser, 2004). The word *process* comes from the Latin verb *procedere,* which contains in its etymology the action of "going forward". It is possible to go *forward* only if there is a goal somewhere in time or space. In theatre work the *process*, however deep and complex, is always going towards the construction of an objective, tangible form, which must be enjoyed by a spectator (the etymology of theatre is rooted in the *experience of seeing*). The fact that, in some cases, the spectators remain virtual (as in many theatre workshops or during training activities, for example) does not diminish their structural relational role during the process.

The reader should bear this in mind and forgive us for keeping the spectator in exile, at least for the current conceptualisation.

The method we made use of is in itself co-creative, dialogical and reflexive. The analytical process started from a thematic dialogue on group theatre as co-creative space. We both drew from our theoretical and practical knowledge of the topic and challenged each other in finding analogies and applications to the context of higher education. Practical and reflexive knowledge focuses on the specific contexts of Odin Teatret and Altamira Studio Teater. Both ensembles are based in Denmark and are of international composition. The former has more than 50 years of acquired experience, the second was founded in 2010, with strong inspiration from the tradition of theatre anthropology, third theatre and theatre laboratory that Odin Teatret's director, Eugenio Barba, has embodied and conceptualised (Barba, 1995). In 2015–2016, Altamira Studio Teater, whose director and founder is Pierangelo Pompa, engaged in a partnership with the Higher Education Research Group at Aalborg University. Tatiana Chemi coordinated the artist-in-residence programme with the Altamira ensemble, given her previous research on laboratory theatre and Odin Teatret. The present chapter is the outcome of co-creative reflection between the two authors, who will formulate their conclusions looking at dilemmas and perspectives on a possible transfer of tools from performative co-creation to collaborative models of learning and teaching in higher education.

THEATRE IS/AS CO-CREATION

Co-creation is a compound word that brings together, on the one hand, a processual element and, on the other, a product-oriented one. The former is represented in *co*, which synthesises the Latin word *cum*, meaning *with*, *together*, a shared process. The latter has its etymological source in the "Sanskrit root *kar-* to be found in the verb *kar-oti*, to do, to make, and the nouns *kar-tr*, creator, and *kri-ja*, action. The same semantic core is identified in the ancient Greek *kraino*, to create, to produce, to fulfil, and in the Latin *creare*, to create out of nothing, to generate, to produce or perform" (Chemi, Jensen, & Hersted, 2015, p. 34). Even though the latter meaning also implies a processual element (the process of creation), this process is, etymologically speaking, tightly linked to the making of a tangible product or experience, an artefact or a work of art. While in the former case the process of sharing is emphasised, the latter term directs the attention to any kind of objective, concrete, tangible result, which corresponds to acknowledged parameters. The core of co-creation, therefore, is togetherness in a common creation, shared by the group of makers and with a group of receivers. Within the tradition of theatre and performing arts, the closeness of relational sharing and collective making is especially meaningful, as it explains the very ontology of theatre as co-creative art form. Far from being a regressive experience of con-fusion, co-creation in theatre happens in a complex dialectic where couples of opposite poles interact without merging or moulding into each other, without causing con-fusion or confusion.

This dialectic occurs by leaving its elements their autonomy, for instance in the different roles of audience or performer, of actor or director. This autonomy runs through the two – only apparently opposed – poles, through their shared process and their objective result, which can be differently and alternatively stressed in the various phases of the work. The specific identity of every co-creative process is the way in which these two poles are addressed and intertwined, but still kept independent.

Because of its material nature, in theatre, the work of art is nothing but a performative moment made of relationships. Interacting human beings in a given space and during a given time-span are the structural core of performances. The work of art *is* the group and its relationships enduring through time and made visible in a tangible form. This is so ingrained in performances that, if relationships do not work or are at stake, then the performance will die. This happens to be true for all kinds of performative genres and historical periods. More than a stylistic observation about specific theatre forms, this is the ontology of theatre as such. However, there are specific creative traditions that have consciously thematised in their practices the correspondence between the theatrical creation and the development of a relational system. This is connected to the explicit choice of specific groups of using theatre work also as a laboratory for social relationships and a channel for personal development, and theatre language also as a collective mirror, where a group of artists publicly performs its social identity as a form of political and cultural activism.

In these traditions, very much oriented around the notion and the myth of the "group", collaborating or interacting actors and directors produce performance materials and participate in the creative process with a set of possibilities and responsibilities which is much wider than in so-called traditional theatre. In such theatre groups the quality of the interaction is even more central to the survival of the ensemble and its repertoire.

Historically, theatre practices such as group theatre (Marwick, 1994), theatre laboratory (Schino, 2009), or third theatre (Barba, 1995), need a collective body that shares (*co-*) compositional and dramaturgical tasks (*creation*). This communal creation is not just juxtaposition of individuals, but a dynamic research dimension. The equation of individuals is not just 1+1=2, but rather a creative result of 1+1=3, meaning that relationships shape a novel, often unexpected result: a third way, which a mere collection of separate individuals would have not provided. Creative collaboration becomes, at its best, a transformational process for each individual, where new relational and technical factors come continuously into play, triggering a self-generating process that multiplies discoveries and possible contaminations. 1+1 can be the beginning of a perpetual redefinition of individual identities, which opens the work to an exponential development. If the collective as a *mystical body* is nothing more than an ambivalent myth, the *group* in its complexity is an absolutely concrete crucible of transformational experiences. On creative collaborations, the works of John-Steiner (2000) and Sawyer (2007) are seminal and we wish to refer to them for further information on the topic.

RE-FRAMING RELATIONSHIPS: FROM DAILY TO EXTRA-DAILY BEHAVIOUR

Anthropologist and evolutionary biologist Ellen Dissanayake has examined the importance that art in general has had in human development (2000, 1995). She found biological and evolutionary evidence for the universality of art-making as an adaptive behaviour, based on the human need of making relationships visible in a given community. As a direct consequence of our ancestors' need for celebrating *intimacy,* reciprocity, *bonding* and *emotionality,* the arts have had the fundamental function of *making special* events, artefacts, roles and relationships. Evolutionary changes in human bodies made human infants more vulnerable and helpless than other mammals for a longer period of time, and emotional attachment became a question of survival. The establishment of social relationships with other human beings became the basis for another essential survival strategy, either in its private mother-infant intimacy or in societies' shared rituals. Rituals or ritual behaviours, which are one of the sources for art (Turner, 1967), are built on the need to make any given element special. According to Turner, people have also used rituals for the purposes of signalling a transition from one condition to another, which the individual and tribe find meaningful: for *liminality,* which Turner intends as the threshold to be stepped over in order to *become.*

The daily routines of relationships do not fully explain the extra-daily work in performances.

Theatre anthropology (Barba, 1995, p. 13) attempts to define the common structural elements that characterise the technique of actors, dancers and performers, independently from cultural differences, context of origin and specific aesthetical conventions. Barba's research recognises a specific set of recurring principles in the different traditions. These principles concern the objective use that performers make of their body and their energy in a situation of organised performance, which is physically different from the use they make of their body and energy in daily life. This difference is condensed in the expression *extra-daily behaviour*, the opposite of *daily behaviour*. Barba in his writings refers directly to the technical level of the actor's work, and based on these it is possible to build a very clear bridge between the *technical* and the *ethical* – referring the concept of ethics to its original etymology, connected to the meaning *custom*, the very pragmatic and material level of human behaviour. Since the work of the actor is an eminently practical one, where values exist almost only in their embodied form, it is possible to say that technique and ethics are almost synonymous, and that the extra-daily behaviour of the actors is their ritual way to *make special*, in the way Dissanayake (2000, 1995) intends this expression.

Barba's extra-daily behaviour is mostly a technique of the individual actor, even if transmitted through generations and shared by a collectivity of contemporary artists. In Barba's terms, extra-daily behaviour is first of all the actor's way to have an impact on the sensorial reception of the spectator, to conquer and keep the attention of the audience. But in more general terms, we could try to apply Barba's conceptualisation and vocabulary to other levels of theatre practice, specifically, to the way relationships are organised in theatre work. First of all, the codification of physical behaviour in acting traditions includes, in many cases, not only individual behaviour, but also the way the actor is supposed to react and adapt to what the other actors are doing on stage. The dynamic of action, reaction and adaptation between various elements of a performance is explicitly thematised in the jargon and the practice of many theatre traditions. At Odin Teatret, for example, *dialogue through actions* is one of the basic skills actors must develop. Barba's transcultural performances, involving actors from different traditions, base their very possibility of existence on the fact that all these traditions share, tacitly or under different terminologies, a common attitude towards establishing objective relationships on the level of physical actions, and a common way of articulating physical behaviour in objective units recognisable by any other professional actor as actions or reactions. Objective and clear articulation of physical behaviour is the condition that grants the possibility of collaborating despite cultural or individual differences.

In this way, the scenic relationship itself is codified and structured in different forms from the everyday one, even if stylized according to the various expressive styles and body cultures. This scenic relational code is objective and individual at the same time. Just like the personal technique of each actor, it is basically connected with the perceptive experience of the spectator. It is first of all an instrument to manipulate the spectator's attention and reception, to make the scenic relationships between actors visible, believable and comprehensible. Nevertheless, just like for the individual technique, this relational code can be observed as the objective correlation of a relational *ethos* shared by the actors belonging to a specific group or tradition, based on their shared artisanal (the professional craft) responsibility towards the spectator.

In addition to this, every sound theatre tradition codifies *not only* the way performers behave on stage, but also the way they behave during training and rehearsals, or while doing any kind of activity in the *working space*, whose entrance is indeed the *threshold* beyond which a different code is active. The reader might look back at our initial image of the shoes left out of the performing space, which indicates the trespassing from the daily (shoes) to the extra-daily (bare feet or stage shoes). Literally the actors leave their daily behaviour behind and transform the very artefact of shoes from a daily to a symbolic object. But why are feet one of the focuses of this ethical shift? It is because the material behaviour of the feet is one of the technical foundations of actors' extra-daily use of the body.

The practice of shifting from ordinary to extra-ordinary is more evident in non-Western traditions, where theatre practices have been connected until recent times with ritual and religion, or in any case have kept a much higher level of formalisation and codification than Western traditions. But this shift is nevertheless recognisable in almost all theatre contexts, even if in much more secular and elastic forms, which are not connected to explicit ideological formulations or formalised learning processes.

This practice includes the way actors use the working venues, the way they dress, the way they speak to each other. It is a practical set of rules, which embodies the *ethos* of the group.

But, given the extra-daily behaviour, how does the actors' performance on stage achieve a verisimilar quality? This happens because actors aim to create *an organic equivalent* of daily behaviour using extra-daily means. Following the same logic, we could formulate the hypothesis that the system of relationships on stage and in the working space tries to create an equivalent of the daily system, but which responds to rules and conventions completely different from the daily ones. These conventions have certainly technical and aesthetical motivations, but they are so strong and so engaging for the body-mind of the individual that they inevitably create an alternative, extra-daily psychophysical and ethical context. They "make it special". These alternative codes concern both the performance itself and the preparation of the performance. They operate a re-framing of relationships by establishing specific procedures and conduct that involve learning and creating.

Altamira Studio Teater is continuing its work demonstration. Now the actors are showing the construction of a complex collective scene, where extreme coordination is required of players, and with the space and music, not only for the aesthetical success of the scene but, in this case, also to ensure the safety of the actors, who run and fall while playing fragile wooden violins in a very small space, just a few centimetres away from the spectators.

Intimacy, reciprocity and invasivity characterise relationships in group theatre. The actors' bodies react to each other and have tangible impacts on each other. The action of one actress hitting another provokes a direct reaction (moving away, running away, crying, surprise) and changes the direction of the whole scene. This confers upon the actors' bodies and actions a fundamental responsibility: the fact of being able to start a chain reaction of concrete and readable responses. This special kind of dilated and formalised reactivity is one of the main focuses of actors' training. As chaos theories well describe, the flap of a butterfly's wing in Brazil can set off a tornado in Texas (Lorenz, 1972) and start nonlinear dynamics. These dynamics, in theatre, are tangible because they are made visible in a performative and dramaturgical form. As the purpose of theatre is to translate ideas into forms (per-*form*), or in other words to translate the ordinary into the extraordinary (Eisner, 2002) or, in theatre anthropological terms, to glide from the daily to the extra-daily, relationships cannot be the same in real life and on stage. The private use of the body has no place on stage – the actor's face wears a mask or make-up or any other device that is signalling the technical and ethical diversity of the stage dimension. Similarly, ordinary or daily behaviour does not have a place in performative work.

Therefore, the first step towards co-creation in group theatre is a re-framing of daily relationships into extra-daily ones. How does the ensemble do that? We can cite the examples of Odin Teatret and of Altamira Studio Teater, where tacit or explicit relational codes of conduct regulate the preparation work of the ensemble. These codes regulate what is almost impossible to regulate – the bodies' intimacy, the reciprocity of actions/reactions and also the invasive dimension of theatre, where actors give all their body and mind to the compositional work. This is done by means of re-framing. In order to make the passage between the daily and the stage dimension, actors might use rituals and rules. For instance, the routine of leaving shoes outside the theatre hall at Odin Teatret is as much for hygiene as for ritual. Or rather, it starts as a cleanliness habit and develops into a ritual act. The *limen* (Turner, 1982) of the door signals the threshold into a different dimension, where other relationships enter into force. Codes of conduct regulate the space of work, how to use it, how to interact with it. But there are also basic routines, such as the rule of leaving mobile phones outside the room or switching them off and hiding them, or verbal rules, according to which actors do not speak to each other in the same way they do as the friends, lovers or antagonists they are for each other outside the theatre. These actions regulate relationships, set limits to individual daily behaviour and by doing so liberate the actors' creativity. The paradox of the theatrical creative process lies indeed in the process of limitation in order to set free.

The myth of theatre as free expression is here heavily challenged. Actors do not create together by being uncritically open to the others and by means of uncontrolled freedom, but rather by means of restricting and reorganising their range of action (from daily to extra-daily), by reframing their behaviour and relationships to the professional context of performance and by including each other in their individual creation (action/reaction). Seeing the actors' and directors' creative process in this light has some consequences for our conceptualisation and its application to higher education. The first one is a different view of participation and leadership as ethically charged.

PARTICIPATION AND LEADERSHIP

The act of creating together – co-creation – is basically participative. Participation means to take part (Latin *partem*, part + *capere*, to take), but also stresses the agency: part-icip-*aCtion*. The action of taking part in group theatre occurs by means of relationships and collective dynamics. As we have seen above, though, these relationships are coded and the freedom that actors might achieve is demanding. Each member of a co-creative ensemble bears the responsibility of the good functioning of the group and of the creative process. This responsibility is directed to the other members and to the leader, the director, and is active in nature. In this sense the actors' freedom is challenging, because filled with active responsibility. In the theatre group there is no place for passive following – followers have (must have) a propositive, actively creative attitude, otherwise the members of the ensemble would experience an imbalance and the chain of actions and reactions would be interrupted. When theatre groups are professional, they cannot allow any disequilibrium to get in the way of creation. Therefore it is vital to co-creating ensembles that relationships function well (by means of agreed and shared codes of conduct and rituals, even when they are established in the complete absence of a common ideology or common explicit beliefs) and that this is a sustained effort. Perseverance in the availability of work energy and sustained commitment to the common project ensure a stable work environment.

How does such a co-creative group come together? How it is possible for a director to lead such a demanding project? Is the management of this demanding freedom at all learnable?

Pierangelo, as director of Altamira Studio Teater, must generate a frame that is stimulating for each individual actor. This frame includes the dialectic between the individual contribution of actors and the director's synthesis. It must include also the space for a spontaneous network of different kinds and levels of collaboration between different members of the group. It must admit a progressive and equal distribution of responsibilities that satisfies individual ambitions and challenges the abstraction of wishful thinking.

How he interacts with his colleagues depends partly on intuition, luck, and chance, but it certainly must be based on a shared – sometimes tacit – agreement to common rules of conduct. This agreement embodies a very concrete and specific cultural choice. It means literally taking a stance in relation to the context in which the group lives. It is a personal and collective answer to the surrounding contexts and their influences. The extra-daily code of the group, its way of codifying and challenging relationships, is its own way of "making it special".

Because acceptance of these codes implies the suspension of the daily ego, the refusal of many previously-learned codes and the establishment of what Barba calls the professional super-ego (see Meyer-Dinkgräfe, 2005), Pierangelo finds it easier to choose actors that are young and not yet socialised in a specific theatrical code, because learning a code of conduct is like learning a language: it is easier to learn a mother tongue than a second language. As the codes of conduct are the mother tongue of the ensemble, which is going to be the internal communication tool, it is fundamental to learn it well and become fluent. It is important to have an affective connection with it, linked to artistically foundational experiences – to the first days of professional work, where every actor receives the imprinting that will mark all his or her professional life.

Metaphors apart, actors are asked to share deeply rooted beliefs on how performance must be created, or at least to believe that the common work gives enough space to everyone's personal needs.

They are asked to share codes that regulate their concrete behaviour as theatre-makers, compositional tools based on the use of relationships, body and space. This professional dimension, which is specific to group theatre and performance, might be in contradiction with the tacit codes of conduct in our Western society, which are ego-centric (Scharmer & Kaufer, 2013), because it aims at suspending the individual ego in a sustained common project.

The role of the leader/director implies a very important maieutic element, between creation and pedagogy. The maieutic method consists of intellectual and artistic midwifery. *Maieutikos* is indeed the Ancient Greek for midwifery and the method has been attributed to Socrates (Hanke, 1990), who used generative questions in order to stimulate intellectual growth and knowledge. So, the question whether this intimate work of the actor can be learned does not exclude the concept of professional (co)creation. The maieutic role of the director and of the colleagues entails the creation of an environment where the individual actor or actress can find his or her own conditions of work as a professional. The leader is at the service of the actor and facilitates the birth or development of his/her autonomy. This is a rigorous and coherent process that is at the core of any leadership of theatre groups and that can be applied to any leadership in creative contexts. The director guides the actors as a pedagogue who is also author and creator himself in a sort of reciprocal maieutic process. His authority derives from his knowledge of aesthetical rules, of the craft of theatre, of the audience, from the responsibility he has taken for the survival of the group. His decisional power is at the service of the survival of the group as well as of the development of each individual, who becomes paradoxically obliged to be free and responsible.

The maieutic process is reciprocal. Not only does each actor have a maieutic role for all the colleagues, but each actor and all the actors together have a fundamental maieutic role towards the director. The director, in the specificity of his or her role, lives his or her own learning process as a theatre director and as a group leader. This process is made of successes and failures, which are even more delicate because they are made on the body of the actors. The actors must contribute positively and creatively to this process, following but challenging the director, accepting his weaknesses but being demanding, creatively opposing their point of view when needed, but always within the frame of the professional code, which implies different roles and responsibilities.

The director is the expert of composition and meaning-making. But at the same time he must leave this dimension open to many different possibilities, where the sensibility of each actor can find its own space.

Similarly to other artistic creations, theatre and performance generate meaning. But unlike other art forms, they generate a complex network of relationships and bodies. They also generate *embodied* meaning (see in this volume Springborg's contribution). The complete relativisation of identity in the body-mind enigma opens up to a process of discovery of self, of own body and own identity. Both ensemble and audience participate in this process, which contains huge development potential, because both parties are engaging in the process, literally, with their entire selves. They are inside the learning process, not just looking at it from the outside.

PER-FORM-ANCE

The structural aspects of theatrical co-creation are several. Some aspects change in the various performative genres, others are common throughout different genres. General characteristics are the fact that theatre has clearly stated purposes, that performance takes place in spaces where the unexpected can happen, and that what happens in front of the audience is an organic process of adaptation. Everything in performances is subject to transformation. Because this happens in ensembles and through relationships, this transformation is always also contamination, and adjustment. Actors adjust to each other, directors adjust to actors and vice versa, audiences and actors adapt to each other and even performances adapt to actors, while they develop their identity and professional knowledge.

Altamira Studio Teater is a group theatre whose practice can exemplify how individuals bring their individuality together in a co-creative project. The single individual brings herself into play: a drive or desire or need or a kind of energy is behind her proposed action to the group. In group theatre, this means a concrete dramaturgical action offered to the group in order to receive a re-action. This objective correlative of a drive can be a song, an action, a dance, a spoken text, anything that can initiate a chain of reciprocal reactions. When this co-creative process is activated, the space-time of performance transforms itself. There is no longer *mine* or *yours* (or not only), but a common flow of actions that is made visible in specific theatrical channels or forms. The fact that relationships become visible because transposed in aesthetic form also makes feedback to each other sustainable and continuous. In other words, if an actor refuses to react through actions to the proposed action of another actor, this will affect the group work in a specific direction and the whole ensemble is then forced to adjust accordingly. The refusal or the recognition of a proposed relationship is an act that deeply affects the organic nature of both process and result. It can limit research and discovery, and can end up frustrating the collective effort to create a space and time where individuals relate to each other according to an extra-daily principle.

In group theatre it is vital that each one of the ensemble members takes the responsibility and risk of being free to create. If one member of the group does not engage in this individual creation of materials and stimuli to the others, the group will not have any shared creation. The individual contribution is fundamental; everyone must be available to be a (re)active party to the proposals of the others. Paradoxically, co-creation is only admitted against the background of individual creation and of deep personal motivation, and only if these are in sustained, dialectic and active relationships with others.

Theatre and performance are structured actions – the tangible form they make use of is action made by actors. The makers of theatre are inside the medium's form. They are at the same time the authors, the material and the form itself. Therefore theatre-makers think in actions when they create. These actions are transformed when they encounter others' actions and shape (per-*form*) the final work of art, the performance. Actors can learn how to think in actions and how to react to actions, but their individual work of composition is constantly unfolding before their very eyes. In other words, what unfolds before the audience's very eyes is a real-time learning process, an adjustment to given conditions that, no matter how often they have been repeated, are always new to the here-and-now of the performer. The skills needed to respond to these challenges are technically improvisational, where the word improvisation, far beyond its basic meaning, implies a fundamentally pedagogical, self-pedagogical and processual aspect. It means that actors must learn how to stay in open processes, where knowledge is emergent and contextual. The way in which an actor is expected to react to given stimuli is always novel and must be appropriate to a given context of actions. In this sense, creative and learning processes are analogous to each other. Constructivist and pragmatic learning theorists conceptualise learning as a basically creative act (Illeris, 2009), just as performance theorists (Schechner, 2002) define the creative process as a basically pedagogical one. Schechner, quoting Goffmann's work on the presentation of self in everyday life, defines performance as the activity that individuals engage in when they participate in given events that are to influence other participants (Schechner, 2002, p. 23). This influence, according to Schechner (2002), is ontological ("being"), active or technical ("doing"), poetic or expressive ("showing doing") and hermeneutical ("explaining showing doing") (p. 22). Each of the elements of performance implies a process of change and transformation, of enquiry, of playful research and of serious play. In other words – they imply learning processes.

CREATION-ACTION

The relational aspect in theatre and performance cannot be denied. The transformative character of theatre relationships unfolds in between a singular and a plural dimension: the personal, unique and delimited body of the individual actor or actress on the one part, and interactions between actors on the other. We have brought the example of Altamira Studio Teater and how individuals participate in the common creation. Sometimes these actors report feelings of togetherness ("you feel that you are together") that can be explained differently according to different disciplines. Neurosciences would explain it by means of mirror neurons, the neurons responsible for behaviours of imitation and empathy (Bråten, 2007), psychology describes it as group flow (Sawyer, 2007) or team flow (Van den Hout, Davies, & Walgrave, 2016).

The psychological state of group flow is well known in collaborative art forms (Chemi, 2016a). In these cases, artists report that they achieve a shared feeling of concentration and focus by converging their attention on each other during performances, as a sort of reciprocal inspiration and focus-keeping.

This is achieved by means of explicit or tacit agreements amongst the members of the ensemble, by deep personal knowledge and knowledge about each other's reactions, together with shared common values, and a common sense of purpose. If these conditions occur, the members of the ensemble may perceive each other as an organic unity and end up experiencing a positive state of self-forgetfulness together – in other words, group flow (Van den Hout, Davies, & Walgrave, 2016). In recent years, Eugenio Barba has been using, in his oral contributions, the expression *collective mind*, giving this name to several Odin Teatret workshops that open the performance-creation process to the active participation of chosen spectators. One concrete example is the ensemble's upcoming performance (present title *The Tree*) and its open feedback workshops, indeed called *the collective mind*. With this expression, Barba refers to the very specific creative process developed by Odin Teatret, which involves actors, dramaturges, assistants and spectators-in-progress in a kaleidoscope of individual contributions, which contaminate each other and react continuously to the new stimulations appearing in the process. In the 'collective mind', the authorial dimension of the director manifests itself in the organic, narrative and poetic selection and composition of an enormous amount of materials and possibilities. Pierangelo, who had been working on the performance *The Chronic Life* (first performance, 2011) as one of Barba's assistant directors, once said to his master: "It's strange. I'm not the director but I feel the performance belongs to me as much as to you and to the actors". Barba replied literally and explicitly: "the performance has one mother: the actors, who offered their bodies. But it has many fathers" (Barba's private dialogue with Pompa).

In this tension between individual and collective, the performative and dramaturgical co-creation is fashioned. Creation is action between individuals and in theatre this is concrete, situated in a given context, specific, bodily. There is nothing abstract or merely psychological in this being together within theatrical co-creation. Theatre is not made of abstract concepts or isolated works of art, but rather of persons and their relationships. Theatre is a system of relationships in action.

This can be pleasurable, but very often it is not. "Being together" in group theatre can exceed personal boundaries on several levels: psychological (suspension of ego), bodily (intimacy and crossing of intimate sphere, breaking of habits, crisis of personal and relational entropy), and emotional (crisis of identity). This process is not necessarily pleasurable, but theatre makes use of the unpleasantness of personal interactions and ignites coping strategies that are essentially developmental and pedagogical. Even though a certain level of hedonistic benefit is necessary to fuel the individual drive to creation, what really moves theatrical research is the challenge of what is unpleasant. We have no intention of reviving the myth of the unhappy or miserable artist, which we believe a legacy of Romanticism (Chemi, Jensen, & Hersted, 2015, pp. 42–43) and of misunderstanding of the nature of artistic creativity, but we have no intention of substituting this myth with a new one based on the belief that theatre is all hedonic expression and free play. We would rather refer to Etienne Decroux (1963), the French master of abstract corporeal mime, who used to say that the real searcher (whom he called mime) "is comfortable in the discomfort" (p. 73, unsurprisingly, quoted in Barba, 1995, p. 24).

Freedom in group theatre is filled with responsibility for each other and risk-taking. What is most unpleasurable is also what allows for strategies of change and learning to be activated, sublimating entertainment, which is one of the fundamental tasks of good quality theatre, into pure research.

LEARNING IN THE ART OF THEATRE

The limits and advantages of creating together are clear in theatre and performance, precisely because they are per-*formed,* sat in aesthetically organised form. The limits are addressed above as the challenges implicit in theatre-making. The advantages are implicit in the strategies that actors and directors activate: change and learning processes within complex environments. However, we wish to emphasise here the concrete rewards that co-creative strategies can bring to their participants. Creating together with others reveals the core of any (well-structured) creative process: the opportunity of discovery. Looking closely at creative breakthrough in group theatre, we can point to specific kinds of discoveries: the re-discovery of the known and the discovery of unknown. Both rely on serendipitous methods and processes (Christoffersen, 2004) but with fundamental pedagogical differences. The former consists of understanding in different ways what is already known, with the consequence of acquired knowledge (accommodative) or deepened level of knowledge. The latter triggers truly innovative processes, allowing for the encounter with the unknown, or as Darsø (2004) puts it, stepping into the learning space where participants don't know what they don't know. This dimension involves contemporaneously learning, creativity and artistry in the same transformative process. The only strategy for navigating through the not-known is to continuously learn how to react to stimuli, because strategies are not given beforehand. It does not merely involve learning, as much as learning to learn, as Barba and Savarese (2011) explain, with reference to the actor's technique, in their chapter focused on the actor's training. This does not simply mean learning improvisational techniques – undoubtedly fundamental in theatre co-creation (Sawyer, 2007) – but hints at more complex and structured learning patterns. It is about learning the improvisational art of continuously learning.

At the same time, actions in theatre happen in tangible forms. This signifies that learning happens while putting learning in aesthetic forms, while creating shapes. Consequently, the serendipitous process might end up redefining the very context of work and its participants. Transformation and change occur in the performers' identities, the relational work of preparation and the performance itself. This creative benefit turns the disadvantages of the co-creative process into tangible advantages. The more articulated and complex the process of co-creation, the more challenging and complex the synthesis of it will be. Concretely, for instance, the more participants in the co-creative process, the more complex and diverse the process itself will be. Synthesising very open and complex processes in artistic form is itself complex. Relationships in group theatre provide the technical continuity for the co-creative processes, no matter how complex they are. The relationships *are* technique.

As already mentioned above, in this almost ideological conceptualisation of relationships reside the very ethics of theatre. Going beyond the logic of individualism, without renouncing its virtues, group theatre develops artistic forms collectively, but the ensemble's co-creation depends on the individuals' own work on themselves, on their own transformation of individual drives into artistic forms and on their mutual capacity of allowing relationships and shared processes to completely transform the individual offerings. The challenging freedom of giving and receiving demands an ethical attitude of personal responsibility for the collective co-creation. When co-creation is truly given space in the ensemble, its existence becomes a political manifesto against ego-centric alienating systems on the one hand, and an artistic statement on the other. But it is a manifesto made of actions. The final product of these processes is a performance as an act of individual and collective autobiography, which is telling the story of a system of relationships in action. The ethical and political strength of this alternative relational model is still to be fully exploited and explained. Doing so would open unknown perspectives not only for artists or theatre-makers but also for fields of humanistic research on the essence of relationships, at work with a common creative project.

CAN WE LEARN FROM THEATRE LABORATORY?

Our concluding remarks consider how theatre laboratory learns and creates and reflect on applying it to higher education.

We will start by summing up the main points we have addressed.

With regard to possible transfer from theatre theory and practices to co-creation and higher education, some fundamental differences must be taken into consideration. First of all, not all aspects of the two contexts can be fully compared, because of the different organisation of their pedagogical practices. For instance, in a higher education context, educators cannot choose their students, as can happen in theatre ensembles and theatre laboratories. An educator who chooses her students in higher education would raise a number of ethical dilemmas about democratic accessibility to education. However, we must admit that the vision of an almost Socratic community of thinkers that choose each other on the impulse of common interests and affinity exercises a strong fascination on us. Our intuitive association goes to apprenticeship practices, where educators could open up their research workshop to their students' legitimate peripheral (or active) participation. Higher education educators are frequently expert researchers in a specific domain and often actively participate in research projects. Regardless of the size, the scientific tradition and methods, the topic or the application, these projects can be looked on as laboratories where knowledge is to be achieved. The legitimate participation of student-novices in these communities of practices could open up to co-creative processes, where experts and novices enrich each other's knowledge and understanding.

One more challenge in making the theatre/higher education link explicit resides in the very concept of transfer and the (im)possibility of transferring knowledge from one domain to another. This topic is complex and we cannot address it in depth in this chapter, therefore we wish to refer to Beach's sociocultural perspective (1999).

As to the question of whether theatre is always co-creative, our reader can legitimately formulate doubts based on a specific knowledge of theatre traditions other than theatre laboratory. Are theatre productions composed by means of a high degree of instruction or direction truly co-creative? If we understand co-creation as reciprocal inspiration and shared effort of creation, it would then be understandable to look at the relationship between director and actors as uneven and unbalanced. The reader might recall the quote from Barba's private dialogue with Pompa above, where he claims that "the performance has one mother: the actors, who offered their bodies. But it has many fathers". If this is so, what is the consequence for authentic reciprocity in these learning processes? To what degree is the director/actor relationship mutually co-creative? Even in theatre laboratory, does co-creation mean that no form of leadership is allowed? In theatre laboratory, co-creating ensembles establish processes based on action/re-action. This means that their creative processes are based on reciprocity, beyond the roles of actor or director. Although the ensemble accepts the decisional role of its director, and his consequent right to make the final decision on which solution to keep, this does not obliterate the fundamental reciprocity of the act of creation. Stretching the consequences of our thoughts further, we might assert that reciprocity is synonymous with co-creation in theatre practices.

Another consequence of the conceptualisation in the present chapter is the very close relationship between learning and creativity. Within co-creative practices of artistic composition in theatre laboratory, creative and learning processes seem to be almost analogous. We have mentioned this close familiarity above by referencing how pragmatism and constructivism think about learning as a basically creative activity. However, the specific elements of this relationship could be advantageously addressed in future studies. If so, theatre laboratory would provide an obvious area for experiments.

At this point of our journey, we cannot give any didactic quick fixes or set answers on the topic. Indeed we doubt the appropriateness of offering formulaic answers at all. True to the open research approach of theatre laboratory, we wish to conclude by formulating the dilemmas and research questions that emerge from our reflections above.

First of all, our reflection stimulates a number of fundamental questions about the nature of theatre and of education in themselves. Is theatre going to be instrumental to education or should it rather defend its autonomy (Chemi, 2016b)? What is the purpose of letting higher education find inspiration in artistic fields? Finding answers or perspectives to these answers involves complex, cross-disciplinary and conceptual work. This focused research should look at the development of theatrical and educational practices and try to extract the pedagogical essence of these practices. This might lead to novel definitions of intent and purpose for both fields. Theatre practices that apply to other non-theatrical contexts carry with them a specific aesthetic statement, which is visible and concrete in these practices (Chemi, 2016b). Higher education practices that seek and find inspiration in artistic fields do not practice academia as in an ivory tower (Barnett, 1990) but aim at renewal, creativity, innovation and openness to cross-disciplinarity. This also might have the consequence of defining the very purpose of higher education as innovative and relevant to society.

Even more specifically, looking at the co-creative practices of theatre laboratory, which elements might inspire higher education? In which way should this inspiration occur? To what extent is the transfer of learning processes possible from an artistic to a specifically pedagogical context? For instance, what would it mean to translate the concept of extra-daily from theatre to education?

Finding answers to these questions not only involves gathering of knowledge and theoretical conceptualisations but also practical experimentation with novel forms of cross-disciplinary co-creation. In other words, a contribution like ours can open paths of reflection, but what will make a difference will be the establishment of experimental spaces, where concepts and hypotheses can be tested, discarded, translated, renewed, and reinvented. Such a space can only be a laboratory, where open inquiry is cultivated and cherished.

REFERENCES

Barba, E. (1995). *The paper canoe*. London & New York, NY: Routledge.

Barba, E. (2015). *The moon rises from the ganges: My journey through Asian acting techniques*. Holstebro & Malta: Icarus Routledge.

Barba, E., & Savarese, N. (2011). *A dictionary of theatre anthropology: The secret art of the performer*. Taylor & Francis.

Barnett, R. (1990). *The idea of higher education*. Buckingham: The Society for Research into Higher Education & Open University Press.

Beach, K. (1999). Chapter 4: Consequential transitions: A sociocultural expedition beyond transfer in education. *Review of research in education, 24*(1), 101–139.

Bråten, S. (Ed.). (2007). *On being moved: From mirror neurons to empathy*. Amsterdam, NLD: John Benjamins Publishing Company.

Chemi, T. (2016a). Distributed problem-solving: How artists' participatory strategies can inspire creativity in higher education. In C. Zhou (Ed.), *Handbook of research on creative problem-solving skill development in higher education*. Hershey, PA: IGI Global Publishers.

Chemi, T. (2016b, July 7–9). Transgressive or instrumental? A paradigm for the arts as learning and development. Full paper at *32nd EGOS colloquium, organizing in the shadow of power*. Naples, Italy: University of Naples Federico II.

Chemi, T., Jensen, J. B., & Hersted, L. (2015). *Behind the scenes of artistic creativity: Processes of learning, creating and organising*. Frankfurt am Main: Peter Lang.

Christoffersen, E. E. (2004). Introduction to peripeti and serendipity. *Peripeti, 2*, 5–15.

Darsø, L. (2004), *Artful creation: Learning-tales of arts-in-business*. Frederiksberg: Samfundslitteratur.

Decroux, E. (1963). *Paroles sur le mime*. Paris: Gallimard.

Dewey, J. (2005). *Art as experience*. London: Perigee (I 1934).

Dissanayake, E. (1995). *Homo aestheticus: Where art comes from and why*. Seattle, WA & London: University of Washington Press (I 1992).

Dissanayake, E. (2000). *Art and intimacy: How the art began*. Seattle, WA & London: University of Washington Press.

Eisner, E. W. (2002). *The arts and the creation of mind*. New Haven, CT: Yale University Press.

Freud, S. (2003). *Beyond the pleasure principle* (Vol. 840). Penguin UK.

Gosse, V., & Moser, R. (Eds.). (2004). *World the sixties made: Politics and culture in recent America*. Philadelphia, PA: Temple University Press.

Hanke, M. (1990). Socratic pragmatics: Maieutic dialogues. *Journal of pragmatics, 14*(3), 459–465.

Hickman, L. A. (2007). *Pragmatism as post-postmodernism: Lessons from John Dewey*. Bronx, NY: Fordham University Press.
Illeris, K. (2009). *Contemporary theories of learning: Learning theorists … in their own words*. London: Routledge.
John-Steiner, V. (2000). *Creative collaboration*. Oxford & New York, NY: Oxford University Press.
Lorenz, E. (1972). *Predictability: Does the flap of a butterfly's wing in Brazil set off a tornado in Texas?* American Association for the Advancement of Science, December 29, 1972.
Marwick, A. (1994). Experimental theatre in the 1960s. *History Today*, *44*(10), 34.
Meyer-Dinkgräfe, D. (2005). *Theatre and consciousness: Explanatory scope and future potential*. Bristol, GB: Intellect Books.
Radbourne, J., Glow, H., & Johanson, K. (2014). *Audience experience: A critical analysis of audiences in the performing arts*. Bristol, GB: Intellect.
Sawyer, K. (2007). *Group genius: The power of creative collaboration*. Philadelphia, PA: Basic Books.
Scharmer, C. O., & Kaufer, K. (2013). *Leading from the emerging future: From ego-system to eco-system economies*. Berrett-Koehler Publishers.
Schechner, R. (2002). *Performance studies: An introduction*. London & New York, NY: Routledge.
Schino, M. (2009). *Alchemists of the stage: Theatre laboratories in Europe*. Poland: Icarus.
Stanislavski, C. (1989). *An actor prepares*. Taylor & Francis.
Turner, V. W. (1982). *From ritual to theatre: The human seriousness of play*. Paj Publications.
Van den Hout, J. J., Davies, C., & Walgrave, B. (2016). The application of team flow theory. In L. Harmat, F. Ørsted Andersen, F. Ullén, J. Wright, & G. Sadlo (Eds.), *Flow experience: Empirical research and applications*. Switzerland: Springer.

Tatiana Chemi
Department of Learning and Philosophy
Aalborg University

Pierangelo Pompa
Altamira Studio Teater
Denmark

CHARLOTTE WEGENER

8. CO-CREATING THE JOY OF WRITING

Creative Analytical Writing Practices

QUESTIONS

"I write in order to learn something that I did not know before I wrote it", Laurel Richardson (1994/2003, p. 501) aptly noted, and this statement also applies to the ideas presented in this chapter. The chapter suggests a way to think about practice and teach creative, co-created writing practices that makes writing a key to learning and identity building for students. In my teaching and supervision of students, I wish for writing to become a way of thinking, learning and being in the world. I am not solely concerned with the final product. I also strive to be a catalyst for each student becoming and being someone who writes. From this perspective, learning is not only a cognitive process of information processing or knowledge acquisition (an epistemological process), but more fundamentally an ontological process, an essential part of becoming somebody, an identity-building process of taking part in a changing social practice (Packer & Goicoechea, 2000). Over the years, I have run writing workshops for students and faculty and developed a writing practice increasingly focused on joy. This is not to suggest that our students can or should always be happy when they write. Nor does it mean that they (or we) necessarily become happier human beings by writing.

Writing academic texts involves decoding of genres, it involves deadlines, feedback from teachers, and evaluations from examiners. However, this does not prevent us from getting involved in creative and co-created writing practices with our students. The chapter suggests some steps to take to merge convention and creativity and suggests that it is exactly the balancing act of these two elements that fosters joy. In a variety of future jobs for which we educate our students, mastering this balancing act between convention and experiment is crucial. The chapter presents academic writing as a social practice through which we continuously create and recreate both the social practice and ourselves as academics, students and teachers. It presents examples from my own practice as teacher and supervisor, based on a model of three drivers for creative, co-created writing practices called *the Toolbox*, *the Building Materials* and *the Building*.

At the beginning of each semester, I always ask the students in my writing workshops about their expectations and wishes. Why have they come? What do

T. Chemi & L. Krogh (Eds.), Co-Creation in Higher Education, 117–130.

they hope to take from the course? The students' responses often take the form of questions such as the following:

- How do I structure my time so I do not just write up to the deadline?
- I am not motivated to get going – how do I embark?
- I would like to get feedback, but my peers might be just as busy as me.
- I keep finding new information and things to read and I can't stop investigating.
- How do I get an overview of the literature?
- How do I get started with the analysis?
- I would like to write so the reader gets on board.
- Am I allowed to write 'I'?
- I have no (good) ideas – what should I write about?
- I have too many ideas – how should I focus?
- Can I possibly write anything that has not been said already?

The various statements and questions are all highly relevant, and there is not one single correct answer to any of them. Some of the students' questions concern academic conventions and genres. Others address the never completed work of investigating, learning and communicating through writing. However, the questions contain more than that. The questions touch on the students' *relationship* to their field, to the art and craft of academic methods and materials, that is, identity work. In what follows, we will examine writing as a social practice and subsequently, I will present the model that I use in my teaching and supervising of students, consisting of three drivers for creative co-creation of writing practices. Then I discuss two cases in which the model was helpful and finally, I sum up on the model and provide a short afterword.

WRITING IS A SOCIAL PRACTICE

If writing is regarded as both an epistemological and an ontological endeavour, we all write as participants in a social practice. Production of text is a prerequisite to pass an exam and move forward in education. Through writing, students show that they are able to control and produce knowledge and that they understand conventions appreciated in the given practice. The more successful they are in doing so, the more fully they participate, as illustrated in Lave and Wenger's theory of situated learning (1991). If they fail, they may conclude that they do not belong to the social practice (to this class, this study, or even to the university in general). Understanding academic writing as a social practice focuses on how students (and we ourselves as researchers) participate in a community through text production. Text is the most important medium through which we express ourselves when we convey "what we know". However, text is equally an important medium to express "who we are". Writing what we know and who we are is constant participation leading to feelings of belonging or isolation.

The text must finally be detached from the person who wrote it and, when it is read by others, these readers bring their knowledge and preconceptions into the encounter with the text, carrying out a kind of "re-writing" (Thomson & Kamler, 2010). In this way, knowledge is constructed through the way we express ourselves, and through the way our expression is received by others. The writing process is part of a much larger social practice in which the subject, the research field and the institutional and political environment represent the possibilities and limitations of what we can express, and how we can be understood and evaluated. Writing practice is therefore fundamentally concerned with learning, communication and identity creation through participation.

No matter how isolated we are or feel when writing (and both students and faculty tell me they often do), writing is a social activity. Our writing is based on the ideas of others and meets other ideas when we send it out into the world. Lave and Wenger (1991) developed the idea that participation in a social practice fundamentally depends on access to activities and technologies. Becoming a full participant in a social practice (in this case a university study) requires that you have access to participation in the production process (in this case the production of texts), and to mastering the technologies used in production (in this case, writing in certain ways). If the manner in which the production takes place in a specific social practice is not transparent and visible, it is difficult or impossible to participate, and it is therefore difficult to learn. To teach academic writing involves helping students not just to decipher what an academic text looks like, but also to decode the processes that led up to its being written – how the text has come to be. Students (and faculty alike) who have difficulty writing academic texts often conclude that they do not "belong" and that they are not suitable for the study (or the job). However, the reason may be that academic writing is a *black box*, whose internal functions are hidden.

To understand and master academic writing, therefore, within a particular professional or methodological tradition is not just a matter of learning some techniques and methods. It is about mastering the traditions and conventions of this practice more fundamentally. Through participation, we enhance our skills and continually get access to participation and thus have the opportunity to both continue and change a practice.

To conceive of academic writing as a social practice provides some pedagogical tools. Instead of concluding that the student and the study (or the employee and the job) are a bad match, we can aim to turn the *black box* of writing into a *glass box*. A black box is opaque. You feed it with information (perhaps a lecture series or data from a research project), and expect a result (maybe a term paper, a report or an article). If the process from input to output is invisible, it is difficult to adjust it, if the output does not live up to your expectations. The result is simply good or bad. Making the text production processes visible is not just about teaching tricks of the trade. If the writing process becomes a glass box, it is then possible to decode the mechanisms in the social practice and begin to understand and create one's own role therein.

A PRAGMATIC APPROACH TO WRITING

To understand writing as a social practice reflects a pragmatic approach, both in the everyday and philosophical sense of the word. In everyday language, the term *pragmatic* is an attitude to ordinary challenges and problems. Being pragmatic means being inclined to find feasible solutions and get things done within the actual framework and with the resources available. This is an important approach to writing. Writing as a social practice, however, is also rooted in pragmatism in its philosophical meaning of cognition through action. According to the American philosopher and educator John Dewey (1859–1952), education should foster critical and reflective thinking so we can act ever more knowledgeably and intelligently in the world (Elkjær, 2005). From a pragmatic perspective, writing is both reflection and action (Dewey, 1916). The simple act of writing can provide new ideas and insights. Additionally, the actual text is a medium for expressing new insights and thus communicating with the outside world. Richardson (1994) says radically that research *is* writing. In the process of writing, one must make a variety of choices that are crucial for the knowledge produced. What to include and what to leave out? What is the focus and what serves as backdrop? Who to cite and who to ignore (Kamler & Thomson, 2014)? Which vocabulary and style is fit for the content, message and reader? These are not choices taken in isolation. Kristiansen (2010) suggests that we must see an academic practice in a broader historical perspective to understand what is at stake in students' writing. Academic genres reflect socio-cultural conditions and we must acknowledge this to create a meaningful pedagogical practice.

The decisions to be taken during a writing process are thus dependent on socio-cultural conditions, and equally, text production affects these conditions. A text makes a (perhaps small, but sometimes big) imprint on the world when someone reads it and is affected. Writing takes place at a specific time, at a specific place within a specified tradition. As touched upon initially, writing involves both questions of knowledge and knowledge production (epistemological questions), and it involves the way we are present in the world, and how we understand ourselves and our relation to the practice we are part of (ontological questions).

If we return to the students' questions and statements in my writing workshops, what they basically express are: What should I do with all the knowledge that already exists? What should I take with me, what should I leave behind, and how do I find the balance between communicating the work of others and pursuing my own question? How do I position myself in the text with my motivation, and how do I argue rigorously for what I claim to know? These questions are not of the kind to which the teacher can respond adequately with a straightforward plan for the writing process or a template for academic texts. Rather, by reading, writing, speaking and listening, we can continuously provide answers together with the students. That is the creative co-creation of writing practices.

THREE DRIVERS FOR CREATIVE CO-CREATED WRITING PRACTICES

Academic writing is a continuation (and perhaps further development) of certain ways of constructing and disseminating knowledge which is not necessarily visible and accessible. Kristiansen (2010) points out how crucial it is that writing pedagogy makes it possible to work explicitly with the relationship between the rhetorical expressions and the underlying understandings of what knowledge is in a specific social practice. I have tried to transform the black box into a glass box by this model. It offers three metaphors for the writing process and three related questions for the writing practice. The model is an alternative to step-by-step writing strategies and offers structured, yet flexible, ways to reflect upon writing together with the students:

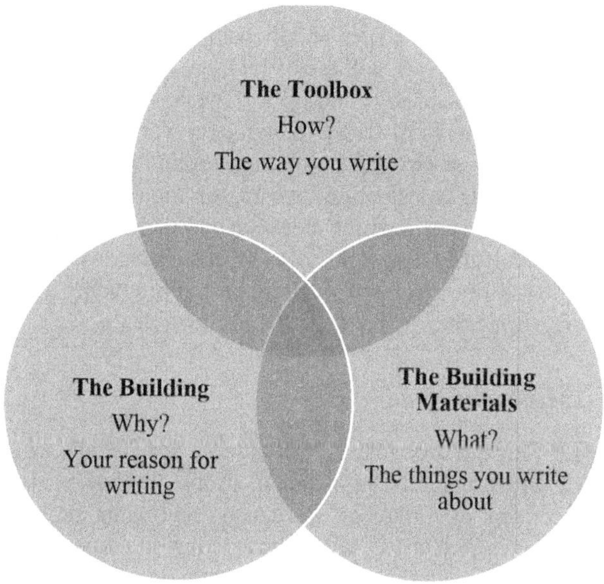

Figure 8.1. Three drivers for writing

The Toolbox regards writing habits and language – how do you write? When I ask students to write with a focus on the Toolbox, I investigate with them how to build writing habits and expand their linguistic repertoire. I ask them to write to practice their writing skills and forget about being clever, being right or the fear of other people's judgements. I ask them to let go and just write what comes to their mind. When I ask students to focus on the Building Materials, we direct our interest towards the content and the work with theory, methodology and data – what do they write about? I ask them to write to investigate and analyse. I encourage them to be curious, bold and persistent. The Building relates to the intent and purpose of writing – why do they write? What is the quality and strength of their work? The focus is to communicate and make a contribution that others will understand and perhaps appreciate. I talk to them about writing for a reason beyond the exam – why is this important to know about for themselves and others?

The model offers a way to separate the three different sets of questions and work with the three drivers one by one. However, they also overlap, and we also work in the subsets. For example, I ask my students which writing habits and linguistic tools they need, depending on the content and purpose of the text. For instance, they must ask themselves which content elements convey the message or intent as best as possible. Finally, I ask them to move into the middle of the model and make all three drivers support each other. The research question is often located here.

In the next section, I will provide two cases to illustrate how the model serves (1) as a start-up tool in a new supervisory relationship and (2) to analyse a situation in which a student is stuck. Here, we will look a bit more into each of the three drivers. Working with the model enhances writing agility. The drivers are not to be understood as phases, in which students first write to practice (to warm up and develop writing skills), then write to analyse (working with theories and data) and finally write to disseminate (to present the contribution focusing on the receiver). Rather, they are three basic drivers to switch deliberately between and with accompanying questions and writing strategies. If the student manages to make them work together, writing with joy is a real possibility, along with the prospect of producing a worthwhile text. I will take them one at a time and then together as a whole.

The Toolbox – The Way You Write

How do we write? This question relates to both the writing strategies and habits and to language, style and structure. The metaphor of the Toolbox is inspired by Lévi-Strauss's (1966) concept of "bricolage". Bricolage represents the kind of creativity that takes place in everyday tasks, when our existing strategies are not sufficient. Bricolage is the use of things at hand (routines, strategies, language) in new ways and in new combinations to solve current problems. The point is that an ongoing expansion and development of the Toolbox provides a wider repertoire and more opportunities to express ourselves through writing. The proverb "If you only have a hammer, then everything begins to look like nails" illustrates it very well. If they have only one writing strategy (e.g. "I just need to pull myself together", which I often hear), students have no choice but to blame themselves if the strategy does not work. Likewise, with the linguistic repertoire – if they have a limited vocabulary and limited ways to construct text, it restricts what they can express through writing.

The Building Materials – The Things You Write about

The Building Materials is the content element of the text. Somewhat simplified, an academic text consists of theory, methodology and data. In the writing process, which precedes the final text, students must get involved with other people's ideas by reading their texts (theory and analyses), producing and processing information (data), and doing this in certain ways (methodology). The metaphor of Building Materials relates to the production and analysis of data and the theories and methods. Work on the theory, methodology and data takes place in a particular social practice, which I encourage students to adapt and contribute to through writing. Thus, they write not just for understanding, interpretation and presenting. They produce something new in the world.

The Building – Your Reason for Writing

The Building is a metaphor for the research field or the discussion that the text aims to contribute to. The former chief executive of SAS Jan Carlzon has been widely cited for the story of two monks who spent their lives working in a quarry. One day a tourist passes by and asks one monk what he is doing. He does not care: "I'm cutting stone." The tourist then asks the other monk, and he responds with a smile: "We are building cathedrals" (Lagerström & Carlzon, 1985). Carlzon's point is that the two monks have two different managers. One boss does not motivate employees by drawing the big picture, while the other can convey the vision. When students write, they are in part their own bosses. The metaphor of the Building, which I have chosen to use here to avoid the religious connotation of a cathedral, concerns where the contribution is directed to. Why is this important to me and to the world? The Building as a metaphor focuses on the broader context of the text – where and how it is to be included and make a difference. Is it a large and complex castle with numerous outbuildings; a bridge that connects two professional fields; or perhaps it is a little cabin still in the making?

The Interaction between the Three Drivers

Although there are advantages of focusing on one driver at a time, none of them can stand alone:

If we focus solely on the Toolbox, we reduce writing to a series of tips and tricks. It may produce a well-written text, but probably without much substance. Most people have had the experience of reading something really impressive and appealing, which on closer examination turns out to be ineffective (an indifferent Building) and perhaps nothing more than nice rhetoric (poor Building Materials).

If we focus solely on the Building Materials, this can result in a text with careful and reverent recapitulation of theory, a polished methods section or endless analyses. The text does all the *right* things with its content elements, but there is no vision of contributing to a larger construction (a vague Building), and/or the language does not support the content (a very small Toolbox). It is a well-written text, but without any potential impact.

If the focus is solely on the Building, the text risks being polemic, without regard to domain-specific requirements (a Toolbox irrelevant to the context) and without convincing use of theory, data and analyses (few or poor Building Materials or poor use of them). The message is there, but the argument behind it is lacking. The student is building a chimera.

The model highlights that academic texts of high quality must balance the three drivers for writing. Writing based on all three drivers is not a structured linear process, but neither is it pure chance or chaos. Instead, working separately with questions based on How, What and Why offers a flexible approach to writing in which language, content and vision can be separated. Students do not have to deal with it all at once. The model also serves as an analytical tool to identify problems in the writing process – does the problem belong to the Toolbox, the Building Materials or the Building? We can start identifying the relevant type of questions. Here is what it can look like in my own practice.

TWO CASES

Esther Starts from Scratch and Finds Her Direction

The following mail correspondence illustrates how I initiated a supervisory collaboration with a student quite openly. Yet, three questions based on the three drivers made the work take a fruitful direction very quickly. Esther had indicated that she would write a thesis on the subject *happiness*. We initiated supervision like this:

> *Dear Charlotte,*
>
> *I am looking forward to having you as a supervisor. I do not feel I know exactly in which direction I should go with my thesis topic, so I want to find a day for the first meeting with you as soon as possible.*
>
> *Regards,*
>
> *Esther*
>
> ---
>
> *Dear Esther,*
>
> *Your subject is exciting, and it is no problem that you are open to different directions at this time. It would be good if you write a brainstorm and send it to me before our meeting. Please, tell me a bit about:*
>
> - *what interests you about the happiness concept?*
> - *what theoretical, methodological and/or empirical knowledge do you have that you might draw on?*
> - *what would you like to know about happiness when you have finished your thesis?*

What do you think?

Regards,

Charlotte

Dear Charlotte,

I have now looked at some literature, and here are my answers to your questions:

What interests me about the happiness concept is that it is much hyped, happiness is measured and compared, many want to achieve happiness and strive for it, for example by using self-help books, but there is still no real understanding of what happiness is. Moreover, who says that we must be persistently happy? This can be a bit of a paradox since people may seek something that might be a misunderstood concept, resulting in a feeling of inaccessibility (I realize that the paradox builds on my own assumption).

Right now, I have not much theoretical, methodological or empirical knowledge, but since Monday, I have found about 30 research articles, three relevant debates, and 20 books I have skimmed. After looking through it all, I have arrived at a greater confusion about the concept than I expected. In many cases, happiness, satisfaction, positive- and negative emotions, and resilience are used interdependently.

I want to understand what happiness is and how to distinguish between being happy and being fulfilled, or whether it might be two sides of the same coin. Further, I want to know either how I as a consultant can help a company to have satisfied employees, or how I as a psychologist can understand and help patients with a psychiatric illness (e.g. anxiety) to live a satisfying life. Also, I wish to uncover "the myth of happiness".

I know that it is messy and undefined so far, but I hope it helps you to understand where I'm going with this explanation. I need to start to be more specific.

Regards,

Esther

I was really pleased as a supervisor when I read Esther's email. Although she wrote that it was messy, her email revealed curiosity about the conceptualisation of happiness, she was critical about the societal relevance, and there were concerns about how she could use her thesis work in her future profession. Esther's Building was complex and interesting. Additionally, she was quickly collecting her Building Materials by skimming and selecting. Esther decided to make a conceptual study of happiness and then pursue her desire to understand and help patients with mental illness to have a satisfying life, thus abandoning the consultancy trail. Her research question ended up looking like this:

> How can the phenomenon of happiness be understood based on a theoretical exploration and an empirical study of two individuals living with psychiatric diagnoses?

With this pairing of happiness and mental suffering, Esther was able not only to uncover the myth of happiness, as she wrote. She actually managed to criticise and refine the myth, because she could point out that the happiness imperative tends to exclude groups such as psychiatric patients. Additionally, she showed how we get to know more about both happiness and mental suffering when we cease to see them as incompatible. Esther's contribution was to establish a new connection. At the same time, she worked with her own professional identity as a future psychologist, but identity work did not overshadow a critical examination of the concept of happiness.

My email to Esther is grounded in the model. The first question addresses her personal drive and invites her to write from the Toolbox. It does not require lines of arguments or theoretical grounding. Rather, what I ask her to do is to write from scratch, to get the writing going without censoring herself. The second question obviously regards the Building Materials and the third question encourages her to look into the future and sketch what she wants. Overall, this short correspondence makes Esther start using her Toolbox, take stock of her actual and needed Building Materials and tell me about the Building she wants to contribute to.

Ann's Writing Crisis and How She Moved on

No matter how smooth the start, however, crisis is quite common during a writing project. Focus disappears. The research question slips through the fingers. The analysis does not go where the students imagined, and everything seems to disintegrate. They wonder what they are doing and it is definitely not what they imagined and hoped for. They ask if the direction has to be changed, and if this means that the previous work is wasted? They may be afraid that the project does not hold water and that it all ends up with nothing of importance. Crisis is evident. Crisis may look like this. One of my students, Ann, wrote this email to me pretty close to deadline:

> *Dear Charlotte,*
>
> *As we agreed, here is some of my writing. It has not progressed as I hoped – I think I've got some sort of writer's block. In any case, I really find it difficult to create the necessary argumentation chain in what I write. It becomes very fragmented. The research question has caused me real trouble – and it is probably here the problem lies. I do know what I want, but I am constantly in doubt whether I should delve more into the concepts and definitions. However, I believe that today I have had a small breakthrough so there is at least some*

kind of coherent research question. I have had several problems with the sections Theory and Methods. When we talked last time, I was quite optimistic about describing the method and how I applied it. As you can see, however, I have no grip on that section now.

In return, I threw my energy into the theory and except for a final sum-up, I think that part is complete. Strangely enough, I cannot get a grip of phenomenology now. This spins in all directions, and I have several unfinished drafts – maybe it's because I'm undecided about the structure – what belongs to the philosophy of science section, and what should I save for the theory section – and maybe I should totally rethink all this?

For the analysis, I have only some notes – so I have a long way to go. This also contributes to my writer's block, I think – I alternate between telling myself that I will succeed and then I fall into despair about the very short time I have left. I must admit that I often think of what might happen if I do not hand in the thesis on time????

So, this is the status, briefly, from here – I'm calling at 4pm as agreed, if it still fits into your programme?

Many greetings from Ann

What is at stake here? A bunch of things. As a supervisor, it is good to get such an email prior to a meeting because both parties get the opportunity to take a step back from all the disturbances and consider the situation. Ann herself is even sensing what we might call the *real* problem in the eye of the storm. Ann is working simultaneously on almost all parts of text, and at the same time, she blocks the writing with her doubts. Maybe she should focus on something other than she actually does, e.g. spend more time and space on the concepts and definitions? Should phenomenology appear in the philosophy of science chapter or in the theory chapter or maybe in both? These questions belong to the Toolbox. She also realises that she has lost knowledge – she did have a grip on phenomenology, but she does not have that any longer. It relates to the Building Materials – where did that go? Ann writes that she actually does know what she wants. This relates to the Building. The three metaphors and their corresponding questions based on How, What and Why can be used to make a diagnosis – and Ann and I did that jointly on the phone at 4pm. We found out that she had control of her Why and that she had doubts about How and What. However, because she was overwhelmed by doubt and time constraints, it was difficult to actually describe her Building. Therefore, we decided to start here, and Ann's first task was to take stock and restore focus. She did it by answering these questions as proposed by Professor Pat Thomson on her blog www.patthomson.net[1]

- Why is my topic important?
- What do I now know that I didn't know when I started?
- What have I done so far?

- How has my understanding of my topic changed as I've gone along?
- What could I write a paper about now?
- What does my existing research question offer and what does it prevent?

Then she rewrote the research question and finally, she made a tentative abstract to get an overview of the text as a whole. Based on these moves, Ann was able to put aside her doubt, stop impeding the flow of the writing and finish on time.

ANSWERS

Finally, we can use the three drivers as quality criteria. Academic texts must comply with formalities; however, inspired by Richardson (1994), we can, in addition to formal requirements, ask our students and ourselves when we review their work questions based on the three drivers:

The Toolbox concerns the aesthetic appeal: Does this text prosper aesthetically? Does it express a creative and analytical practice, which opens the text for the reader and invites reflection or thought? Does the text have rhythm and momentum; is it satisfying, complex and not boring?

The Building Materials concerns reflexivity: Does the text contain appropriate self-criticism, does the writer position him- or herself in the text so that the reader can assess his/her perspective and standpoint? Is the text properly balanced between sober presentation of theory, methodology and data on the one hand and appropriate selection and creative and analytical thinking on the other hand?

The Building concerns the contribution and potential impact: Does the text affect me emotionally and intellectually? Does it inspire new questions or encourage change in practice?

The model has proved to be a tangible tool for continually keeping the dialogue with my students open. It helps them investigate what it takes to master academic writing within their choice of research area and methodological tradition. It helps me facilitate their learning not just as a matter of techniques and methods but also – more fundamentally – as identity work through participation. Through this, they enhance their skills and, consequently, their opportunity to continue and change the practice they are part of.

Now that we have covered all the questions that the students asked in the beginning, it is time to stop. None of the questions can be answered once and for all, but with the three-driver model in mind, we can work creatively and co-create writing practices with the students that create less confusion and more joy.

AFTERWORD: IT'S ALL ABOUT YOU

Dear reader, perhaps you think that something is missing. It is. I have not touched upon the question of 'I' and the students keep asking. In some disciplines and fields of research, it is widely accepted. In others, it is not. In provisional texts written to expand the Toolbox or examining the Building Materials, I always encourage the students to use 'I'. What I tell them in addition is this:

You are the writer, and if you cannot use 'I' due to conventions, you must study your research field for well-written texts to serve as usable templates. Creative, co-created writing practices are aimed at enriching the final text. Thus, you cannot wait until the last revision to find out about 'I'; you must practice in relation to essential requirements and conventions to make them yours and maybe expand, twist or abandon them cleverly. Conventions have to be incorporated into our own writing practice so that they become familiar and serve the purpose of the text. You must make conventions serve as a framework that supports your work and your aim and not let them ruin your joy.

- That's fine, they say, but you did not answer the question: are we allowed to write 'I'?
- Maybe not, I reply, nevertheless, it might be useful to remember that the work is carried out and the text is written by – you.

Pelias (2004) says that, no matter how an academic text is written, basically it is always a first person narrative. Even the most traditional text is someone's story and it goes like this:

Literature Review: I have studied this topic for a long time. As I read, I found out that I could divide the topic into several categories. When I was done, I saw many more unanswered questions.

Research Question: I would really like to find out more about this particular thing. Therefore, I asked the following questions: …

Method: I decided to gather information on the subject. I talked to these people and studied these documents.

Results: I collected all the information, made some analyses and they indicated what I expected (or: I was really surprised).

Conclusion: I can explain this in many different ways, but I think that this way makes most sense. I have many more questions to ask, but it feels good now that I have some answers to some of them.

It's all about you – expand your Toolbox, select and treat your Building Materials wisely, and take your contribution to the Building seriously. Then it's not about you any longer. Let go.

NOTE

1 https://patthomson.net/2015/07/08/writing-to-get-unstuck-phdknowhow/

REFERENCES

Dewey, J. (1916). *Democracy and education: An introduction to the philosophy of educationMacmillan.* New York, NY: McMillan.

Elkjær, B. (2005). *Når læring går på arbejde: Et pragmatisk blik på læring i samfundslivet*. Copenhagen: Forlaget Samfundslitteratur.
Kamler, B., & Thomson, P. (2014). *Helping doctoral students write: Pedagogies for supervision*. Oxon: Routledge.
Kristiansen, B. (2010). Tekstproduktion og vidensproduktion. *Dansk Universitetspædagogisk Tidsskrift, 9*.
Lagerström, T., & Carlzon, J. (1985). *Riv pyramiderne ned! – en bog om chefen, lederen og det nye menneske*. Copenhagen: Gyldendal.
Lave, J., & Wenger, E. (1991). *Situated learning: Legitimate peripheral participation: Learning in doing: social, cognitive, and computational perspectives*. Cambridge: Cambridge University Press.
Lévi-Strauss, C. (1966). *The savage mind*. Chicago, IL: University of Chicago Press.
Packer, M. J., & Goicoechea, J. (2000). Sociocultural and constructivist theories of learning: Ontology, not just epistemology. *Educational Psychologist. 35*, 227–241.
Pelias, R. J. (2004). *A methodology of the heart: Evoking academic and daily life*. Walnut Creek, CA: Altamira Press.
Richardson, L. (1994). Writing: A method of inquiry. In N. K. Denzin & Y. S. Lincoln (Eds.), *Handbook of qualitative research*. Thousand Oaks, CA: Sage.
Thomson, P., & Kamler, B. (2010). It's been said before and we'll say it again-research is writing. In P. Thomson & M. Walker (Eds.), *The Routledge doctoral student's companion: Getting to grips with research in education and social sciences* (pp. 149–160). London & New York, NY: Routhledge.

Charlotte Wegener
Department of Communication and Psychology
Aalborg University

LOTTE DARSØ

9. CO-CREATING MEANING THROUGH ARTFUL INQUIRY

INTRODUCTION

The purpose of this chapter is to point out the need for aesthetic and artful methods for reflection, learning and co-creation. The context is management education focused on developing innovation competency. The main arguments are that Artful Inquiry affords deeper layers of knowing which would otherwise remain tacit and non-conscious. Co-creation with art may happen between people, e.g. by having verbal or nonverbal conversations using art materials, but co-creation may also happen between one person and the art material and the artistic process. The material 'speaks back' in surprising ways, metaphorically and symbolically. The data derive from observations and written reports.

An imperative question asked in this book is: how do we best prepare students for the challenges of tomorrow? I will argue that if students have developed innovation competency they will be able to deal with pertinent issues and challenges and furthermore they will be able to create a desirable future for their children and grandchildren. Briefly defined, innovation competency is "the ability to create innovation by navigating together with others under complex conditions" (Darsø, 2012, p. 110). The concept will be unfolded and elaborated later. A relevant question would then be how developing innovation competency corresponds to the educational reality of today? Even though there are many examples, including those in this book, of educational experiments and innovation, education, in general, is falling behind societal evolution. Systems such as schools and universities are hard to change. At universities all over the world professors still teach large audiences in auditoriums, using mainly one-way communication. Interestingly, this is repeated in the so-called disruptive education called MOOCs, Massive Open On-line Courses. Certainly, this may be seen as an advantage to reach larger quantities of students, who would not otherwise be able to attend, but is this really the best way for people to learn? The advantage is that much knowledge can be conveyed to many people in a short time. It is economical and efficient. But the question of how students learn throws a shadow on the concept. Some can assimilate some of the knowledge, others cannot. When the subject is innovation, a lecture for introducing the topic of innovation is fine, but for developing innovation competency a different approach is needed. People need to try out the process together with others, have the direct experience and make it happen in real life.

T. Chemi & L. Krogh (Eds.), Co-Creation in Higher Education, 131–149.

Another issue of significance is the paradigm of traditional academia, which is basically critical, analytical and in some instances reflexive. This stands in contrast to a newer trend of design thinking, which places more emphasis on creating and seizing possibilities. Whereas academia seems bound to the past (of what is), design thinking is turned towards the future (of what might be) (Friis, 2016). Likewise, innovation is, by definition, tuned into creating the future. My point here is not to dismiss academia, but rather to argue for balancing academia with the newer trends, i.e. to add alternative approaches to learning, such as problem-based learning, practicing innovation and design thinking, and working with creativity and Artful Inquiry. Irgens proposes balancing "the eye of science" with the "eye of art" in order to get a binocular perspective in education (Irgens, 2014). Building on the work of philosopher Ernst Casirer, Irgens explains that science tends to simplify and reduce complexity through a process of abstraction. Art, on the other hand, tends to complexify and intensify its object of study, layer by layer, through a process of visualisation and concentration. The former works through conceptual interpretation while the latter works through intuitive interpretation. Both are needed for understanding the world we live in. Both are needed for creating the future. The problem in education is that the balance is skewed. We need more art, more creativity, more design, and more innovation in order to bring the world of education up to the needs of global society (Pink, 2006).

The context for this chapter is executive management education, the teaching approach of which is in general mostly traditional, with lectures and discussions on theories and cases. According to Mintzberg, management involves science, art and craft; however, traditional MBA courses are too tilted towards abstraction and theory (Mintzberg, 2009). Mintzberg emphasises the gap between abstract management education and learning from experience and practice. This has also been criticised by Cunliffe (2002, p. 35): "Advocating the systematic application of theory and techniques to every situation, it fails to consider that practitioners deal with ill-defined, unique, emotive and complex issues." In my chapter on *Authentic Leadership and Co-Creation*, it is concluded that: "… management faculty must leave the expert role of educating people by only introducing theories about management and leadership. Management faculty also needs to embrace emergence and uncertainty by creating pedagogical and social learning spaces for stimulating transformation conducive to authentic leadership and co-creation" (Darsø, 2014, p. 110).

The empirical case concerns an international executive Master programme, LAICS: Leadership and Innovation in Complex Systems (www.laics.net). This is not traditional education in the sense described above. The content is traditional as it leads to an academic degree with a syllabus of around 4,000 pages on theories of innovation, leadership and complexity. What makes it different from, e.g., an MBA, is the teaching and learning approach, which includes arts-based methods, a variety of social technologies, learning through direct experience, zen walks and learning journals. In addition, apart from professors the faculty includes artists, such as actors and a theatre director, musicians (both classical and jazz), a visual artist, a sculptor, a dancer, a yoga-nature practitioner, and a graphic facilitator.

This chapter has the following structure: after the introduction, the research method, empirical case and data generation are presented. This is followed by an introduction to the key concepts of innovation competency with the analytical sub-categories of socio-innovative and intra-innovative competency. These notions are related to Co-Creation and Artful Inquiry, respectively. Then the concepts of Co-Creation and the model called the Diamond of Innovation will be presented and discussed, together with examples and data from the executive master programme (LAICS). After this the concepts of intra-innovative competency and Artful Inquiry will be unfolded and discussed by introducing a recently developed model (Darsø, 2016). This is interwoven and analysed using data and examples from LAICS. Finally the findings will be summarised.

METHOD, EMPIRICAL CASE AND DATA

The empirical case is the executive Master programme, which has existed for 10 years at the time of writing. I am one of the founders and have been the programme director since its inception. As the name LAICS implies the focus is on leadership, innovation and complexity. The format is four modules. The first three modules consist of three seminars each (nine seminars in total), and the fourth is mostly a writing module (master thesis). Each seminar lasts 3½ days and for each module one seminar takes place abroad. On module 3 the participants travel to Banff in the Rocky Mountains of Western Canada. We stay at the Banff Centre and work with their faculty of artists and with a management professor, who is also a visual artist. This seminar concerns reflection on personal leadership and authenticity. The participants are highly diverse. They all have at least a Bachelor degree and 2 years of practical experience, but most of them have higher degrees and many years of practice. They come from both public and private organisations and their background can be anything from teacher, consultant, midwife, engineer, scientist to architect, designer or artist.

The research question was: how do leaders develop their own leadership? The method was partly action research, partly observations and conversations. One of the advantages of action research is getting direct experience together with the participants. Participation and experience add the aesthetic qualities of the sensing process that qualitative interviews would often miss, such as facial expressions, sounds like laughter or sighs, and silences that can be awkward or heart-warming. The sensing process is one of the main characteristics of the field of aesthetics, which involves our senses: seeing, hearing, feeling, tasting and smelling (Strati, 2000). The subjectivity of this approach, which some critical voices would object to, can be balanced by inquiring into other people's opinions and sense-making of what took place. Another way of counteracting subjectivity could be through reflexivity aiming at becoming aware of and questioning underlying assumptions. In addition, theoretical concepts and frameworks can be applied in order to build alternative or complementary interpretations. This is attempted both by the researcher and the students.

The data include 14 written reflection reports and 2 master theses. Here the students themselves make sense of their learning journey by reflecting on, among other things, the methods, processes and theories that have supported their journey.

KEY CONCEPTS

The key concepts of Co-creation and Artful Inquiry will be defined by relating them to Innovation Competency and, as indicated in the introduction, innovation competency can be understood as dynamic meta-competences of socio-innovative and intra-innovative competency (Darsø, 2012). This distinction is analytical in order to create a better understanding of what is involved in developing innovation competency in practice. It should therefore be emphasised that the two sub-categories are intertwined in lived life and that they cannot be developed by reading about them; they can only be learned through experience and practice.

Co-creation concerns creating something together and is therefore related to the sub-category of socio-innovative competency. Socio-innovative competency is defined as “mastering social interaction that enhances innovation” (Darsø, 2012, p. 110). The difference between co-creation and socio-innovative competency is related to the purpose and content. Co-creation does not necessarily have to be about innovation, which, according to the original definition by Schumpeter is novelty that creates economic value (Schumpeter, 1934). Co-creation can involve many other aspects, such as groups writing reports for passing exams, restoring and decorating a common environment, cooking together, etc. The common feature is the ‘co’ which means doing or creating things together and ‘socio’, which means social. In the present chapter, however, the content will involve innovation and consequently will be interlinked with a conceptual model called the Diamond of Innovation (Darsø, 2003). Socio-innovative competency involves communication, leadership and facilitation.

Artful Inquiry is “the skill of inquiring into something of importance through body, mind, heart and spirit.” (Darsø, 2016). This form of inquiry is related to the sub-category of intra-innovative competency, which is defined as “consciousness and sensitivity into own and others’ talents, preferences and potentials for development and innovation” (Darsø, 2012, p. 111). Artful Inquiry is a process that can be generative for developing intra-innovative competency. However, Artful Inquiry can be used in other contexts, such as problem solving, prototyping and art work; it is not bound together with intra-innovative competency only. Intra-innovative competency involves attention, empathy and authenticity.

Co-Creation

According to Bason co-creation characterises “a creation process where new solutions are designed *with* people, not *for* them” (Bason, 2010, p. 9). This definition is based on design thinking (Kimbell, 2012). Darsø defines co-creation as "a process of interpersonal interaction, involving relations, communication and leadership, aiming at creating new value" (Darsø, 2014, p. 113). It may sound simple, but this is far from the case. Human interaction is usually what makes or breaks successful innovation. The social aspect matters more than one would imagine. Social innovation was first coined by Peter Drucker as arising from human needs, rather than from technology, and therefore focused on societal issues such as health, education and job creation (Drucker, 1985). Later Darsø defined social innovation more specifically as new forms of interaction, behaviours, constellations or functions. Interestingly, the innovative 'product' is here not only the resulting innovation. Rather it is something that is normally neglected: a new human infrastructure that can yield continuous creativity and innovation (Darsø, 2011) as well as new practice (Aakjær, 2013). The focus is on the human factor and on the quality of the innovation process. This was prompted by PhD research, which took place in a pharmaceutical company and focused on identifying the cradle of innovation (Darsø, 2001). How does innovation begin? How could the early innovation process be initiated, improved and supported? In order to illustrate and map the innovation process, Darsø created a model, the Diamond of Innovation. The model displays two important dynamics that take place simultaneously, a knowledge dynamic and a communication dynamic. The knowledge dynamic moves between what people know and what they do not know. The communication dynamic moves between relations (which are tacit) and concepts (which are explicit). Two findings from this research project will be emphasised here (ibid.). Firstly, data showed that innovation was triggered when people asked open-ended questions regarding what they did not know, contrary to what was expected, namely, that innovation would be triggered by knowledge. The second finding concerns the importance of creating relations of trust and respect between the participants of a co-creation process in order to access the space of not knowing, i.e. ignorance. This may seem trivial. However, time after time people seem to forget this. They are too busy hunting for fast results. However, the quality

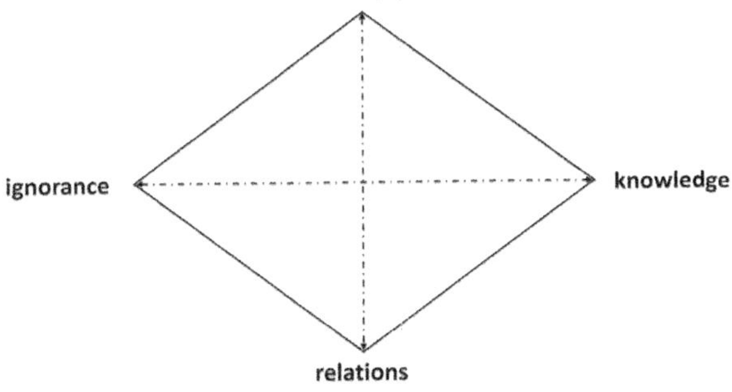

Figure 9.1. Diamond of innovation model

of people's relations is crucial for a successful communication and, ultimately, co-creation process.

Co-Creating Learning Space

In executive education it is often underestimated how important it is to create a safe learning space. A learning space is defined as "a psychological safety net, constructed by relations between people for creating broadness and community" (Darsø, 2012, p. 118). On most MBA courses this is supposed to happen by itself, as simple socialising. Socialising is the first step in Nonaka & Takeuchi's knowledge creation model (the following steps are externalising, combining and internalising), and in their interpretation it concerns sharing tacit knowledge (Nonaka & Takeuchi, 1995). This is supposed to happen when employees are staying together at a venue for some time. Slowly people get to know each other and thereby build empathy. At LAICS we have developed a more conscious and deliberate process of creating an inspirational learning space. In fact, one of the learning objectives of the very first seminar is to understand how learning spaces can be built. The participants learn this by doing it in practice. Of course, this is underscored by theory and literature with explanations. One of the building blocks is the Diamond of Innovation with a special focus on building relations of trust and respect. We work with playful outdoor presentations, we create a common codex in order to build optimal learning conditions, and we ask two volunteers to be "gardeners", a leadership role of the Diamond of Innovation, which means taking responsibility for all the participants' wellbeing during the seminar (Darsø, 2003). We also work with storytelling in order to get to know each other and we offer a master class with an entire day of theatre rehearsal techniques, which involve lots of physical exercises as individuals, in pairs, small groups and in plenum. In addition the participants get learning journals and are given time for reflection as well as questions to reflect upon.

The Concept of Artful Inquiry

> If the arts are about anything, they are about emotion, and emotion has to do with the ways in which we feel. Becoming aware of our capacity to feel is a way of discovering our humanity. Art helps us connect with personal, subjective emotions, and through such a process, it enables us to discover our own interior landscape. Not an unimportant achievement. (Eisner, 2008, p. 11)

I have already briefly defined artful inquiry and I have related it to intra-innovative competency. Here I shall broaden and develop the concept by presenting a recent model (Darsø, 2016). But first I will argue why inquiring and reflecting through artful methods is relevant in leadership education. The main argument is to make learning conscious by 'digesting' experience. Experience tends to be layered in the body as sensations or pre-verbal images (Damasio, 1999). "You know more than you can tell" is a famous sentence from the work of Michael Polanyi (Polanyi, 1983, p. 4), who coined the concept of "tacit" knowledge. Interestingly, Polanyi suggests that it is possible to access tacit knowing "provided that we are given adequate means for expressing ourselves" (ibid, p.5). Here the main argument is that Artful Inquiry can provide 'adequate means'. Another argument in favour of surfacing tacit knowing is that being conscious about what we know makes us better equipped for applying it in practice. Developing competence is exactly about becoming able to judge situations and apply relevant knowledge. Below I will present the model.

Artful Inquiry is about inquiring through aesthetic or artful methods. It is about crafting inspirational questions and finding relevant and suitable methods. In order to craft relevant questions, the situation and context must be taken into consideration as well as the purpose. As the present context is a leadership seminar with the purpose of reflecting on personal and authentic leadership, the questions are designed accordingly.

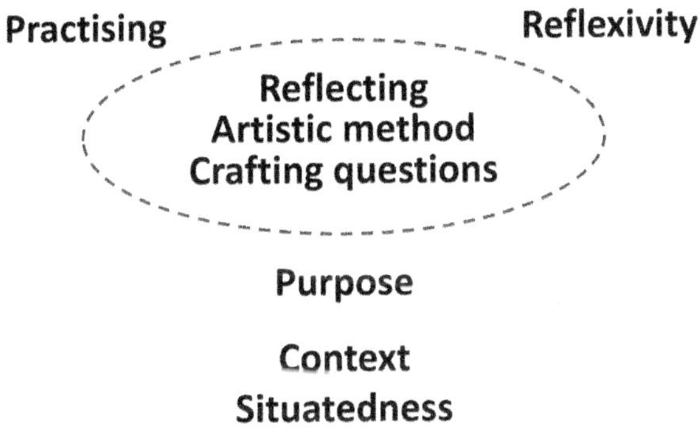

Figure 9.2. Artful inquiry model

Crafting Artful Questions

A well-crafted question outlines subject, focus and direction. Questions can be immensely powerful because questions have an irresistible and highly attractive force of making us curious. Questions can be categorised as open versus closed, and as divergent versus convergent. An open question can have a multitude of answers whereas a closed question can be answered by yes or no. Divergent versus convergent questions can be understood as the degree of openness/closedness. Divergent questions such as 'why' or 'how' lead us towards what we do not know, whereas convergent questions such as 'how many' or 'which' are directed towards getting facts and information. Palus & Horth describe powerful questions as having three characteristics: they invite exploration, resist easy answers and invoke strong passion (Palus & Horth, 2002, p. 22). Exploration is one of the main qualities of divergence as a way of looking into the space of possibility. Invoking strong passion is a different and important feature of powerful questions. This is related to identifying a purpose that is deeply meaningful to the respondent. An illuminating example of such a question is described in the "World Café" by Brown (Brown & Isaacs, 2005, pp. 84–85). Hewlett Packard was working to develop a vision for the HP Labs and began a global network conversation with the question: "How can we be the best industrial research lab in the world?" At some point an engineer suggested changing the question slightly so that it would really energise him and his colleagues: "How can we be the best industrial research lab *for* the world?" The change is only one small word, a preposition, from 'in' the world to 'for' the world. However, that made a huge difference for the conversation. The former underscored a purpose of competition, whereas the latter pointed towards a purpose of contribution. It is a seminal example of a powerful question as it invokes strong passion.

Constructing Powerful Questions

Question construction is an important leadership skill. Vogt, Brown and Isaacs suggest that powerful and strategic questions can be built by attending to 3 dimensions: architecture, scope and assumptions (Vogt, Brown, & Isaacs, 2003). The architecture is similar to the taxonomy above, but more specific. Here the taxonomy is related to which interrogative word is used. From 'very powerful' to 'not very powerful' the sequence is: why, how, what, where, when, who, which. For example there is a qualitative difference between the question 'Why did you become a leader?' and 'Which leadership tasks do you prefer?' The why-question invites many possible answers, whereas the which-question limits the answer to selecting a few tasks. Scope indicates proportion or extension. In the HP question the scope is the HP industrial research lab in the world. A larger scope would involve the whole HP organisation. A smaller scope could be to involve only one country. The scope is thus dependent on the direction of the purpose and the subject. In this chapter the scope involves personal leadership. Paying attention to assumptions is a noteworthy point, as questions always have assumptions and we often fail to notice these. The HP question and the change of the preposition mentioned above illustrate this eminently, going from an assumption of competition to one of contribution.

Another way of constructing powerful questions that evoke passion is through Appreciative Inquiry (Cooperrider & Whitney, 1999). This is a method for organisational change and development that builds on strengths, on what works and on possibilities instead of the traditional approach of deficiency, focusing on problems, weaknesses and what does not work. The assumption is that human systems develop in the direction they continuously ask (appreciative) questions about.

What are the criteria for a question to be artful? Here we have to add the spiritual dimension of what is deeply meaningful. Theory U is an appropriate framework for identifying such criteria as it involves four fields of attention: surface, mind, heart and will (Scharmer, 2007). Briefly, Scharmer and his colleagues have developed an archetype for creation, based on 150 interviews with scientists and leaders from all over the world. The idea is that for real change or innovation to happen, we need to go to the bottom of the U to connect with "the future that wants to emerge". We start at the surface level, which is characterised by our habits ('downloading'); move into 'seeing' (mind level), which means discussing the subject with others from different perspectives; then into 'sensing' (heart level), which means trying to empathise with others in order to understand the whole system including our own part of it; and lastly move into 'presencing' (will level), which means trying to let go of our ego in order to lean into the future that wants to emerge through us. This takes an attitude of humility and stillness, like meditation or mindfulness, slowing down and being open to what comes. From the bottom of the U something might 'crystallise' (heart level), usually a small seed, a vague idea or an image; this is 'prototyped' (mind level) in order to understand it better through drawings, images, or small theatre plays; and finally embodied (surface level) into small steps of action.

To summarise, an artful question is an open and divergent question. It is powerful in relation to evoking strong passion. The HP question is an artful question. However, for it to be artful inquiry, artful methods must be applied in searching for answers. In relation to leadership development, the question should be deeply meaningful and as the participants are heterogeneous the question must also be personalised and relevant. In executive programmes with a diverse group, one way of doing this is to present a few questions to choose from. An example of an artful question for personal leadership is: what do you offer to the world? Repeatedly, this question has triggered important reflections and insights from LAICS participants. This question fulfils the criteria of being open, divergent and evoking passion. And it is purposeful and meaningful. However, the power of the question also depends on the context in which it is asked (Darsø, 2014). In the case described here, it is asked during a meditative hike in the Canadian Rocky Mountains as a question to reflect upon. There is time available, wild nature and a community of compassionate people. The participants are invited into "presencing mode" to let go of the old, slow down, and let the inner knowing emerge. The same question could be asked in a traditional board room and it might work with good facilitation, but nature does have healing effects, for example, on lowering blood pressure and reducing stress (Williams, 2012).

Artful Inquiry

From artful question to artful inquiry relates to the method chosen. An artful question can be used for ordinary reflection, which is expected in the students' written reflection reports. However, it is emphasised that other channels of reflection, such as images, drawing and artwork are more than welcome. When this happens, we can talk about artful inquiry. Artful inquiry uses artistic methods to explore the not yet known, i.e. the emerging tacit knowing that can be called forward through these processes. In some instances the artistic method merges with the reflection process. It becomes the reflection process. One example is from a person working on a self-portrait through prototyping. He set out with the intention "to see myself as a product that, through an innovative process, will be re-designed" (p. 5). Interestingly, he discovered during his prototyping process that the value lies in the process more than in the product. The question of "who could I be?" becomes one with the artistic process of reflection.

> Drawing prototypes has opened a new world – a world of reflection and new ideas. Prior to my experiments with drawing, my focus was on the result of drawing and I evaluated my drawings by the premise – does the picture look nice? I now enjoy the process of drawing and evaluate the result by the premise – has it changed my perceptions and given me new ideas? I'm sure I will use this as a tool to ask, approach, answer questions and solve work-related tasks. (p. 30)

Artistic Methods

The following account is rather general in order to provide a basic overview. In my earlier research, based on over fifty interviews with artists, researchers and managers, I have provided an overview with eight cases of artistic intervention (Darsø, 2004). For more recent examples, see e.g. (Sköldberg, Woodilla, & Berthoin Antal, 2016). One of the major surprises from my research was that each artist applied artistic processes slightly differently. Theatre exercises were used in many different ways, and so was storytelling, prototyping, and all other arts-based methods that I came into contact with. The creativity and inventiveness in applying artistic methods is overwhelming. The what-works-for-what catalogue of artistic methods is still missing. The what-works-for-whom issue is another challenge, which was expressed by one of the participants as: "some things work for you while others do not".

Artistic methods produce tangible as well as intangible results. The former applies to journal writing, morning pages, drawing and painting, sculpting, textile work, as well as prototyping. These methods have a lot of potential as the emphasis can be either on the making process, or on the result, or on both. Often the result will be a physical reminder of the process, and perhaps also of the context and the participants. The latter applies to theatre rehearsal, Image Theatre and Forum plays, as well as other forms of embodying, exploring movement and sensing. Also listening to different types of music can be explorative as a form of reflection (Darsø, 2004); and presencing, through breathing exercises, zen-walking (which is walking very slowly and trying to be empty of thoughts) or meditation, allows tacit knowing to surface to consciousness. The reminder of the process is more elusive, in the form of memory, photos or notes in a journal.

Reflection

According to Cunliffe and Jun, reflection is defined as "a mirror image – an objectivist ontology based on the idea that there is an original reality we can think about and separate ourselves from" (Cunliffe & Jun, 2005, p. 226). This means taking time to step back from the busyness of organisational and social life in order to think more deeply about what is happening and what is important to focus on. According to Adler, reflecting is one of the three competencies (together with leveraging and framing) that Howard Gardner found distinguished extraordinary leaders from ordinary ones (Adler, 2007). As explained earlier, reflection can also be imbedded in the artistic process as direct sensing or even communion with the material. This is often a wordless experience and can be deeply meaningful and awe-inspiring. How do we deal with such experiences in a respectful and ethical way in order to retain and make sense of them? It seems that the experience would need some kind of translation afterwards for it to be memorised. For most people reflection would be in written form in order to make sense of the experience. This adds another layer of knowing, as this is a process of surfacing tacit knowledge. In particular, this concerns the intangible. When there have been tangible outcomes, these may serve the purpose by themselves. The risk, however, of translating and making sense of experience is that the magic dissipates. On the other hand, if not recorded in writing, the whole experience may dissipate, depending on the recollective skills of the creator. The reflection process is a way to discover and harvest new insights, which helps in making the learning process more conscious.

Reflexivity

Reflexivity adds distance to the reflection as it calls for a critical perspective. Cunliffe & Jun explore two forms of reflexivity, self-reflexivity and critical reflexivity, as an approach towards more critical, responsible and ethical behaviour in organisations. They define self-reflexivity (Cunliffe & Jun, 2005, p. 229):

> […] as the conscious act of an existential self, wherein we examine our values and ourselves by exercising critical consciousness. It is a process that depends on an idea of a transforming self, continuously emerging and changing as we interact with others and our environment.

Critical reflexivity, on the other hand, "offers a way of critiquing ideologies, normalized practices, and their consequences. It offers a way of reformulating and expanding the bounds of social and organizational practice by highlighting systemic control structures that reproduce themselves in our discourse and practices" (Cunliffe & Jun, 2005, p. 232).

Both of these forms are relevant in management education as they may help in suggesting alternative interpretations to what happened and what was learnt. Obviously, self-reflexivity is involved when the topic is personal leadership. In relation to the reflection reports, we suggest a "reality check", where the person involved asks other people's opinions or applies different theoretical concepts and perspectives for interpretation.

Application of Artful Inquiry

In this section I shall apply the Artful Inquiry model to the reflections of one particular participant and all quotes below are from her reflection report. The italicised words relate to the Artful Inquiry model. This person was an internal consultant in a Danish municipality, who wanted to reflect upon her leadership.

> The *purpose* of working with leadership at this very moment in this *context* has to do with my experience with this master, my work and my personal life. I basically wonder – how I can activate my sources and beliefs in the best possible way with the purpose of creating new value with the people around me [*question*]. (p. 6)

Her leadership story was very touching and could best be described as one long poem. She explains how this came about:

> The leadership narrative emerged as a result of five days' hard mental and physical work in Banff. We worked with drawings of leadership, reflections on our most admired leader, meditation in the forest, leadership icons in clay, theatre work such as using your voice to communicate a message, using your body to incarnate a most admired leader [*artistic method*], etc. (p. 9)

She also *reflects* afterwards on her learning:

> I have worked with facilitation for many years having a deep belief in a conceptual approach to innovation, meaning using models, schemes, structures, tools, etc. But I have learned that an artful approach is related to direct experience that involves feelings and touches the person profoundly. I have observed that when the feelings are activated, e.g. through common tasks that involve the body in different ways, it diminishes the voice of fear, which must be the overall purpose, and opens you up for other people and other solutions. The writing of the leadership narrative is an example of how an artful approach through many channels made me let go of the control and made me produce a narrative that I would not have with another approach. (p. 17)

She created a new *practice* for herself: running reflections, which she uses continually:

> The learning journal is an important tool for reflection in the LAICS programme. Using the learning journal consistently has taught me the value of ongoing reflection on experience and learning and it has inspired me to work with running reflections. I have noted a significant coherence with my self-reflections and how grounded I appear at work. It is a very positive experience and it has given me an urge to continue with my reflections. (p. 19)

As it appears from the above quote she uses *self-reflexivity* for becoming more grounded at work. In addition she applies *reflexivity* in the form of theories in order to understand her learning from alternative perspectives, including those of (Drucker, 1999), (Boland & Collopy, 2004) and (Scharmer, 2007).

This example gives an indication of how the Artful Inquiry model can be applied. It works both for planning an Artful Inquiry process and for analysing empirical data.

ANALYSIS

There are various ways in which tacit knowledge can surface and become meaningful. Here follow some examples of what has worked for the participants: drawing or writing with dominant and non-dominant hand; new perspectives and insights on themselves; the impact of the leadership icons; co-creation with materials that "talk back", and co-creation with tangible materials. The following quotes are from reflection reports and master theses.

Drawing or Writing with Dominant and Non-Dominant Hand

As part of searching for generative methods to support the U-process (based on the work of Scharmer, 2007, described earlier) my colleague and I tried out a new method. It is based on Ph.D. research by Lucia Capacchione, who has been experimenting with writing and drawing exercises using both hands. Interestingly, Capacchione found "that writing or drawing with the non-dominant hand directly accesses right-brain functions" (Capacchione, 1991, p. 17). Findings from neuroscience and brain research can be summarised briefly as follows: right-brain functions are holistic, colourful, emotional, aesthetic and artful, whereas left-brain functions are rational, logical, sequential and analytical. The brain is undoubtedly much more complex than that, but the point here is that Capacchione recommends dialoguing with both hands for self-development and healing.

At the seminar we let the LAICS participants experience the U-process (instead of only talking about it) by working on the question: how can I create innovation in my organisation? After going through the first four steps, we designed an exercise of 30 minutes for the step of *crystallising*, for which we have struggled for many years to find an appropriate method. We used 10 minutes to instruct and explain and then let the participants take 10 minutes to draw with dominant hand and 10 minutes to draw with non-dominant hand. Much to our delight, this exercise had some surprising results for some of the participants, who could not believe all the interesting details that the non-dominant hand had drawn. Using the dominant hand one person had drawn tall buildings in the background and a path leading to a bridge, but then did not know what was on the other side. With the non-dominant hand, this person could suddenly draw what was on the other side: a nice garden with flowers and butterflies (a lot of details). 2–3 others had similar experiences. Since then we have used the method every year and it seems to work for several of our students.

Writing with the non-dominant hand can be instrumental for helping tacit knowledge to emerge. One participant wanted to find out about her strengths and competences. She could not do so by thinking (left-brain), but writing with the non-dominant hand resulted in important insights:

> My work with left/right attention and the exercises with both my dominant and non-dominant hand have really been exciting and rewarding … The making of the report has helped me see my strengths and competences in a new light. … I now realise that my strengths are very much related to who I am and the way that I think, act and work. This is new and valuable knowledge to me. How my joy is a personal asset is very much a part of this realisation. However, I can also see personal competences which I have gained and trained by my left mode attention such as analytical and strategic capabilities. (p. 16)

New Perspectives and Insights on Themselves

Some of the artistic processes have effects similar to art therapy. Generally speaking, art therapy is applied as a healing process, which is accomplished through art work. There are several different schools of thought, going from a psychiatric perspective to a spiritual one. The work of Pat B. Allen corresponds well with my research data, as she claims that "Art therapy, … , is mostly about getting other people to know themselves through art making." (Allen, 1995, p. xv). In several reflection reports there are indications of healing effects from the artistic process, mainly as new insights and perspectives on themselves, as also found by Sutherland (Sutherland, 2013). An example from a reflection report: "It is therefore a gift suddenly to become aware of all the deeper knowledge and emotions which are actually already present in me and to have discovered a way to get in contact with them."

The same person continues:

> This report has clarified as well as catalysed a process of personal change and I see that I am in the process of developing new perspectives of being me. … The new me is more circular than linear and is more jazz than classical! And I feel and sense, as well as I think and know, how to integrate personal strengths and professional competences to take personal leadership towards valuable change in my life and in my organisation. (p. 17)

The Impact of Leadership Icons

Another finding regards the role and impact of the leadership icons, which the participants make in clay on the first day of the Banff seminar. The icons are fired and on the fourth day the participants get to glaze them. Later the same day the icons are fired in a Raku kiln, taken out and cooled off with everybody standing around the kiln. Several participants mention their icons as incredibly meaningful and as important reminders of the process. Here is an example:

> The work I did during the days in Banff gave me an important insight. I believe that especially the artistic processes helped me to a new and necessary insight. My leadership icon – the link[1] – turned out to be the materialisation of what I suddenly knew I needed, but do not have access to. This icon now has a prominent place at home to remind me that I need, deserve and have the right to claim *connectedness*. (p. 4)
>
> Furthermore, working with My Leadership Story also contributed with insight regarding connectedness and cooperation. (p. 5)

Another example of the significance of an icon together with a profound experience derives from a master thesis on psychological innovation (Kunze, 2011, p. 4):

> First practice after arriving in Banff was shaping "my personal leadership" in clay. There were time constraints and no time for reflection. Just do it. I chose the first thing that came into my mind – the symbol of a thriving heart. Afterwards I was surprised that this simple little symbol contained the essence of all the questions I had. It was as if things were fused into a single expression. ...
>
> My next question was about how I got on with the insights I had gained through the heart metaphor. My experience was that I got in touch with nature and that it replied back with a speed and accuracy that was surprising. The answer was meaningful, profound and surprisingly rewarding. As if the answer unfolded from an immanent truth emerging through my wordless question and my intense listening for meaning. My response was clear – aha! – that things fell into place in my consciousness. This was a very rewarding and moving experience...

Co-Creation with Materials That "Talk Back"

The above is not only an example of the value of creating icons, but also a description of how materials "talk back". This is a way of co-creating meaning with artful and natural materials. Another participant, who had great difficulty working with clay, felt that working with nature was easy: "Later we went making land art with Ed. With only a vague idea in your mind on the story you are going to tell, it was easy picking up stones, branches, pinecones and flowers and arranging it all in patterns – and meaning emerged into telling a story. I'm amazed by the ease with which these materials were talking to me compared with the clay." (p.15) and he later adds "all I had to do was to let my story emerge from the parts available to me." (p.16)

Co-Creation with Tangible Materials

An example of co-creation is from a master thesis that investigated the moment of the innovation process when a group generates a concept that has transformative value. The empirical case involved a Danish kindergarten that was ordered to make a specific contract. The leader of the kindergarten could have filled in the formula herself, but instead, she decided to develop this contract together with the employees by engaging a facilitator from outside. After some exercises and discussions, the facilitator asked them to form groups and to transform their visions into cake boxes[2] by using a variety of tangible materials. Working in groups with the cake boxes as part of creating the contract was described as "a moment of deep concentration and yet of fun; of hands and materials forming a shared space for interaction; of individuals losing their egos and realizing their amazing influence on their collective future" (Schumann, 2009, p. 50). This can also be understood as communication through prototyping, which according to Schrage means creating a shared space for conversation and demonstration of ideas (Schrage, 2000).

CONCLUSION

Developing innovation competency is needed for creating the future we desire. This cannot be achieved through traditional lecturing. Students must be activated to experience and learn in practice. The focus of this chapter has been on Co-creation and Artful Inquiry in a context of management education. As demonstrated above, Artful Inquiry can help in surfacing tacit knowledge in various ways. The "eye of art" produces intuitive interpretation and intuition is related to tacit knowing. Furthermore, neuroscience points to right brain thinking as holistic, aesthetic and emotional. For some people, writing and drawing with both hands work surprisingly well in relation to accessing inner knowing, hidden emotions and unexpected creativity. The data shows that this method has rendered many important insights and has provided healing effects as well, similar to art therapy where people get to know themselves better by making art. The artistic process itself can provide a way of immersing oneself and reflecting with it. But also the artistic product has a lot of both symbolic and 'reminder' value, as we saw with the leadership icons of clay. Another interesting feature is how 'materials talk back' to people and become activated in a silent communicative process that brings new perspectives and insights forward. In the examples of co-creation, verbal as well as non-verbal, visualising and prototyping show great potential for accessing people's non-conscious inner images and for sharing and creating meaning. Artful Inquiry followed by self-reflexivity can be transformative.

As a leader it is important to know oneself, but in today's organisations time is scarce and people's attention is drawn towards tasks, meetings, deskwork, other people, not to mention social media. As Adler recommends, time for inner contemplation and reflection should be on the leader's agenda and prioritised – or it will easily be invaded by all the other "stuff" (Adler, 2016). As argued earlier, crafting questions of significance is an important leadership skill. Powerful questions are open, deeply meaningful, and invoke passion as the HP example illustrates. Appendix A presents a list of powerful questions that have been formulated by both faculty and students. Artful Inquiry, however, not only involves powerful questions, but also *how* the inquiry will be performed. Which artistic approach will be used? As demonstrated in the examples above, this depends on the type of question, the purpose, the type of person, the context and the time available. As the data suggest, what works for one might not work for someone else. This implicates trying out various art forms in order to find out what is suitable for each particular leader. At LAICS we try out a variety of artistic methods in order for each participant to find their preferred method and materials. In the best of worlds, a potent question matched with an appropriate artistic process merges with the reflection process into an intense experience of revelation and new insights that lead to improved or transformed practice. Usually transformation happens as people become more conscious about their values and potential, more innovative and more courageous towards making a difference.

NOTES

1 'The link' consisted of two linked clay circles.

2 Cardboard boxes that bakers use when selling cakes to customers.

REFERENCES

Aakjær, M. K. (2013). *Reconfiguring boundaries in social innovation.* Aarhus, Copenhagen.

Adler, N. J. (2007). Organizational metaphysics. Global wisdom and the audacity of hope. In E. H. Kessler & J. R. Bailey (Eds.), *Handbook of organizational and managerial wisdom* (pp. 423–458). Thousand Oaks, CA: Sage Publications.

Adler, N. J. (2016, January 13). Want to be an outstanding leader? Keep a journal. *Harvard Business Review.*

Allen, P. B. (1995). *Art is a way of knowing: A guide to self-knowledge and spiritual fulfillment through creativity.* Boston, MA & London: Shambala.

Bason, C. (2010). *Leading public sector innovation: Co-creating for a better Society.* Bristol, GB: Policy Press

Boland, R., & Collopy, F. (Eds.). (2004). *Managing as designing.* San Francisco, CA: Stanford Business Books.

Brown, J., & Isaacs, D. (2005). *The world café: Shaping our futures through conversations that matter.* San Francisco, CA: Berrett-Kohler Publishcers, Inc.

Capacchione, L. (1991). *Recovery of your inner child: The highly acclaimed method for liberating your inner self.* New York, NY: Simon & Schuster.

Cooperrider, D. L., & Whitney, D. (1999). *Appreciative inquiry.* San Francisco, CA: Berrett-Kohler Communications, Inc.

Cunliffe, A. L. (2002). Reflexive dialogical practice in management learning. *Management Learning, 33*(1), 35–61.

Cunliffe, A. L., & Jun, J. S. (2005). The need for reflexivity in public administration. *Adminstration & Society, 37*(2), 225–242.

Damasio, A. (1999). *The feeling of what happens: Body and emotion in the making of consciousness.* San Diego, CA & London: Harcourt, Inc.

Darsø, L. (2001). *Innovation in the making.* Frederiksberg, Denmark: Samfundslitteratur.

Darsø, L. (2003). [Is there a Formula for Innovation?]. *Børsen Ledelseshåndbøger: Innovations- og Forandringsledelse.*

Darsø, L. (2004). *Artful creation: Learning-tales of arts-in-business*. Frederiksberg, Denmark: Samfundslitteratur.

Darsø, L. (2011). *Innovationspædagogik: Kunsten at fremelske innovationskompetence*. Frederiksberg, Denmark: Samfundslitteratur.

Darsø, L. (2012). Innovation competency – an essential organizational asset. In S. Høyrup, C. Hasse, M. Bonnafous-Boucher, M. Lotz, & K. Møller (Eds.), *Employee-driven innovation* (pp. 108–126). Basingstoke, UK: Palgrave Macmillan.

Darsø, L. (2014). Setting the context for transformation towards authentic leadership and co-creation. In O. Gunnlaugson, C. Baron, & M. Cayer (Eds.), *Perspectives on theory U: Insights from the Field* (pp. 97–113). Hershey, PA: IGI Clobal.

Darsø, L. (2016). *Artful inquiry as a leadership skill*. Paper presented at the The 8th Conference of Art of Management and Organization, IEDC, Bled, Slovenia.

Drucker, P. F. (1999, January). Managing oneself. *Harvard Business Review, Best of HBR 1999*, 100–109.

Eisner, E. (2008). Art and knowledge. In J. G. Knowles & A. L. Cole (Eds.), *Handbook of the arts in qualitative inquiry: Perspectives, methodologies, examples and issues*. Thousand Oaks, CA: Sage Publications.

Friis, S. A. K. (2016). The 6C model: The contribution of design to open, complex, problem solving. *The International Journal of Design in Society, 10*(3), 13–30.

Irgens, E. J. (2014). Art, science and the challenge of management education. *Scandinavian journal of Management*.

Kimbell, L. (2012). Rethinking design thinking: Part II *Design and Culture, 4*(2), 129–148.

Kunze, K. (2011). *Development of human causality: LAICS Master in Leadership and Innovation in Complex Systems*. Copenhagen: University of Aarhus.

Mintzberg, H. (2009). *Managing*. San Francisco, CA: Berrett-Koehler.

Nonaka, I., & Takeuchi, H. (1995). *The knowledge-creating company: How Japanese companies create the dynamics of innovation*. New York, NY: Oxford University Press.

Palus, C. J., & Horth, D. M. (2002). *The leader's edge: Six creative competencies for navigating complex challenges*. San Francisco, CA: Jossey-Bass.

Pink, D. (2006). *A whole new mind: Why right-brainers will rule the future*. New York, NY: Riverhead Books, The Penguin Group.

Polanyi, M. (1983). *The tacit dimension*. Gloucester, MA: Peter Smith Publisher Inc.

Scharmer, C. O. (2007). *Theory U: Leading from the future as it emerges: The social technology of presencing*. Cambridge, MA: SOL Press.

Schrage, M. (2000). *Serious play. How the world's best companies simulate to innovate*. Boston, MA: Harvard Business School Press.

Schumann, K. (2009). *Communicate to innovate – Facilitating innovative processes in complex systems: sLAICS master in leadership and innovation in complex systems*. Copenhagen: University of Aarhus.

Schumpeter, J. A. (1934). *The theory of economic development*. Cambridge, MA: Harvard University Press.

Sköldberg, U. J., Woodilla, J., & Berthoin Antal, A. (2016). *Artistic interventions in organizations: Research, theory and practice* (Vol. 4). London & New York, NY: Routledge, Taylor & Francis Group.

Strati, A. (2000). The aesthetic approach in organization studies. In S. Linstead & H. Höpfl (Eds.), *The aesthetics of organization* (pp. 13–34). SAGE Publications.

Sutherland, I. (2013). Arts-based methods in leadership development: Affording aesthetic workspaces, reflexivity and memories with momentum. *Management Learning*, 1–19. doi:100.1177/1350507612465063

Vogt, E. E., Brown, J., & Isaacs, D. (2003). *The art of powerful questions: Catalyzing insight, innovation, and action*. Mill Valley, CA: Whole Systems Associates.

Williams, F. (2012). Take two hours of pine forest and call me in the morning. *Ourside Magazine*. Retrieved from http://outsideonline.com/newsletters website

Lotte Darsø
Department of Learning
School of Education
Aarhus University

APPENDIX A: POWERFUL QUESTIONS FROM THE LAICS PROGRAMME

1. Why did I want to become a leader in the first place?
2. What is my relation to nature and to the place where I come from?
3. What do I offer to the world?
4. What gifts am I here to give?
5. What does life call me to do now?
6. What bigger story am I a part of?
7. Who am I?
8. What is my story?
9. What is my voice?
10. What inspires me?
11. What is my contribution?
12. What deserves my attention?
13. What is my core leadership question right now?
14. Where does my joy come from?
15. What does it mean to give an A?
16. What is the fire in me that can spark other fires?
17. What is my leadership style and what are my weak and strong sides?
18. What are my core values?
19. What tools do I draw upon in my leadership?
20. How can I use my self-portrait as a tool to grow as a leader?
21. What do my hands know about leadership?
22. How might I reflect innovatively on my leadership?
23. How am I innovating as a leader in the LAICS programme?

JULIE BORUP JENSEN

10. ARTS-INVOLVING BURNING MAN FESTIVAL AS CO-CREATION IN SOCIAL EDUCATION STUDIES

INTRODUCTION

The present chapter addresses the topic of co-creation in student learning processes concerning democracy and citizenship in social education studies at a Danish university college, Northern Jutland. The co-creational effects of experimenting with an arts-involving festival, inspired by the Nevada Desert event "Burning Man", in collaboration with pedagogical staff and residents of local refugee and immigrant institutions and local communities, are investigated by means of socio-cultural and cultural-psychological perspectives on learning processes. Original data is drawn from a qualitative action research project that aimed at developing practice and knowledge about arts involvement in the local social education studies programme. The study revealed potential and challenges in respect of using artistic and aesthetic expressions, methods and activities as a way of framing the co-creational aspects of student learning within the content area of democracy and citizenship. The findings show that working with co-creation in teaching may lead to community building, building of relationships within the local community, visibility in society and, last but not least, student learning and development of understanding of democracy in practice. The findings also indicate that there are challenges in respect of scaffolding a co-creational process that requires a great deal of negotiation of responsibility and participation.

BACKGROUND: "BURNING MAN" FESTIVAL AS ADULT PEDAGOGY FOR CO-CREATION?

Why Focus on Co-Creation in the Educational System?

The world seems be changing rapidly, becoming increasingly complex and unpredictable with, for example, regular economic crises, fast global communication and a changing world order deriving from wars, climate change and socio-economic inequality, all followed by migration and large flows of refugees. Paradoxes arise, as new technologies and the creation and expansion of local and global networks lead to increased opportunity for citizens to influence their own life situation, while at the same time the gap between rich and poor is growing. It becomes increasingly difficult for individuals and communities to

T. Chemi & L. Krogh (Eds.), Co-Creation in Higher Education, 151–166.

deal with this growing complexity in ways that develop democratic citizenship, as the answer to complexity seems to be to turn to more nationalist, authoritarian rhetoric, practices and persons (expressed in, for instance, Brexit, the election of Donald Trump as American president, and the decrease of freedom of the press in the former Communist societies in Europe). It therefore seems crucial for societies to strengthen the human ability to handle this type of challenge, in ways that lead to development, human flourishing and democratic community building. Given this, there seems to be a need for concepts like democratic capacity building (Banyan, 2015; Stringer, 2013; Noya & Clarence, 2009), community building (Foster-Fishman et al., 2001), collaborative innovation (Lewis et al., 2014; Halvorsen et al., 2005) and co-creation (Degnegaard, 2013). These concepts are framing a wide range of research and development in many arenas of Western societies. In this chapter, however, I will focus on the educational system and its potential to contribute to democratic development in society. To do this, there seems to be a need for new ways to provide students with opportunities to experience how democracy can be enacted at micro-level in concrete relations and collaboration with other people.

The aim of this chapter is to conceptualise micro-level democratic action as pedagogical *co-creation*. This conceptual combination of co-creation and democracy as pedagogy will be examined through an empirical example concerning an educational experiment in a course on democracy and citizenship within the social education studies programme at a university college in Northern Jutland, Denmark. The experiment was exploring the co-creative learning potentials of including an arts festival, the "Burning Man", in a course on democracy and citizenship. Before describing the Burning Man philosophy and the concrete experiment, the social education profession and education will be briefly outlined in order to understand the importance of focusing on co-creation in an effort to develop the students' competences within democracy and citizenship as part of their professional approach to social education practice.

Democracy and Citizenship: Why Are They Important in Social Education Studies?

The core competency of a social educator is to work with relational aspects of learning processes and learning environments in three areas:

1. 'normal pedagogy': nursery/pre-school and day care;
2. 'school pedagogy': school and after-school activities in schools and youth clubs, and
3. 'special education': physically, mentally and socially challenged children, youths and adults, including refugees, diversely abled, psychiatric patients and elderly.

In all of these areas, a democratic ethic is required in meeting with the user groups, because they are all, to different extent, dependent on the approach of the professional caregivers in order to maintain integrity and dignity in what are often asymmetric power relations (Hvidtfeldt, 2003). This is why the co-creational aspect is seen as highly relevant for the social education profession. Especially in the 'special pedagogy' field, issues of power relations in interaction with at-risk children and youths, disabled persons, immigrants, refugees, socially marginalised persons and groups call for students to develop competences of professionally informed co-creation of meaning and action in order to maintain the democratic professional framework (Callewaerth, 2003).

In relation to this, it is relevant to ask the question: what is co-creation in a pedagogical framework? This question will be addressed below.

Co-Creation

According to Degnegaard (2013), there seem to be several ways to conceptualise co-creation within an educational context, most of them concerned with digitalised and virtual teaching methods and learning environments. However, for this chapter, the most relevant understanding of co-creation in the context of learning within social education studies is that of co-creation as *negotiation of meaning* and co-creation in respect of *building inclusive learning communities*. This definition derives from the therapeutic understanding of co-creation as a way to treat malfunctioning communication patterns in, for instance, at-risk families or to create new opportunities for action for challenged youth (Degnegaard, 2013). In the context of education, however, the way to understand co-creation taps very much into the socio-cultural learning aspect of negotiation of meaning. Therefore, in this chapter, co-creation is conceptualised as a means and an end of negotiation of meaning within the learning setting, environment, culture or community. In this way, co-creation may function as, and also result in, *learning community building*. This creates a strong relation to the concept of educational inclusive teaching and learning in order to embrace all participants in the co-creative process of learning.

Inclusion

In order to support co-creative processes in education with the aim of building democratic competences, *inclusion,* understood as a 'sense of belonging' (SOB) must be of strong interest (Prince & Hadwin, 2013). SOB is correlated with signs of social integration of students in a learning environment. The sense of belonging develops from an emotional experience of being accepted, respected and supported by the social environment (Prince & Hadwin, 2013). Prince and Hadwin refer to psychological studies suggesting that, in general, a sense of belonging is crucial for human development, collaboration and learning from infancy onwards. Consequently, one should consider possibilities for every student to develop a sense of belonging in any educational setting, from pre-school to higher education.

In our particular case of social education studies, the aim was to support students in developing a sense of belonging in the profession of social education. In this perspective, co-creation must be understood as a continuous process with focus on the concurrent participation and learning of every student in class, however diverse and different their learning styles or learning preconditions may be (Prince & Hadwin, 2013). In the end, this way of conceptualising co-creation lays the foundations for participation in democratic action and negotiation of meaning (Degnegaard, 2013), and the way students experience co-creational participation in educational activities may affect the way that they practice co-creation in professional life.

Cultural Psychology

This psychological view of SOB as a social process makes the co-creative aspects of the educational concepts of Jerome Bruner relevant, as his socio-cultural, cultural-psychological perspective on education correspondingly focuses on educational environments as significant for students' building a sense of culture (Bruner, 1996), and thereby a sense of belonging and professional identity. Bruner's understanding of individual learning as correlated to educational culture contributes to understanding co-creation, when students, with their diversity of pre-dispositions, social backgrounds, personalities etc., are met with demands for learning in the school system (Bruner, 1996).

Bruner sees the development of a sense of belonging and cultural identity as dependent on school cultures and their ability to acknowledge that students are different, and therefore should be provided with a variety of possible ways of participating in the educational community, and learning subject matter and curricula content (Bruner, 1996). If learning environments are created with various opportunities for participating and learning, the potential diversity and variety of the students' learning pre-dispositions, conditions for learning and learning styles can be embraced as valuable fundamentals for co-creative processes of negotiation of meaning in a democratic dialogue. This means that learning cultures that invite, allow and reward more than just one or a few ways of learning and participating create the potential to encompass diversity and increase the probability of co-creative processes. All of these considerations relate to differentiated instruction, teaching and learning, a research field that has enjoyed focus over the past fifty years (Smith & Throne, 2009).

Vice versa it follows that a school culture that invites, facilitates, and rewards only one or a few ways of learning and participating may be at risk of creating exclusive learning environments, where only those pupils meeting the specific ways of participation and learning can develop a sense of belonging, and develop the belief that they can contribute to co-creation within the educational culture (Bruner, 1996; Prince & Hadwin, 2013; Smith & Throne, 2009).

A visualisation of the above arguments is attempted in the figure below:

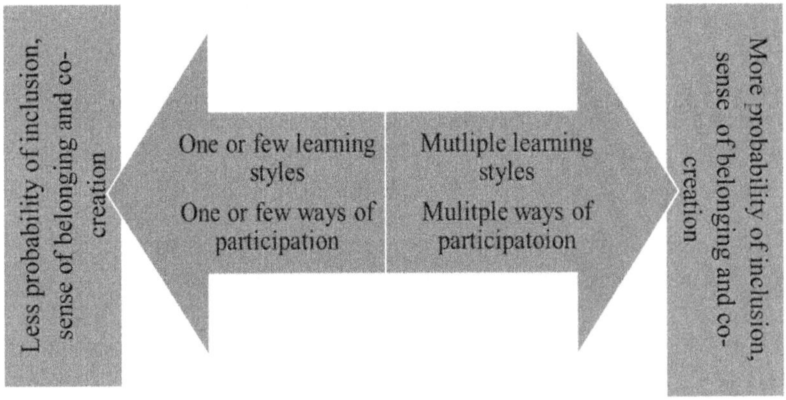

Figure 10.1. Sense of belonging and co-creation approaches to learning and participation

METHOD AND THEORETICAL FRAMEWORK

But how is it possible to study co-creation in an educational context? This chapter builds on an action research approach to knowledge production, based on the assumption that, in order to study social change processes, research must initiate change (Reason & Bradbury, 2008). The Burning Man festival was a part of a larger action research project aiming at creating social change within social education studies at a professional university in Denmark, Northern Jutland, by developing methods and knowledge about arts-involvement in the study programme. The project has been going on since 2011 and it is still – at time of writing – active, with eight current sub-projects within the over-arching action research project framework. The main project is carried out in monthly action research workshops, where the participants from the eight sub-projects work with collective reflections on the developmental work within a socio-cultural theoretical framework (on this way of doing action research, see also Reason & Bradbury, 2008). The participants of the sub-projects are educators within the social education studies programme and they function as co-researchers in the project (McCormack, 2008). The co-researcher approach entails the educators, in pairs or small groups, formulating their own research interest and teaching experiments in their own courses, and documenting and investigating their experiments. In order to develop collective and more general knowledge, the monthly workshops with the university researcher are used as a resource to reflect on, understand and develop knowledge from the data from their teaching experiments. Furthermore, the co-researcher approach means that, over the years, the research focus has moved from an interest in welfare innovation through professional development into an interest in developing student identity within a profession.

The research that forms the empirical basis of this chapter was a sub-project carried out in 2014. This specific project therefore had its own research question, its own data collection process and analysis framework (McNiff, 2014). Data was provided by means of the educators' logbooks, pedagogical plans, written student portfolio-testimonials, a focus group interview with five students, and a qualitative questionnaire. In this chapter, I will analyse excerpts from this data within a cultural-psychological theoretical framework in order to capture the co-creative aspects of a Burning Man festival. It took place in a specific course for students studying within the area of 'special pedagogy'. The title of the course is *The social educator in an ethical, local and global perspective*. The content is theories of democracy, citizenship and empowerment. The teachers operate with the hypothesis that only through collaboration with the user groups, in this case refugees, will the students be able to learn what competences are needed to develop society and communities in a democratic manner among diverse groups of citizens.

Burning Man Festival

The idea,[1] therefore, was to bring the arts-based Burning Man festival into play as a method for the students to experience co-creative, democratic collaboration with institutions, citizens, refugees and immigrants in a socially-challenged area in a small town in Northern Jutland. The Burning Man philosophy puts strong emphasis on embracing and communicating cultural and ethnic diversity by means of multi-cultural artistic expression (Gilmore, 2005). At the outset, this philosophy was seen as highly relevant for the purpose of working with citizenship and democracy in a co-creational manner, since the area of the town involved housed a refugee centre and accommodation for immigrants. The explicit focus for 'our' Burning Man festival was community building, encompassing a wide extent of collaboration on culture-and-arts expressions and activities between all participants regardless of position, role, background and abilities, such as the Burning Man philosophy entails (Gilmore, 2005). This focus on diversity and cultural and artistic expression was expected to provide both students and citizens with various ways to participate and learn, as outlined above.

The Burning Man festival was therefore interpreted as a co-creation approach to learning for social education students that allowed them to explore and learn co-creation (1) by doing it in practice, (2) by collaborating with 'real' diverse citizens, (3) by means of artistic activity, thereby understanding citizenship and democracy from a co-creation perspective with various possibilities of participation and learning. This background allows for an investigation of the festival's data through the following research question:

> How can a Burning Man festival contribute to the development of social education students' competences within democracy and citizenship as co-creation?

Before I describe the co-creational effects of the Burning Man festival, I will briefly outline the logic behind the idea that the Burning Man concept could create spaces for co-creation. The idea was developed within the main action research and development project, by three of the co-researchers. They worked under the same main research motivation embedded in the main project, where the hypothesis is that arts-involvement and arts-production can create spaces for learning processes that leads to identity building among the social education students. Such arts-based learning processes are well-researched in elementary school contexts as identity-building, bodily and emotionally anchored and experience-based, but only randomly explored in higher education contexts. These more personal learning processes are important because students in higher education – and especially in professional education – often experience a lack of meaningfulness and cohesion between their different study activities (Pahuus & Eriksen, 2011). They also experience a lack of social and collective meaning in relation to the profession in general, because the conceptual teaching activities and the professional concepts seem distant, delineated and out of sync with the practices that the students experience when doing practical training (Rasch-Cristensen, 2011; Simons & Hicks, 2006). In this challenging environment, the involvement of arts in teaching seems to have potential for bridging and framing learning processes in a way that creates personal meaning for the students by connecting conceptual, professional and identity-building learning processes with collective, social learning processes (Chemi & Jensen, 2015). Over the years, it has become increasingly clear to the project participants that this learning potential and outcome of arts involvement can be meaningfully interpreted as a co-creational learning process. Moreover, the co-creational aspects of teaching and learning in certain ways derive from the arts involvement and, finally, co-creation is connected with inclusive teaching in a cultural-psychological perspective. These theoretical aspects will be outlined below as:

- Arts involvement
- Aesthetic learning

Arts Involvement

The co-creative dimension of arts involvement in teaching and learning is related to the social and communicative aspects of artistic production, where the students' individual understanding of conceptual, professional-cultural knowledge is expressed and visualised by means of a collective artistic form, and connected with fellow students' personal, bodily and concrete experiences within the professional practice. In other words, arts mediate meaning, when individuals work together and collaborate on artistic activity, giving their individual reflections and perspectives on the professional world collective, artistic shape and form. In this chapter, these characteristics are conceptualised as *co-creation of art-works* and *co-creation of meaning*. Artistic activity is therefore seen as a way of teaching in which artistic expression and collective creation – co-creation – are interwoven in multiple processes of knowledge exchange and learning, because:

- Artistic activity is rooted in bodily and sensory experience, providing opportunities to activate and articulate bodily-embedded knowledge forms in the artistic work (externalisation).
- Artistic activity synthesises different forms of knowledge and knowing by connecting thinking and verbal articulation with bodily and emotionally rooted knowledge forms.
- Externalisation makes the student able to express his or her bodily and emotional experience through artistic means. Externalisation thereby communicates personal knowledge and constitutes the basis for reaching out to others when participating in co-creation of meaning together with other students.
- Artistic activity can serve as metaphor for previous and present experience and knowledge and form new metaphors in the sensory-based encounter between the individual and the work of art, which also has a meaning-building learning effect in co-creation processes.
- The art emphasises own and others' bodily connectedness, which otherwise is 'stored in the body', again serving as a means of connecting to other students in a co-creating, meaning-creating learning process (Jensen, 2017; Cole & Knowles, 2008; Eisner, 2008; Langer, 1961; Weber, 2008).

Aesthetic Learning

In order to substantiate further the idea of arts involvement as a co-creative identity-building framework for teaching and learning in social education studies, the project's arts-involving methods for co-creation in teaching borrow insights from the field of aesthetic learning theories and practices. Aesthetic learning can be defined in various ways. In this chapter, aesthetic learning is understood as learning processes happening when the student is actively involved in an environment with concrete activities that can be sensed in cooperation with other students, when they co-create artworks that express professional experience and knowledge. The chapter draws on the following definitions, where aesthetics is seen as:

- From the Greek *Aisthesis, aisthetá* "what can be sensed": *Aisthánesthai*=sense, feel, perceive, and *techne*=learning by means of sensory perception.
- Symbolic forms that provides an interpretation of ourselves and the world perceived though senses, and which communicates *from*, *to* and *about* feelings (Austring & Sorensen, 2006).
- Human creation with conscious and intentional form, which contains a symbolic dimension and communicates beyond its immediate appearance – often "what cannot be expressed by means of words" (Hohr, 1994).

Over the years, the sensory and emotional basis for learning has become increasingly clear to the project participants. The fact that the arts have a strong sensory point of origin, combined with emotional and experiential associations has led to the assumption that arts can play an important role in co-creative processes, where students need to develop relational and empathic competences with each other and their user groups.

THE BURNING MAN FESTIVAL AS CO-CREATION WITHIN DEMOCRACY AND CITIZENSHIP

The Burning Man festival was held in autumn 2015 with the participation of 300 citizens of an ethnically and socially diverse part of the town, a group of professional social educators, a class of social education students, four educators from the professional school and leaders and staff from 3 local institutions. The festival took place in a small park in the middle of the area.

For one week, the participants collaborated on creating a sizeable wooden figure representing a human being. At the same time, other participants did other kinds of activities, such as cooking food from their original local cuisine, playing music, singing songs, dancing or doing paintings and many other activities of a cultural, sensory and artistic nature. At the end of the week, the activities culminated in a procession through the neighbourhood, a dance performance, a meal, and music performance. To close the festival, there was the burning of the wooden human figure. After it was burned away, every trace of the festival was removed.

The artistic and aesthetic point of this was, according to the project management, that:

> the participants get an extraordinary experience, which they will remember for a very long time. The fact that you burn the figure is making the experiential nature of the collaborative and relational process very clear for the participants. The figure only exists in the memory of the persons who have been present at the event. (Educator, project manager)

The educators were building on the concept and philosophy of the original festival in the Nevada desert that started out on the beaches of California as a liberation project, afterwards growing and moving to the more spacious Nevada Desert. The original Burning Man festival rejects any theological, religious or political ideology, but builds on a strong, multicultural philosophy that "clearly [delineates an] ideology of ethics and culture, encompassing principles of personal, social and environmental responsibility" (Gilmore, 2005, p. 46). These principles are reflected in the so-called 'dogmas' below. The term *dogma* seems like an intentionally paradoxical way to put forward a philosophy that strives to be as non-dogmatic as possible. The dogmas below derive from the educator's log book, describing the local philosophy behind the Burning Man concept. They are formulated by the local project management, whose main emphasis is on participation, and on the rule that a Burning Man festival has "no spectators". The dogmas were handed out to the social education students when starting preparations for the festival (translated and modified by the author):

> *Radical Inclusion:* Anybody can be part of Burning Man. We rejoice over and respect strangers. There are no conditions for participating in our collective.
>
> *Giving gifts (barter):* The value of a gift is unquestionable. Barter does not entail an expectation of trading with something of the same value.
>
> *No commodification:* To maintain the true spirit of Burning Man it is important to create communities and social environments unaffected by commercial sponsorships, transactions or advertisement. We will protect our culture from such exploitation. We transform consumption into participation and experience.
>
> *Help oneself, take care of oneself and see oneself:* Burning Man encourages individuals to discover themselves mentally and physically, and trust or discover their own resources.
>
> *Aesthetic action:* Self-development derives from the uniqueness of the individual. The individual or community are sovereign deciders of the content of the work. The work is offered as a gift to others. In this spirit, the giver should respect the rights and freedom of the receiver.
>
> *Collective effort:* Our community values creative and other collaboration. We aim at creating, supporting and protecting social networks, public spaces, artworks and methods for communication that support such interaction.
>
> *Citizenship and responsibility:* We value the civil society. Citizens organising events should accept the responsibility of public welfare and strive to communicate civil responsibility to the participants. They should also accept the responsibility of own and other's participation within the frames of the local, regional and national law.
>
> *Leaving traces:* Our community respects the environment. We are committed to not leaving physical traces of our activities where we gather. We clean up after ourselves, and try, as far as it is possible, to leave places in better condition than when we found them.
>
> *Participation:* Our community is committed to a radical participatory ethic. We believe that transformative change, in the individual or in society, is only possible by means of deep personal participation. We become by doing. All are invited to work. All are invited to play. We make the world real through actions that open the heart.

> *Spontaneity and straightforwardness:* Straightforward and spontaneous experiences are in many ways the most valuable in any culture. We seek to overcome the barriers between us and acknowledgement of our inner selves, that keep us from reality and the people around us, from participation in society and contact with the natural world that extend beyond human interference. No idea can replace this experience.

During the project week, these 'dogmas' were put into practice by the 300 participants, in the activities described above. The co-creational aspects seem clear, since the elements of participation, barter, welcoming strangers etc. require development of a strong competence of negotiation of meaning – one of the core aspects of co-creation within a democratic framework. The students responded positively to the activities (quotes are from the qualitative assessment focus group interview):

- My learning process was supported, since I dared to speak during group discussions
- I learned how to take responsibility for my own learning process
- [I got] insight into citizenship and democracy
- [I got] the insight that social educators are different
- [I realised that] free frames require responsibility
- It supports learning to look at the project in a positive manner
- Learning a lot on seeing the product at the town square at the end of the week – a visible result.

The negative responses were formulated like this:

- Too little teaching in the classroom
- Many participants did not take responsibility
- Some students are not comfortable with too wide frames and rules.

The student quotes are meaningful and dense statements about their learning process and the challenges and potentials of working with democracy and citizenship in such a co-creational, arts-integrating teaching experiment. This will be analysed and understood in a cultural-psychological perspective below.

ANALYSIS: CULTURAL PRODUCTION AND CO-CREATION OF MEANING

In respect of co-creation, the statement of "daring to speak during group discussions" in correlation with the insight of "taking responsibility for my own learning process" indicates that there are some dynamics in the interaction between the collective, the group and the individual entailing a strong aspect of *responsibility.*

This taking of responsibility for your own learning process in order to be able to contribute to the collective process merits further exploration. Vice versa, the responsabilisation of the collective in order to contribute to co-creation may also be relevant:

In a cultural-psychological perspective, artistic and cultural production as carried out in a Burning Man festival shapes the students' experience of time and space. It also provides sensory form, in which people can learn and create meaning. This meaning will be individually expressed, but still socially and culturally shaped, communicated and interpreted, in processes and 'products' (the wooden sculpture, dance performances etc.). If we return for a moment to the original rituals and 'dogmas' of Burning Man, we see that people gather to form an interim community based on strong idealistic beliefs, free of religious dogmas. Participants are encouraged to make of the experience whatever meaning or interpretation is available to them (Gilmore, 2005). In a learning setting, arts shapes every single individual's expression, voice and body within the structure of the art form, providing them with a shared and negotiated space for interaction and recognition. This time-and-space-shaped reification of common experience makes multiple ways of participation possible, giving the participants an experience of participation and contribution to a shared whole. In other words, inclusion in a co-creational process of experiencing citizenship and participation in democracy.

In an artistic perspective, the Burning Man activities illustrated above function as a structure in the collaborative room, a structure which is sensorially perceived and emotionally interpreted, and in which social relations among the participants can be developed. It can also be seen as a *cultural product*, as a 'thing' created by sound, movement, time, sculpture, activity, interaction and space. In this shift in perspective, there is a move towards pedagogy with a socio-cultural viewpoint. The cultural approach to pedagogy as a social activity mediated by cultural 'tools for meaning-making' was initially formulated by Jerome Bruner in his further development of the ideas of Vygotsky and Piaget. In relation to including artistic and cultural activity in a learning setting, Bruner's preoccupation with the phenomenon of cultural works, or *oeuvres,* brings further support to the idea of putting arts into play in the higher education context, such as in a Burning Man festival. The idea of *oeuvres* and their pedagogical significance is closely related to the idea of externalisation, which Bruner, supported by Meyerson, sees as the main function of any collective cultural activity. This means that culture generates canonical works that externalise, make visible and express its art and science, its institutional structures, laws and markets, as well as history at large. When the 'work', such as a wooden figure of a human being, is produced on a smaller scale in a local community (similar products could be made in the classroom, too), the small group's externalisations of 'everyday arts' contribute to the product, in what can be termed a process of co-creating meaning. The externalisations in the co-creational process thus become available for sensing – for example, by means of building and shaping a figure or creating a dance or an artwork. So the individual and collective co-creational effort becomes sensible for all participants through hearing or seeing and the product, so to speak, constitutes the process. What happens is that the 'everyday-artistic' knowledge and skills of every student, citizen, refugee, immigrant or social educator are externalised when solving tasks in the process of producing a figure, a dance or a product, which the whole group of participants contribute to and can hear or see. According to Bruner, the product or the work in this co-creative process gives rise to diverse activities of the participants:

- Scaffolding for each other through the negotiation of meaning.
- Creating and sustaining group identity and solidarity.
- Making division of labour visible in a group, providing opportunities to recognise diversity and thus help individuals to become more aware of their own strengths.
- Illustrating collective rather than individual progress.
- Creating common and negotiated ways of thinking in a group during the creative process.
- Inspiring metacognition about the work and, therefore, learning.

In the student quotes above, we see some of these learning benefits expressed in statements like "I dared to speak during group discussions", which can be interpreted as an effect of the group identity and solidarity created, and the visibility of division of labour and competences. When these basics are present, the individual student finds the courage to speak up and thereby contribute to the co-creation of learning and meaning. Since the statement indicates that this particular student does not always dare to speak in group work, it seems as if multiple ways of participation and learning were present in the activities of the festival, recognising diversity and thereby contributing to inclusion, democracy and co-creation. In addition, learning effects like metacognition and scaffolding can be interpreted as present in statements like "I learned how to take responsibility for my own learning process". The students also say that they "learned democracy and citizenship", which may be perceived as an effect of the way the wooden figure represents a collaborative and co-creational process between students, citizens, professional social educators and teachers from the institution. As Bruner states, works (*oeuvres*), in this case a collectively created figure, "achieve an existence of their own" (Bruner, 1996, p. 22). The *oeuvre* generates a cultural, negotiated sense of belonging in the group – co-creation of meaning and inclusion of multiple perspectives and ways of participation and learning. Moreover, the work is visible as indisputable evidence of externalised knowledge and reflection, whether it be bodily, mental, cognitive, emotional or experiential. If creating an artwork together is seen in light of collective production using cultural tools (e.g. visual arts tools – colour, strokes, motives etc., musical means (rhythm, sounds, notes etc.), the cultural production characteristics have potentials for learning on at least three different, but related levels:

- Individual (the individual participants contribute to the figure, the dance, in multiple modes of participation and learning).
- Group (attuning individual expressions to the others in the group and scaffolding for each other by contributing and suggesting expressions within the artwork, sometimes even without speaking).

- Community (a figure, a dance, a theatre performance, a concert or an arts exhibition, where the group contributes to the whole artwork and expresses a community's diversity and multiple-expressed participation).

CONCLUDING REMARKS AND PERSPECTIVES

If co-creation is seen as a process of negotiation of meaning, the above insights with the socio-cultural and cultural-psychological concepts may shed new light on the aspects of co-creation that are related to a pedagogy that supports the development of democratic competences in social education studies. This can meaningfully be conceptualised as *pedagogical co-creation.*

However, the student quotes also revealed a more ambivalent experience of the Burning Man festival, where they felt abandoned in the learning process, and where they missed 'normal' teaching with lectures and more conceptual work with theories ("too little teaching in the classroom"), which can be interpreted as a very common challenge when experimenting with untraditional ways of teaching. As Bruner states, folk pedagogy can often impede cultural-psychological pedagogies, since the way in which students are accustomed regarding schooling and teaching creates certain expectations of frames, content and roles in the classroom. These expectations convey meaning to the situation, and make it unnecessary to negotiate the learning setting, creating a feeling of security and predictability (Bruner, 1996). As the Burning Man festival moves pedagogy and the student learning process from the classroom to the local community, the students may be uncertain of their roles, expectations of learning outcomes and tools for studying. This is expressed in statements like "…some students are not comfortable with too wide frames and rules" – or they may experience a lack of meaning, which seems to be the case when they experience that their fellow students are not taking responsibility in group work, learning processes and interactive processes with citizens – "many participants did not take responsibility". Such outcomes of the Burning Man festival point to a potentially excluding effect of the artistic activities, which may impede a meaningful and co-creational learning process for the students. This is worth considering when bringing co-creation into the core of teaching citizenship and democracy in social education studies, for instance by means of a Burning Man festival or similar learning activities. When looking at more recent research, this is a common experience for teachers and educators when teaching in a co-creational way in higher education (Bovill et al., 2016; Elsharnouby, 2015; Young & Collins, 2014).

Even though a Burning Man festival is a very spectacular event, the findings indicate that some of its components are still relevant and manageable in respect of working with the co-creational dimension of teaching. The participating educators all agreed that the Burning Man festival demanded a great deal of work: organising, collaborating with external parties, negotiation within and between institutional logics etc. However, they also agreed that the work pays off in respect of community building, building of relationships within the local community, visibility in society and, last but not least, student learning and development of understanding of democracy in practice. The findings also indicate that there are challenges in respect of scaffolding a co-creational process that requires a great deal of negotiation of responsibility and participation. However, this seems to be a challenge worth working with in future developmental projects in social education studies, since the student evaluations seem to convince the educators that the majority of the students obtained the intended learning outcomes in a way that generates deeper, bodily and emotionally anchored knowledge on citizenship and democracy in a co-creational practice.

NOTE

[1] Aknowledgments for the idea to Morten Lykkegaard, Holger Kjærgård, and Pernille Sams, all lecturers at University College Northern Jutland, social education studies.

REFERENCES

Austring, B. E., og Sørensen, M. (2006). *Æstetik og læring: Grundbog i æstetiske læreprocesser.* Copenhagen: Hans Reitzels Forlag, Socialpædagogisk Bibliotek.

Banyan, M. E. (2015). *Capacity building.* Retrieved from http://academic.eb.com/EBchecked/topic/1904179/capacity-building

Bovill, C., Cook-Sather, A., Felten, P., Millard, L., & Moore-Cherry, N. (2016). Addressing potential challenges in co-creating learning and teaching: Overcoming resistance, navigating institutional norms and ensuring inclusivity in student–staff partnerships. *Higher Education; the International Journal of Higher Education Research, 71*(2), 195–208.

Bruner, J. S. (1996). *The culture of education.* Cambridge, Massachusetts, MA: Harvard University Press.

Callewaerth, S. (2003). Profession og personlighed – to sider af samme sag? In I. Weicher & P. Fibæk Laursen (Eds.), *Person og profession: En udfordring for socialrådgivere, sygeplejersker, lærere og pædagoger.* Værløse: Billesø & Baltzer.

Chemi, T., & Jensen, J. B. (2015). Emotions and learning in arts-based practices of educational innovation. In B. Lund & T. Chemi (Eds.), *Dealing with emotions: A pedagogical challenge to innovative learning* (Electronic ed.) Rotterdam, the Netherlands: Sense Publishers.

Cole, A. L., & Knowles, J. G. (2008). Arts-informed research. In J. G. Knowles & A. L. Cole (Eds.), *Handbook of the arts in qualitative research* (1st ed., pp. 55–70). Thousand Oaks, CA: Sage Publications Inc.

Drotner, K. (1991). *At skabe sig – selv: Ungdom, æstetik, pædagogik.* Copenhagen: Gyldendal.

Eisner, E. (2008). Art and knowing. In J. G. Knowles & A. L. Cole (Eds.), *Handbook of the arts in qualitative research* (1st ed., pp. 3–12). Thousand Oaks, CA: Sage Publications Inc.

Elsharnouby, T. H. (2015). Student co-creation behavior in higher education: The role of satisfaction with the university experience. *Journal of Marketing for Higher Education, 25*(2), 238–262.

Foster-Fishman, P. G., Berkowitz, S. L., Lounsbury, D. W., Jacobson, S., & Allen, N. A. (2001). Building collaborative capacity in community coalitions: A review and integrative framework. *American Journal of Community Psychology, 29*(2).

Gilmore, L. (2005). Fires of the Heart. In L. Gilmore & M. van Proyen (Eds.), *Afterburn: Reflections on burning man* (pp. 43–64). Albuquerque: University of New Mexico Press.

Halvorsen, T., Hauknes, J., Miles, I., & Røste, R. (2005). *Innovation in the public sector: On the differences between public and private sector innovation* (Publin Report No. 9D). Oslo: NIFU Step.

Hohr, H. (2010). "Aesthetic emotion": An ambiguous concept in John Dewey's aesthetics. *Ethics and Education, 5*(3), 247–261.

Hvidtfeldt, K. (2003). Eksistentielle grundvilkår i det professionelle. In I. Weicher & P. Fibæk Laursen (Eds.), *Person og profession: En udfordring for socialrådgivere, sygeplejersker, lærere og pædagoger.* Værløse: Billesø & Baltzer.

Jensen, J. B. (2017). *Using musical activity as a way to build supportive learning environments in higher educational contexts.* Booklet. Aalborg: Aalborg Universitetsforlag.

Langer, S. K. (1961). *Reflections on art: A source book of writings by artists, critics, and philosophers.* Oxford: Oxford University Press.

Lewis, J., Ricard, L. M., Klijn, E., Grotenberg, S., Ysa, T., Albareda, A., & Kinder, T. (2014). *Innovation environments and innovation capacity in the public sector: Report no. 1 in the LIPSE project (work package 1).* (European Commission Report No. 1). LIPSE.

Noya, A., Clarence, E., & Craig, G. (2009). *Community capacity building: Creating a better future together.* Paris: OECD Publishing.

Pahuus, A. M., & Eriksen, C. (2011). Akademisering av profesjonshøyskolerne. In M. Blok Johansen & S. Gytz Olesen (Eds.), *Professionernes sociologi og vidensgrundlag.* Aarhus: Via Systime.

Rasch-Christensen, A. (2011). Hvad er teori, og hvad er praksis i læreruddannelsen? In M. Blok Johansen & S. Gytz Olesen (Eds.), *Professionernes sociologi og vidensgrundlag.* Aarhus: Via Systime.

Reason, P., & Bradbury, H. (2008). In P. Reason (Ed.), *The SAGE handbook of action research: Participative inquiry and practice* (Electronic ed. 2nd ed.). Los Angeles, CA: SAGE.

Simons, H., & Hicks, J. (2006). Opening doors: Using the creative arts in learning and teaching. *Arts and Humanities in Higher Education, 5*(1), 77–90.

Stringer, P. (2013). *Capacity building for school improvement: Revisited* (Electronic ed.). Rotterdam: Sense Publishers.

Weber, S. (2008). Visual images in research. In J. G. Knowles & A. L. Cole (Eds.), *Handbook of the arts in qualitative research* (1st ed., pp. 41–53). Thousand Oaks, CA: Sage Publications Inc.

Young, M., & Collins, M. K. (2014). Value co-creation through learning styles segmentation and integrated course design. *Journal of Instructional Pedagogies, 13.*

Julie Borup Jensen
Department of Learning and Philosophy
Aalborg University

SUNE GUDIKSEN, SØREN BOLVIG POULSEN, MADS KUNØ, SØREN IVERSEN, JOAKIM GLERUP, KLAUS GREVE TRUE, EMILIE HOLST, NANNA SCHMIDT, HELLE TETZSCHNER AND KLAUS GREGERSEN

11. BIZCHANGE

Co-Design Meetings to Enable Stakeholder-Supported Design Moves

INTRODUCTION

Over the years, we have experimented with several course set-ups in which master students collaborate with companies on a specific service design problem or opportunity. This has resulted in – at least at the outset and based on feedback – inspiring service design concepts that the company decision makers could bring into the organisation. However, the design concepts were rarely supported by attention to stakeholder attitudes and existing work procedures, which was ultimately, in some situations, the primary reason for the decision maker to reject the entire concept or major parts of it. It is not our goal for the students' design to be implemented as such and we do not consider ourselves to be competing with the local consultancies. Instead, we consider our activities as *cultivating* the local labour market towards more innovative practice, with a greater likelihood of adopting our candidates after graduation. Through these master courses and experiments we also observed the following two tendencies:

(1) When students work with industrial partners, we, as course organisers and subsequently co-design researchers, observed that company partners would like to be more involved or at least have significant influence on the conceptual development when involved. This can also be viewed as a move from expecting solutions to be delivered by students, to working directly with them on the subjects at hand, and in this way to co-create a solution. We suspect that this might be because the industrial partners – if choosing to be involved – prefer to have an impact and ensure that certain vital perspectives are part of the process. As organisers we also highlight this co-creation endeavour as an expectation before the start of the collaboration.

(2) We also noticed that those groups who took into consideration the viewpoint and attitude of decision makers and vital stakeholders, as well as challenging them even in the fuzzy front end of the project, were most successful in getting their concept across to a case partner. In various other company collaboration projects, we have likewise demonstrated how co-design interventions can be fairly powerful in enabling shared communication and mutual understanding, and can initiate

T. Chemi & L. Krogh (Eds.), Co-Creation in Higher Education, 167–203.

reframing. This suggests there would be benefits in arranging these interventions continuously and systematically (Gudiksen et al., 2014; Gudiksen, 2015).

In previous courses we have explored how students themselves can be equipped with the competences to create the means for co-creation through guidance; that is framing, preparing and using co-design tools and techniques to support constructive co-design meetings with business case owners, decision makers and other stakeholders. Rather than just placing the students in a design workshop, we wanted to build up their skill in creating their own co-design situation and facilitate the event as well. We tend to call this *stone skimming* designer roles – moving from design workshop participant to tool maker and facilitator (Gudiksen, 2015 and see Figure 11.1). Now, one can consider the first ring in stone skimming to be positioning a student as a workshop participant, where the goal is to approach a specific problem and develop a product/service solution. Each time the students are exposed to new projects, new contexts, or new domains, a ring is added. The experience of dealing with different problems is important in overcoming a student's habits of understanding problems, as workshops can help develop new ways to approach problems. If successful, such workshops could include new ways of structuring the design process in subsequent design projects, or applying tools to the process in new ways. However, students do not experience a completely new designer role.

Positioning students in different roles enables them to stone-skim to experience problems from different angles, which results in reflections on the design of the process. Additionally, stone skimming is an approach that 'takes the students by the hand' first and then gradually provides more design role opportunities to experiment with. This enables the students to have a higher degree of reflective thoughts on how a design process can, for example, open up design space, challenge assumptions, and elicit surprises (Gudiksen, 2015). Also, it seems to significantly improve the students' communication and negotiating competences.

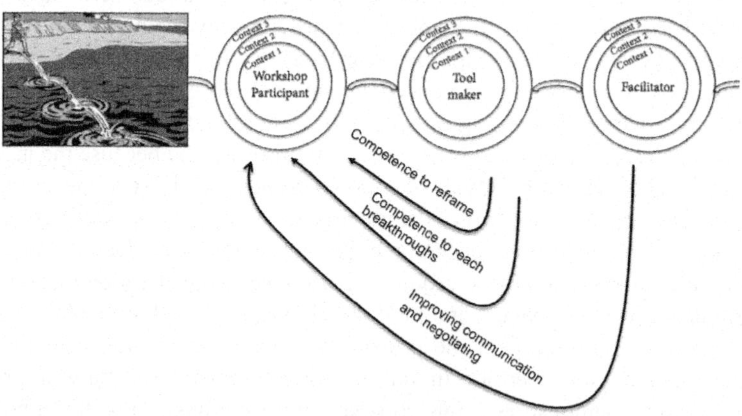

Figure 11.1. The stone-skimming model illustrating student designer roles in the course

Based on these initial observations and the co-design research conducted, we wanted to further explore how to assist students in raising the probabilities of organisation decision makers' adopting a new service design, as well as successfully increasing stakeholders' willingness to play along with the new concept. In this chapter we therefore investigate one main question and three sub-questions through three student-industry collaborations:

> How do students manage to get across design ideas, concepts and in general suggestions to decision makers and stakeholders?

We see the following sub-questions as a way to further focus on the overall research question:

- The use of co-design tools in strategic settings is still in a preliminary stage. When more diverse stakeholders are involved, these tools need to be adjusted or adapted. Therefore we ask, what kind of effects does the application of co-design tools in the process produce, in relation to the specific stakeholders involved?
- Along the way, the group encounters new stakeholders and the circle of stakeholders to be considered expands, which means attention to new constraints in a dynamic ever-changing process. How do the groups choose to deal with these constraints?
- The student groups always choose to involve experienced 'peers' from the industry, but at varying stages of the process and in different roles. Therefore we ask, what are the effects when students choose to involve experienced 'peers' at specific times in the process?

The chapter is structured as follows. (1) We take a short co-creation history tour to explain why we see co-creation as a particularly interesting vehicle for collaboration in general and more specifically for design negotiation. (2) We go through three student-industry case collaborations focusing on the co-design meetings and the kind of design action done in between the meetings. (3) We take a cross-comparison look at the cases to discuss revealing issues and answer the sub-questions, followed by initial results on the overall question.

CO-CREATION: FROM CONSUMER NEED TO DESIGN NEGOTIATION

Currently, we see a conglomerate of various research and praxis approaches manifesting itself with a focus on the benefits gained by involvement of the manager, designer, marketer, partner, end-user or other stakeholders. They all overlap but the purpose or discourse differs to some degree.

(1) Toffler, in the 1980s, foresaw the co-creation trend in his description of the consumer quickly becoming a 'prosumer' – that is a producing consumer (Toffler, 1980, 1984). The discourse here was related to the wants and desires of the consumer to have an influence on the creation of the product in order to create a unique edition. A widely known industry example is the *Build-a-bear* concept

developed by Maxine Clark that in the beginning had a huge success by letting children create a rather unique bear through a series of steps and choices. However, the degree of involvement is open to discussion, as the children were only involved in creating the bear, not directly in designing the shop. But at the time it was something new that many other companies had not thought of, which tapped into a flourishing consumer trend. In the digital age, we can see that this extends into various online communities in which user content and participation is the core of the business (Kim, 2000). Nearly all the content in these online communities is created by the users, and in some communities users can also give inputs to the platform design, although in most cases this is still guided by the producer, who also sets up general rules. The major platform operators – Facebook, Twitter, niche-oriented communities etc. – have great influence and power in our digital age. In terms of design, we can learn from them what enables users to participate in content creation. These communities, in which users become more connected, informed and empowered, have for a decade or so challenged the traditional production process. One of the ethical problems related to this is when this is seen from a capitalist viewpoint as free labour, without any crediting or royalties to the co-creators (Ritzer & Jurgenson, 2010).

(2) In another line of research, management literature points towards co-creation as a potential market differentiator. Prahalad and Ramasvamy coined the term co-creation in 2004 and described it as: "the joint creation of value by the company and the customer, allowing the customer to co-construct the service experience to suit their context" (Prahalad & Ramaswamy, 2004, p. 8). They also pinpointed that the interaction between company and consumer would increasingly become the locus of value creation. They further highlighted four aspects to consider in co-creating business strategies with the acronym DART: (1) *D*ialogue – conversation between customer and firm. (2) *A*ccess – consumer access to information. (3) *R*isk-benefits – consumers are increasingly getting access and information is shared beyond company walls. (4) *T*ransparency – information barriers should be limited so that consumers gain trust. Nowadays companies are struggling with many issues related to co-creation, many of which lead back to the overall aspects mentioned by Prahalad and Ramaswamy. There are new issues, however, like rights, ownership and crediting as part of the process and joint value creation.

In the management discourse co-creation is seen mainly as a business advantage. Perhaps the sharing economy is the newest addition to this direction, but this also has a resource ideology agenda attached to it in some cases, in the sense that if we share resources we reduce resource waste and more people will gain a portion of the resources. We see how companies like Uber and AirBnB challenge existing markets and traditional business models. All these new companies essentially build on a platform design that enables easy interaction between parties.

(3) In politics and, more and more, in municipalities, citizens are considered to be a potential data and idea resource for the advancement of services in the public sector

(Rosted, 2005). Political parties are increasingly trying to attract voters through involvement and transparency. Many municipalities have a focus on what is called in Danish *den samskabende kommune* (Co-creating municipality). Citizens have higher demands on the public sector; problems and challenges are more complex and reach beyond divisions, units etc. There is intensified economic pressure on the public sector's ability to deal with the many tasks at hand (Pestoff, 2012).

Table 11.1. Co-creation discourses

	Consumerism	*Management*	*Policies & politics*	*Strategic co-design*
Why co-creation	Consumers want influence.	Customers and partners can be active contributors.	Citizens want influence. Public sector under economic pressure.	Design/innovation processes involve a circle of stakeholders.
Co-creation reasoning	Consumer influence on products/services.	Value and market differentiator.	Resources, ideas, ownership, collaboration.	Stakeholder ownership and organisational embedding.
Potential positive effect	Consumers receive unique products. Companies have unique products/ services.	New value creation/ capturing for both parties.	New policies and politics in line with citizen experiences. An active population.	Effective concepts that take into consideration stakeholder constraints.
Potential negative effect	Consumers become a free labour force.	Customers as idea bank with no real effect.	Pseudo citizen involvement only to support political agenda.	Stakeholders are stuck with old system of thoughts. Stakeholder communication overload.

(4) In design and innovation circles co-creation plays an increasingly vital role. For instance *participatory design*, with a very Scandinavian flavour, began to involve workers in system development. They criticized traditional development for not involving the workers who were going to use the system in their everyday work life. Early arguments in this research were related to the 'users having a say', operating with more democratic development set-ups and creating ownership for those who were going to incorporate the system into their daily work life (Ehn, 1993; Bødker et al., 2000). As design problems and challenges become increasingly more complex and involve a circle of diverse stakeholders, it has been argued that, if design concepts are to have a chance of surviving the early design phases, stakeholder involvement throughout the process is vital (Buur & Matthews, 2008). When design and designers move closer to crucial decision-making in companies, new toolkits and approaches need to be adopted and adapted to fit situations with

stakeholder negotiation, but in a manner that complements the 'power' qualities that the designers are already equipped with (for instance, visualisation and tactility competences, and working in situations of uncertainty and ambiguity).

From a design research viewpoint, all of the above-mentioned directions influence how one can consider approaching the development of new products and services. The proposition is that we have to aim for the positive effects of co-creation and as far as possible reduce the risk of negative effects.

ZOOMING IN ON STRATEGIC CO-DESIGN

Influential design thinkers Tim Brown and Roger Martin in a recent article discuss the importance of design interventions within organisations as part of the development of new product-service design projects. They particularly express the need to initiate "iterative interaction with the decision maker". They further elaborate by calling these interventions with the decision makers "more critical to success than the design of the artefacts themselves" (Brown & Martin, 2015, pp. 58–61). Dorst, too, in a seminal work on designers' *frame creation process* notes that a key issue is to "crack open and investigate assumptions" of stakeholders (Dorst, 2015, p. 52). However, Brown, Martin and Dorst provide few concrete examples of how and when to approach this and, in earlier books by influential IDEO-related authors, this was not an explicit concern (See Kelley & Littman, 2006; Brown, 2009; Kelley & Kelley, 2013).

Considering the viewpoint of the various stakeholders and the organisational change perspective in general has been an afterthought for design research over the years. It might be first addressed when the new service design concept is presented, or briefly dealt with separately or, at worst, be considered as 'implicitly addressed'. This might leave it up to the service design concept itself to create all the changes in the final delivery to the company.

However, various organisational change researchers emphasise that creating successful, transformative, organisational change involves challenging fundamental stakeholder assumptions, beliefs and values as part of the organisational culture (Argyris et al., 1985; Rosseau, 1995; Argyris, 2010). Likewise Junginger and Sangiorgi argue that service designers need "to re-think the organisation elements around the new service experience" (Junginger & Sangiorgi, 2009, p. 8).

As a consequence of the under-explored intersection between service design and stakeholder involvement as a first step to organisational change, we developed an ambitious, four-month, master's student collaboration with companies, in which we relied on both service design approaches and strategic co-design interventions. Each group selected a service business case. With our point of departure in design as a negotiation agenda between stakeholders with a variety of intentions and interests, we searched for those approaches – tools, techniques, set-ups – that seemed to gradually loosen up fixed stakeholder viewpoints and subsequently work around constraints in the development process.

RESEARCH METHOD

Our research methodology was research-through-design (Frayling, 1993; Archer, 1995), which, as pointed out by Archer, relates to action research as it is a "systematic investigation through practical action calculated to devise or test new information, ideas, forms or procedures and to produce communicable knowledge" (Archer, 1995, p. 6). Following this line of thought, practice-oriented research can be conducted with inspiration from various research traditions depending on the objectives (Archer, 1995). This is also the case here.

The cases conducted for this research derive from an educational constellation, BizChange, at Aalborg University. BizChange is a course designed to give students of Experience Design and Interactive Digital Media strategic co-design competences. By strategic co-design competences we mean the ability to apply design thinking in a business, organisational and use context that, more often than not, includes a wide circle of stakeholders to be considered. To facilitate this learning process the organisers make agreements with local companies to ensure relevant cases and the necessary level of engagement. The companies involved commit themselves to participating in collaborative design meetings throughout the project.

The empirical material for this paper originates from such design meetings and the course set-up (described in detail in the next section). Research-through-design acts as a methodological framework, allowing academic reflections on the methodological and intuitive choices of students and industry partners (Koskinen et al., 2011) before, during and after the design meetings.

The design meetings can be described as intervention experiments, where students facilitate design workshops, based on guiding principles, thus engaging the stakeholders. In so doing, the students are challenged with the potential stakeholder mindset shift and organisational change consequences of the service design initiative. This type of intervention experiment is in the same family as Schön's notion of exploratory experiments, in which an action is undertaken only to see what follows, as well as move-testing experiments, in which there is a possible end in mind (Schön, 1983).

The experiments did not follow any research agenda, but were instead directed by the design challenges that the students faced as designers, in the given moment and context. The students' design of the different interventions can be described as an experiential inquiry cycle composed of four steps (Kolb, 1984): (1) designing the interventions, (2) conducting design interventions through design tools in the design meetings, (3) observing the action and (4) reflecting based on relevant theory with the purpose of extracting design intervention principles and propositional knowledge.

When the various design project cases from the students are connected and brought into the same paper, we get a chance to make cross-comparison between case incidents. Here we look for differences, similarities and above all interesting nuances rather than generalisation, which is rarely a goal in case studies. As Flyvbjerg (2006, p. 221) argues, only context-dependent knowledge exists in the study of human affairs. Concretely, case studies were selected with the intention to develop 'a metaphor or establish a school for the domain that the case concerns' (Flyvbjerg, 2006, p. 230) and because the work from the students was systematically developed, resulting in quality academic project work.

COURSE SET-UP

Over the years the course organiser group has developed various courses that see knowledge, above all, as something we obtain together as teachers, researchers, students and companies. If we work in silos, we miss out on the practical, holistic, everyday human experiences and, in general, on experiential learning (Dewey, 1936; Kolb, 1984).

The educational set-up and the overall intervention design is the responsibility of the researcher. The aim is to design and facilitate a constellation where all stakeholders involved benefit from the collaboration. The constellation is rooted in an Engaged Scholarship paradigm, where the central mission of scholars is to conduct research that both advances a scientific discipline and enlightens practice in a professional domain (Simon, 1976).

It has been pointed out that scholars fail to inform practitioners in a suitable way and that practitioners fail to keep scholars updated on new knowledge and practices. Involving students in such a constellation can be turned into a valuable asset, because they can become the glue of the Engaged Scholarship collaboration.

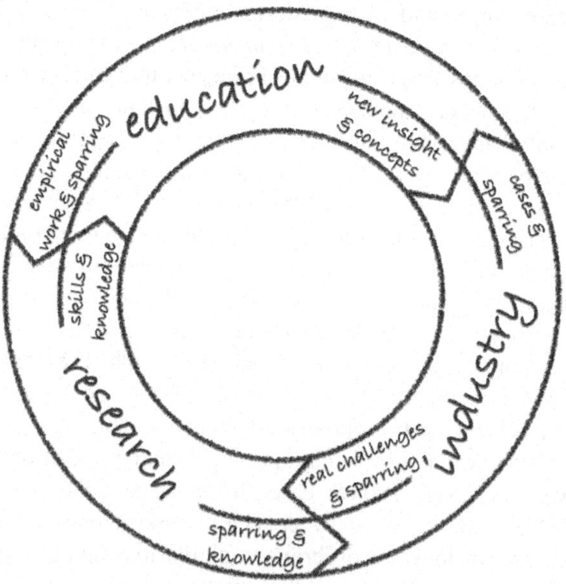

Figure 11.2. The Engaged Scholarship approach is designed to ensure that all partners involved benefit from the engagement

The parties involved engage in the collaboration by both offering and receiving something. In this sense there is mutual benefit from the collaboration.

The researcher offers knowledge to students, in terms of methods and theory. Students, in return, offer industrial practice insights and an empirical basis for understanding the application of the methods.

The company involved offers a practical case with context-based knowledge to the students, who in return offer a facilitated space for reflection, together with a conceptual design proposal. The researcher offers a facilitated process for the company involved and knowledge about new theories etc. In return the researcher receives information about the practical dimensions of a given theory and thereby has the opportunity to look for new ways to improve it.

The four-month collaboration between the students and the companies in the BizChange course was divided into four (or more, for some student groups) design meetings with time in between to investigate, to develop the service design concept and the supporting change actions.

We work with the terms *sense-making* and *sense-giving* to illustrate the flow in the meetings. By sense-making we mean 'meaning construction and reconstruction by the parties involved'. Sense-giving is understood as "attempting to influence the sense-making and meaning construction of others towards a preferred state" as defined by Gioia and Chittipeddi (1991, p. 10). In the co-design meetings there is a flow from mostly sense-making in the beginning to, later on, more sense-giving, as ideas manifest into fully-fleshed service design concepts.

(1) Early co-design meetings – Mutual understanding & shared communication (primarily sense-making). The first co-design meetings focused on the establishment of common understanding between the service business case owner and the students. The students were presented with various communication and mapping tools that they could use to help move the first dialogue along.

The first meeting is central to reach shared communication and create an initial framing of both the service design initiative and the past and current organisational business aspects and culture. The groups were introduced to several visual mapping tools that they could use with the business case owners to frame the project together. These tools fall into the category of a simple framing tool to reach a vital common understanding (Dorst, 2011). In relation to the stone-skimming model presented in the introduction, the first design meetings are less about designing tools from scratch and more about finding a common ground.

(2) Middle co-design meetings – Framing & reframing (sense-making & sense-giving). Before the middle meetings, the students were introduced to co-design tools that are vital for reframing a specific design and for exploring and explicating otherwise tacit knowledge (Polanyi, 1966). The co-design subfield of design games was used at this point as inspiration, as these games have proved useful in challenging a specific frame and in initiating reframing in previous research

(Brandt, 2006; Gudiksen, 2015). The student groups developed their own design games based on design principles presented by the organisers.

(3) Later co-design meetings – Conceptualising & sustaining (primarily sense-giving). In the later meetings, the students used digital platforms and mediums that can showcase concepts and establish a strong frame, as well as persuasive points. In those meetings, the focus was more on sustaining and furthering the work through 'sense-giving' than through 'sense-making' so that the company owner could understand the service design concept and the underlying organisational consequences.

(4) Final meeting and handover (sense-giving). In this meeting between students and stakeholders, students hand over design concepts and process understanding. As the students are not employees of the company, a handover will eventually occur. Students need to let go and companies must take over in the way they think best. How the companies choose to proceed after handover is beyond the scope of this research, and also seems to be a quite difficult, if not impossible, longitudinal tracking exercise.

In the scheme below we have mapped out the different interventions and illustrated the move from organiser-facilitated processes to student-directed processes in the co-design meetings.

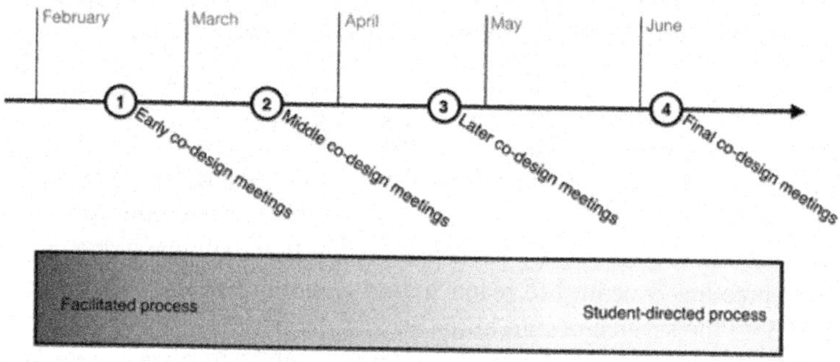

Figure 11.3. Co-design meetings in BizChange course and group cases

CASE ONE: DIGITAL BANKING SERVICE FOR HOUSE BUYERS

The case concerns a local bank who felt that many property buyers are uncertain about the purchasing process – they find it just too complex, it contains too much information and has too many variables for a non-professional to comprehend. Subsequently, the buyers experience a lot of frustrations and worries when purchasing a new home. The bank operation wanted to make the buyers feel safe and comfortable in the purchasing process. Therefore, as a part of their business strategy, they wanted to develop a concept that complied with this aim. The bank expected the student group to cover the buyer's needs and from these develop a concept, and additionally supply 'proof of concept' via a prototype.

(1) Early co-design meetings. Before the group explored the bank's main customers, they needed to get to know the bank organisation better. In order to do so, the group arranged a meeting with the business case owner. Here they decided to apply the mapping tool Business Model Canvas (BMC) to clarify the bank's business aspects and value propositions, together with their readiness towards implementing a new product.

As preparation for this meeting, the group printed out the model's nine subjects and placed them on A1 paper, to guide the topics of the conversation with the business case owner. At the meeting, the BMC was filled in with information provided by the case owner. The procedure was write keywords and key sentences on Post-its and place them onto the right topic within the canvas. Both parties wrote and placed Post-its on the canvas. The group decided not to critically question them, but rather to aim for a positive and unfolding dialogue, which all together contributed to a casual, open atmosphere.

As a next step, fairly soon after this preliminary meeting, the group together with the bank decided to conduct a series of interviews in collaboration with other associated groups of master's students, to investigate user needs during the process of buying property. A design agency hired by the bank supported the group, in order to further qualify the interview collection and interpretation. The design agency arranged a workshop with the student group (see Figure 11.4 for the setting in the workshop).

Figure 11.4. Design agency workshop with the student groups

During the workshop the design agency introduced the group to an interview method, which they framed as the IDEO Approach (IDEO, 2015).

The workshop was organised in four steps:

1. Instructions on the interview method
2. Devising an interview guide
3. Testing the interview guide
4. Instructions on the download method

After receiving instructions on how to use the IDEO approach, the group were to devise an interview guide. Thus they brainstormed on different themes, created questions that covered each theme, and structured these accordingly. Subsequently, the group tested the interview guide twice to make sure it enabled them to cover all the themes thoroughly and collect the desired data. When testing the interview guide during the workshop the group needed to build a scenario as genuine as possible. Therefore they decided to have two teams of two persons – each team was to conduct one interview. In the teams one person was the interviewer and one was taking notes on Post-its (Figure 11.5). The interview was documented in a video recording.

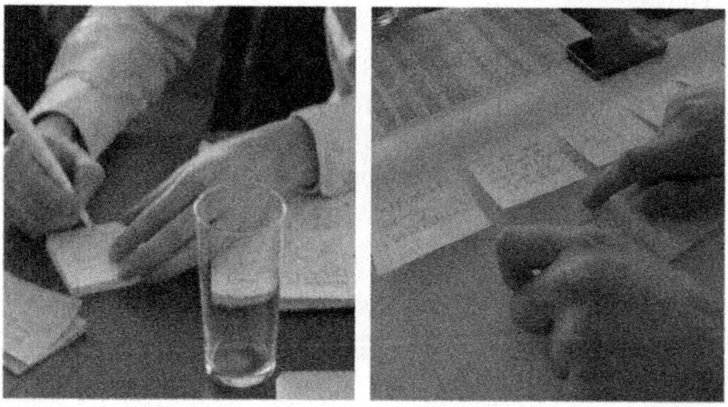

Figure 11.5. Groups working with post-its notes as a first step

The groups were then introduced further to the IDEO approach – this time concerning the method for *downloading* the interview. They did this by selecting the 24 most important notes from each interview and placing them on a poster together with a picture of the person interviewed.

Through the workshop the group obtained an understanding of how to structure and conduct an interview and condense the data collected. The result of the workshop was a thoroughly prepared and tested interview guide and two interviews condensed into *downloads*. The agency, the bank and the various student groups agreed to conduct a total of 36 interviews. After the workshop the group began the search for respondents, scheduled the time frame, and decided who would conduct which of the interviews.

The next step for the group was a second workshop arranged by the agency with a focus on dealing with the newly gathered interview data. This workshop was organised as a compressed design process and divided into four steps:

1. Presenting our downloads
2. Brainstorming on generic themes
3. Devising opportunities for design
4. Making prototypes

The group condensed the insights from each interview by doing downloads as demonstrated in the first workshop, to bring to the second workshop. At the workshop each of the associated groups presented their downloads. Subsequently, the groups were asked to brainstorm on the generic 'themes' in each group – themes that covered the findings and statements given in the interviews.

Figure 11.6. Wall with opportunity clusters

The workshop resulted in three different design opportunities.

1. *Trust is important for my choice of bank*
   From the data it emerged that personal meetings with an adviser resulted in trust (if the adviser had a genuine interest). We found that this trust was important for the respondents' choice of bank. This especially applied to couples who where in the process of choosing which of their banks to move to. Here we found that it was the person with the strongest relationship with their adviser who stayed – their partner moved bank.
2. *I ask for help among friends and family*
   Many of our respondents asked for advice from friends or family who had recently bought a house, or had professional experience somehow (carpenters, bricklayers, etc.).
3. *I came across many surprises during the process of buying my house*
   We experienced that many of our respondents found the process complex, time-consuming, and confusing. They had a tendency not to acquaint themselves with the process before meeting an adviser.

The student group were then asked to design for one of the opportunities and create a rapid paper prototype (Warfel, 2009). As there were multiple groups working on the case, a lot of design opportunities had been created. After the workshop the group therefore needed to merge the numerous design opportunities into a manageable number. To do this, the student group met with the associated groups of master's students and renegotiated the themes. In the discussion it became clear that they could merge many of the themes without altering them, as the foundations for the themes were the same. Thus a lot of the points made in one theme could be transferred to another.

From this renegotiation the group ended up with five design opportunities. Subsequently, the group sought to find the design opportunity with prime potential for innovative design. They found a way to score how well the respondents matched each of the five design opportunities. The scores ranged from 1–5, where 1 was given to the respondents who did not match the opportunity for design, and 5 was given to the respondents who matched it very well. From this, the group discovered which of the opportunities for design scored the highest, which the lowest, which had an extensive effect on few respondents, and which had a significant effect on many respondents. This enabled them develop a concept for the design opportunity that would potentially have the biggest impact on most users.

The BMC approach had given the group an opportunity to get to know the bank from the inside, their values, etc. and to discover things, which the group would not otherwise have been able to discover from their website or other information material. This approach also helped in opening a positive dialogue with the case owner, as the questions asked related to subjects the case owner knew well. The IDEO approach enabled the group to collect and process a lot of data quickly, which was essential to the time limit of the project. The IDEO approach also provided the group with an overview of the data.

(3) Middle co-design meetings. For this workshop the group invited the business case contact from the bank to join them in the next co-design meeting where they sought to identify the potential of two selected design opportunities. They further sought to establish the probability of these potentials being implemented into the business and line of work within the bank. Before this meeting they chose the two opportunities for design with the most potential (according to multiple design criteria): (1) I want to be seen and heard, and (2) a close relationship with my adviser is crucial for my choice of bank. Subsequently, the group decided on some notes and statements for each opportunity to help accelerate the brainstorming process, such as 'I know my adviser', 'Buying a house is a big decision', and 'My bank needs to understand my dreams' (part of Figure 11.7). These themes and notes were put on a poster.

The workshop itself took one hour, of which 30 minutes were spent on co-brainstorming on each of the two opportunities for design. The notes prepared for the workshop formed the basis for the brainstorm, but as the process took off the group together with the bank case owner were able to cover other areas. For example, the group learned about specific work processes in the bank that supported ideas and concepts (how often customers have meetings in the bank, which platforms they were using, how the advisers' system could integrate other systems, etc.).

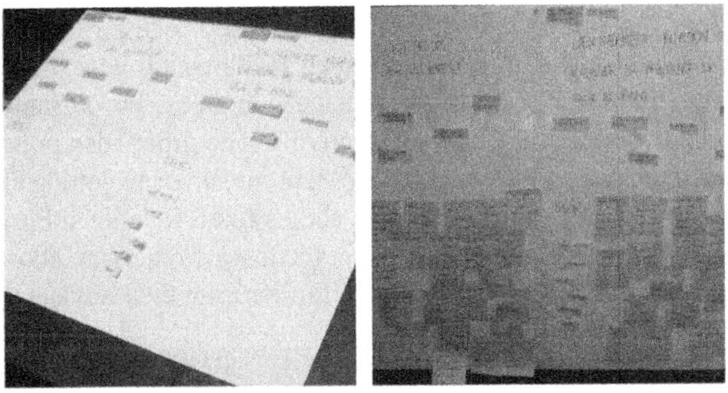

Figure 11.7. Central notes and statements as beginning point

This later co-design meeting gave the group insights into the company's wishes and capabilities and thus helped guide the group in their final design. Furthermore, it ensured that the group developed a concept in close collaboration with the case owner and consequently adjusted the concept according to the needs and potentials of the bank.

After this workshop the group developed the final concept based on their findings during the interviews, the workshops with the design agency and the two co-design meetings with the case owner. Next, a prototype was built and tested (see Figure 11.8).

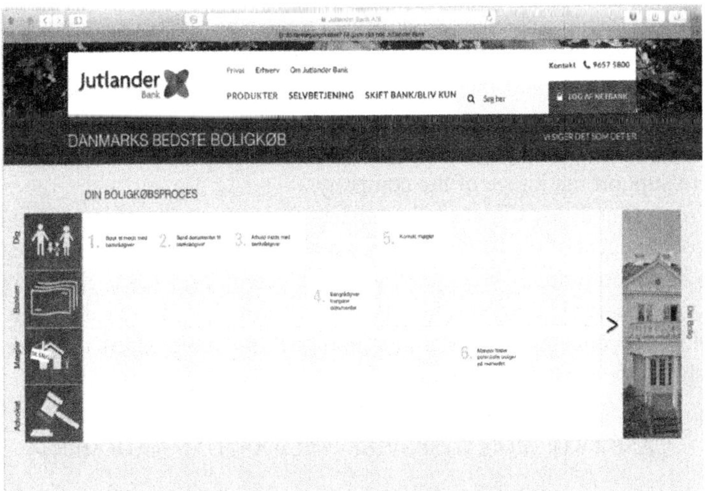

Figure 11.8. Prototype of the buying process

(4) Final meeting and handover. At the final meeting the group was invited to present their findings and concept to the management of the bank, who had not previously participated in meetings or presentations. The group prepared a presentation for this meeting that showcased the final prototype. They focused on explaining their approach and methods. The group also wished to showcase how the concept could contribute to the value proposition and business strategy, by presenting the value gained by the bank and its customers respectively. The group also presented an idea on how to market the concept in order to land new customers by letting all have access to the system, but only allowing customers access to all functions. Furthermore, the group suggested how the system could collect feedback from users, allowing the bank to use this feedback to adjust the system and further train their advisers.

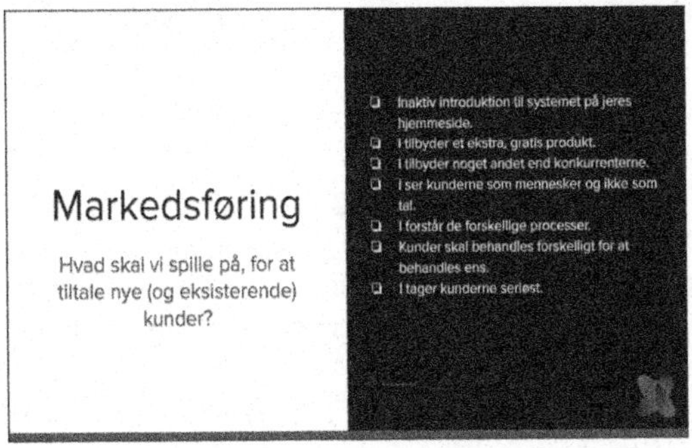

Figure 11.9 Example from proof of concept presentation

The result of the concept can be categorised through three overall and interdependent themes; *knowledge, concept* and *design*. The *knowledge* is the result of the information the group retrieved from 39 different house buyers through qualitative interviews, and themed through the second workshop with the design agency. The *concept* is the overall design criteria and features developed from the knowledge, and the *design* is the different icons, colours, shapes and pictures selected to support the image of the company.

The group found that the overall feedback from the bank was positive in many ways. The managers of the bank asked questions about specific parts of the concept, but were in general mostly concerned with subjects not related to the design of the concepts or its specific functions, e.g. they asked how long it would take to develop and employ the concept, how much it would cost to develop, how the development process should be approached, etc.

CASE TWO: DIGITAL SERVICE FOR WASTE MANAGEMENT

This case was presented and developed by the waste management department of the municipal office of Randers, a fairly large town in Denmark. The case focused on a redesign of the mobile application for waste management called *AffaldRanders* (Waste Randers), as a service. The student group was interested in this particular case because of the apparent lack of user involvement in the design and development process of the current app. The current design was developed without the involvement of the users – the citizens of Randers. The assumption and point of the departure for the group was therefore to increase user involvement as a way to contribute positively with a user-centred approach to the redesign of the service. The group began by obtaining an understanding of the current design and the background for the design combined with user needs, in order to develop an improved service. The general framing of the casework was based on, and inspired by, IDEO's design thinking: a framing for the interrelatedness of people, business and technology perspectives (Brown, 2008). Through the case, the student group aimed to prototype the service with a redesigned app, based on empirical insights from the app developers, potential users and an understanding of the technological possibilities.

(1) Early co-design meetings. The first design meeting focused on gathering insights into the previous development process of the digital service for waste management, as well as gaining an overall understanding of the Randers waste management department. To do this, the students combined an interview with the use of two co-design mapping tools.

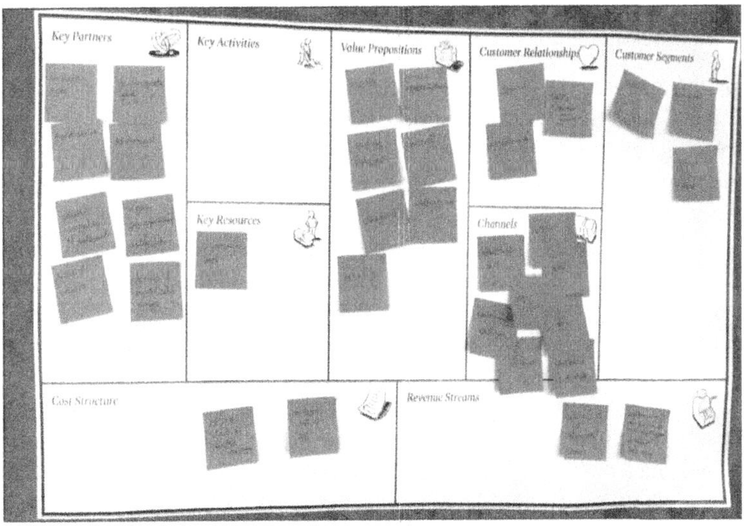

Figure 11.10. Waste management case – Business model mapping and framing

The student group wanted to involve all participating stakeholders. Due to the complexity of a municipality with a range of different departments, there was a need for a simple, but effective mapping tool to help structure the first part of the initial meeting. The group decided to use the BMC (Osterwalder & Pigneur, 2010).

During the meeting the stakeholders showed some difficulties in completing the BMC and expressed a need for additional insights into the municipality of Randers in order to complete the canvas.

> *Project manager*: "Well, if we start at the – yes – very beginning... About two years ago we got a visit from at man (referring to the owner of the app development company), here at the municipality of Randers. In fact, I can't really remember how he was, uhm..."
>
> *IT-manager*: "Hmm, I had met him several times in other contexts, and then I met him at a fair in Odder where we came to talk about it (referring to the development of a waste management app). We agreed that he could come to Randers to talk about its possibilities. And the..."
>
> *Project manager*: "So he came. And he presented us with a very impressive Power Point presentation to demonstrate how we could improve our communication, and pointed out that we should be heading in a more digital direction.... In fact, we were clapping our small hands in excitement. We found it was fantastic to be able to reach out to the citizens' right where they actually are. There is a problem with our site (ed. the website), it is not always easy to reach citizens at the right moment, when they really need us, and this is why they grab the phone instead of going to the website".

Through the canvas, the student group gained key insights regarding the waste management department's value propositions. The group also obtained a better understanding of the different subcontractors who act as key partners for the department of waste management. More importantly, the group achieved insights into the complexity of the municipal office and how the stakeholders involved were unable to fully explain all aspects of the canvas. The BMC became a structural base for talking about the waste management department and did so in a very successful way. A deep organisational insight from the participants is required when dealing with a complex organisation, in order for them to be able to discuss all relevant aspects of the canvas.

The student group also wanted, by involving the stakeholders, to be able to visualise the development process, in order to better understand those parts of the process they had not been involved in. Initially, the group had the idea that the stakeholders should draw the development process, but considered that this could potentially make the participants uncomfortable, as not everyone feels comfortable with drawing, which might have an effect on the results. Instead, the group decided to use a framing tool resembling a domino game with high tactility. The design game introduced an approach that only required the participants to talk and write down as they rearranged the existing bricks (see Figure 11.11). Roos argues that these three-dimensional figures, besides providing a visual overview, are effective "figurative ways of speaking: metaphors, analogy, synecdoche, irony and paradoxes are the most common" (Roos, 2006, p. 78). The student group started the activity by setting up blocks in the order they believed was right. However, before the student group finished, the participants started to correct them, or rearrange the blocks in the 'correct' order. As the stakeholders moved a block they gave the group an explanation for doing so and therefore the group got significant additional insights into the previous development process.

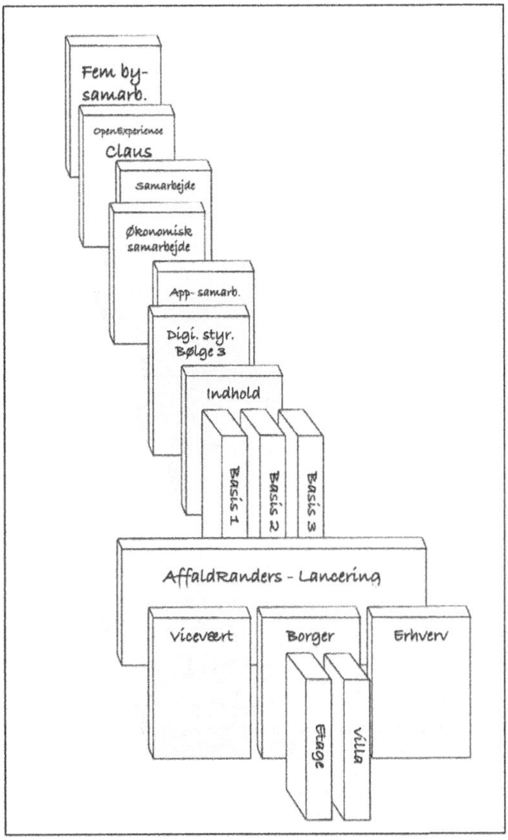

Figure 11.11. Domino game visualisation of development process

Reflections on Co-Design Meeting Set-up

Visualising the previous design process turned out to be a great exercise for the participants and made the process discussion easy and approachable. Also, following the first meeting, the group discovered some limitations in the use of the BMC that, if investigated further, could help them organise the next meeting. The group needed deeper insights into the particular department and the foundation for the developed service. The visualisation of the previous process provided the group with a vital overview and insights concerning a very complex development process with different stakeholders entering and leaving the process at different times.

The dialogue in the first co-design meeting prompted the students to prepare for the next meeting: as they needed further insights into the target audience and the actual development process of the current service alongside the value base of the service, they worked on a game design to help the participants specify the missing information.

(2) Middle co-design meeting. The second design meeting was focused on getting additional insights into the underlying choices made in the earlier development of the service. The group found that the stakeholders from the first meeting were unable to clearly articulate the value propositions or the target audience for the service. Therefore the group decided to involve a new stakeholder who had the necessary technical insights into the development process and preceding design choices. The meeting was structured around a new design game consisting of several steps, specifying the basis for the service value proposition along the way (see Figure 11.12). The student group wanted the participants to focus on one step at a time and decided to keep the following steps more or less hidden until relevant. Information was revealed in steps according to the progression through the *Fog-of-war* game technique (LeBlanc, 2006). This enabled the student group to control the communication, easing the game play and in a way reducing complexity.

During the game the participants were able to be far more precise concerning the values for designing the waste management service and thus ended up with a qualified selection of a specific target audience.

The end result of the game process with the municipality contacts was specific concepts for new features to be potentially developed, but these were mainly included in the game to resemble a goal for the players.

After the meeting the group were able to take the different results from the game and use these in the redesign of the service. The redesign was also based on a user experience evaluation of the current service in order to pinpoint crucial elements for redesign. The values combined with the understanding of the target audience and the evaluation proved to be insightful and useful knowledge, and helped shape the design process and the final prototype.

(3) Later co-design meeting. The third meeting took place as part of a small conference which the stakeholders were invited to attend. This meeting was based on the presentation of a prototype combined with a presentation of the insights obtained from the preceding design meetings. Before the meeting the student group developed a clickable high fidelity prototype (see Figure 11.13), a demonstration video and

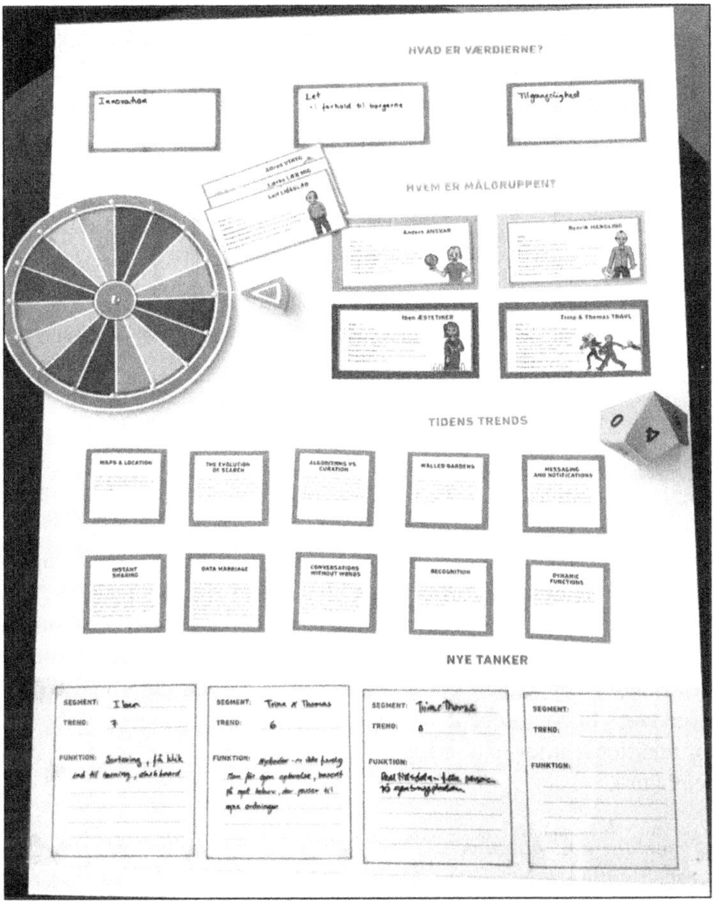

Figure 11.12. Design game revealing information in steps

two roll-up posters with key insights. The preparation was mainly concerned with communicating the concept developed on both a visual and functional level, as well as the design insights upon which the concept was formed.

Again, the student group aimed at involving the stakeholders, which was one of the reasons for bringing a hi-fi clickable prototype and a demonstration video to the table. The prototype closely resembled a finished service, as the student group wanted to give the stakeholders an impression of the role of the service, combined with the look and feel of the finished service (Houde & Hill, 1997).

Afterwards, it was clear to the student group that the use of a hi-fi prototype has some clear benefits. The stakeholders could easily imagine the purpose and role of

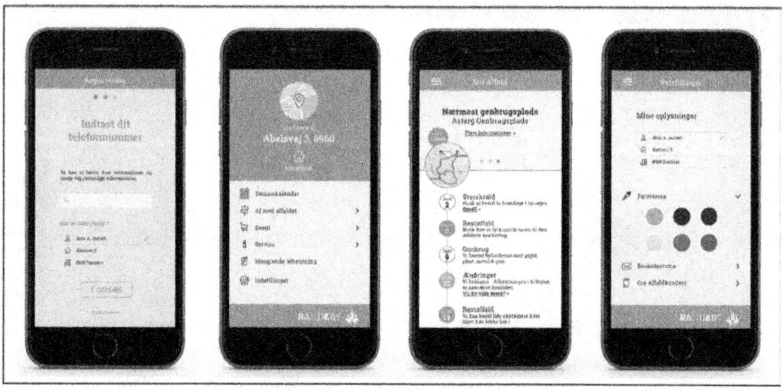

Figure 11.13. High fidelity, clickable prototype

the developed service and the fidelity of the interface level made design choices easy to explain (supporting source). The demonstration video made different use cases clear and showed various improvements made to the user flow of the service (supporting source). By presenting the prototype to the stakeholders, together with other interested conference participants, the group gained insights concerning presentation techniques and what kind of information potential users may need in order to fully comprehend a concept. Specifically, the student group learned that both the demonstration video and the clickable prototype needed additional explaining for the potential users to comprehend the concept. For example, most of the users were in need of additional information regarding possible use cases in order to imagine the service in use.

(4) Final meeting and handover. The final meeting, unlike the other meetings, was concerned with presenting the concept to primarily new stakeholders from the municipality of Randers. The student group reused the demonstration video and brought an improved clickable prototype along with a presentation.

After the presentation the stakeholders were given the opportunity to interact with the prototype. During the presentation there were some questions regarding different flows through the service and some of the stakeholders were concerned about the user experience when using the application. After they had tried the prototype and were able to try out the different interactions for themselves, their concerns seemed to be resolved.

Towards the end of the meeting, the stakeholders provided the student group with some initial feedback and comments on the next steps in the process. The concept provided new perspectives on the navigational structure of the service, along with different visual user interface improvements. The student group provided the stakeholders with inspiration regarding future possibilities from a user-centred design perspective on both an abstract and practical level, which they acknowledged to be missing from the current service.

CASE THREE: SERVICE EXPERIENCE SUPPORTING CITIZENS' SUSTAINABILITY

Green Agents (GA) is a project in the Environmental Department of the municipality of Aalborg, Denmark. The department focuses on civic- and company-aimed initiatives within the environmental sector. For instance, they organize an annual sustainability festival in Aalborg City. GA has existed for two years and has a small project team in the department consisting of only two employees – a project manager and a communication employee.

GA wanted to involve citizens in sustainability agendas to push conversion towards a more sustainable municipality. More concretely, they were looking for a digital solution to engage and commit citizens towards a sustainable agenda and, in general, towards acting in a more sustainable way. The group investigated, therefore, how an interactive, experiential service design might engage and commit citizens towards a sustainable agenda.

The group focused on developing an IT-based service design solution through an iterative design process. These iterations were aimed at developing a concept design and prototypes to be tested and evaluated continuously. During the work, the student group wanted to examine how facilitating part of co-design and co-creation could be a part of the on-going design process.

Previously, the Green Agents had mainly channelled communication through small events by means of education and active learning. From the student group's point of view, this was a 'top-down' strategy, where the communication and activities had already been framed. The group wanted to challenge the established approach to communicating about sustainability by examining how an experiential service design might communicate and frame a sustainable development.

(1) Early co-design meeting. The main purpose of the first design meeting was to acquire an understanding of the organisation and working procedures. The student group applied the BMC as point of departure (Osterwalder & Pigneur, 2010). While preparing the co-design meeting the student group had considered if it was appropriate to use this model, which has typically been applied more to the private sector. They were doubtful whether it was useful in a municipal setting with no paying customers in the traditional 'direct sale' sense.

Before the meeting with the project manager the group printed a hardcopy of the BMC and gathered sticky notes in 3 colours to illustrate each area of the model. The purpose was that the project manager should place Post-its with words or sentences on each building block of the canvas as the dialogue kept going (see Figure 11.14).

First, the group presented the purpose of the workshop to the project manager and described the mapping tool to clarify the agenda. The activity started from the left side and moved slowly to the right across the canvas, explaining each block to the project manager. At the customer building block on the right side of the canvas, the group made it clear to the project manager that he should not see this block as paying customers but as the segments, or target groups, he was trying to engage.

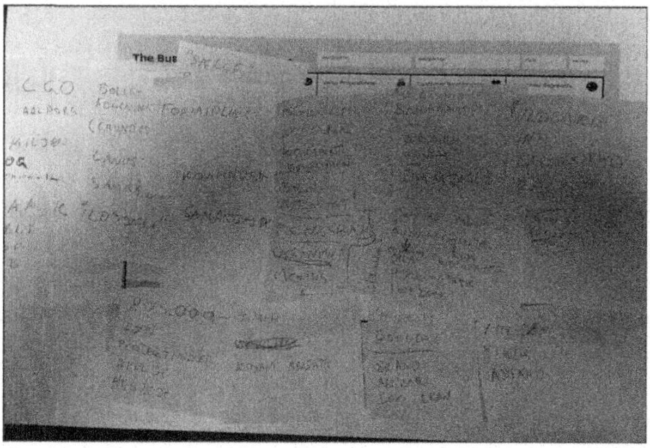

Figure 11.14. Business model canvas mapping

The group felt the workshop was successful in the way that it developed insights and thereby equipped the group with fresh knowledge about how the GA worked, whom they worked with and what their main purpose was. The BMC enriched the interview as it succeeded in articulating otherwise tacit knowledge (Polanyi, 1962). In particular, the group learned about the strengths and weaknesses of the GA. However, they also found that there were occasionally situations where the blocks were difficult to place and they questioned a few times whether or not the project manager had the intended understanding of the canvas section under scrutiny. But overall the student group was satisfied with the workshop and they could clarify or adjust the preliminary doubts and customise the canvas to the situation.

One of the student group's doubts was whether the project manager was capable of projecting his knowledge onto the canvas for the block 'Key Resources'. Here, the group wanted him to describe the resources he had to offer and how to deliver the needed Key Activities, however it became clear that the canvas was not yet a mapping tool that resulted in complete shared understanding:

> *Project manager*: "This is all about competences. It is all about process and supporting this ongoing process. I do not know how to describe it but these are some competences to accomplish projects or processes".
>
> *Student 1*: "So, as you see it, it is about managing a project and a process. But it is also about knowledge and know-how regarding sustainability?
>
> *Project Manager*: "Yes, that is the next part, which is a big part of the department. Knowledge about the plan and which way to go".
>
> *Student 1*: "So it is all about strategy, know-how and project management?"

Project Manager: Yes, knowledge about process, organising knowledge and then it is also about communication again. What do you say? Those are the 3 most important things. How to do processes, knowledge about sustainability and something about communication in different ways. Both a platform of communication, as well as a help to communicate the results".

Student 1: "Do you have anything else?"

Project Manager: "Oh yes, we do also have a great network. Often it is all about making a connection between the housing associations and the person with true commitment. So it is also about cooperation. To know the right people and organisations and what they can bring to the table".

The purpose of the block was apparently not clear to the project manager, which reflects on the challenges that may occur when the collaboration is tied to a certain framework that is familiar to some of the participants, while new to others.

The student group did not manage to keep the project manager focused correctly. In this reflection, the group also found that the project manager mentioned subjects that fitted to the Key Resources block.

Later, when they reached the Customer Segments block, at first the project manager placed a few different Post-its on this block, however soon after he mentioned that they could be placed on the Key Partners block as well.

Project Manager: "What is in common is that they are all persons with true commitment. And they are interested in sustainability."

Student 1: "So that is the denominator?"

Project Manager: "Yes, that is the denominator. And if I have to separate them further there are students, the elderly, homeowners' associations and similar".

And later on in the workshop the talk went back to the Customer Segment block:

Student 1: "Earlier you mentioned cooperation with your customers, so could they become partners or do you see them as customers only?"

Project Manager: "No, we do see them as partners".

Student 1: "So these Post-its you placed on the Customer Segment block could be placed on the Key Partner block as well?"

Project Manager: "Yeah, but I think that they should be placed on the Customer Segment block in the beginning and then they might become partners when we have cooperated on a common project…"

The group found that the project manager seemed to be confused at this point, which might reflect the BMC format, since he found it difficult to differentiate the subjects of these two blocks – mainly because the municipality does not have traditional paying customers. It is worth considering if another, more platform-oriented canvas would have been appropriate to facilitate the collaboration,

In its reflections the group was satisfied with the workshop, which did manage to generate results for the design process. However, as the dialogue above shows, there were challenges and some parts of the method were difficult to place according to the original commercial agenda of the canvas. However, this resulted in new issues and further reflections during the process as well as new learning. For instance, there seemed to be an interesting issue about defining the stakeholders' positions. Regarding the method, the group found that it is important to be very specific at each block and describe it very carefully in terms of generating useful as well as valid data.

The student group decided to use the *KJ-Method* developed by Spool (2004), as it was perceived to be an effective method of categorising and prioritising subjective opinions and subjective data. This method resulted in three design challenges; (1) a missing strategy of communication; (2) a missing definition of the term *Green Agent*; (3) a missing definition of the term *sustainability*. These challenges helped the group to define the direction of the future examination.

The group, however, did not find the current concept satisfying. The communication related to the sustainability agenda was too diffuse and too open. Therefore, the group found it necessary to sharpen the focus further to stronghold a converging process (Buxton, 2007, p. 147) by involving the *10 plus 10 Method* by Greenberg et al. (2011, p. 27). This way, they could concretise the issues from the workshop into a specific concept idea. The group realised, based on the first meeting, that they had not managed to achieve controlled convergence (Buxton, 2007, p. 147).

The workshop showed that the Green Agents work with sustainability in a very wide frame, and the term Green Agent is used in several different connections. To narrow the issues, the group found it necessary to understand the complexity of the questions above. The group used Brinkmann and Tanggaard's thoughts on epistemology as a starting point (Brinkmann & Tanggaard, 2010, p. 57). They had to understand the phenomena of sustainability and Green Agents to develop a service

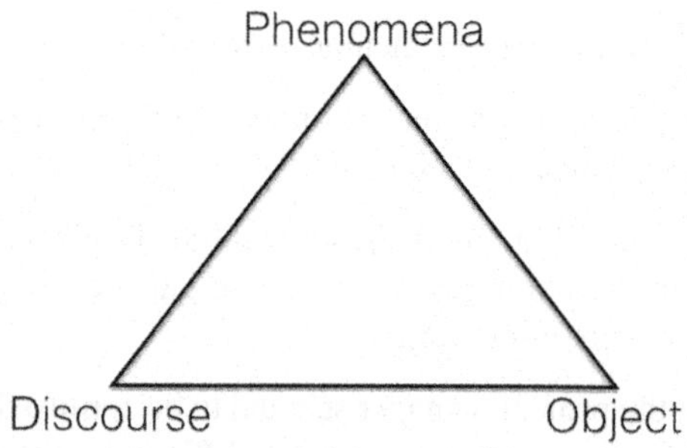

Figure 11.15. The ontological triangle (Brinkmann & Tanggaard, 2012)

design that would be useful within its social context. The Ontological Triangle gave them the opportunity to analyse and answer the questions above from 3 different positions – object, phenomenon and discourse.

These 3 ontological positions meant that the group could define the following questions for their research:

What does sustainability mean for the inhabitants of Aalborg? (the phenomenon)

What does it mean to be a Green Agent? (the object)

How is sustainability spoken about in general, by the Green Agents and among the inhabitants? (the discourse)

These questions helped the group in defining the future direction for their field of research. From here the group explored the concept of sustainability as a phenomenon, as well the discourse that it is subjected to. After this the group used co-design to learn more about the term Green Agent.

(2) Middle co-design meeting. To fully understand the term Green Agent the group decided to facilitate another workshop where the Green Agents would be participating as co-creators. The challenge with the term Green Agent, seen from the student group perspective, was that it was being used diffusely by the organisation. Both the people that work in the organisation and the citizens taking part in the project applied it in very different manners.

By examining the object, Green Agents, the group would obtain an understanding of who they are. This allowed the group to identify the difference between a Green Agent and an ordinary citizen in Aalborg. With this knowledge in mind, the students would be able to obtain an understanding of what elements motivated the current Green Agents, and what they should focus on to engage new stakeholders of the project.

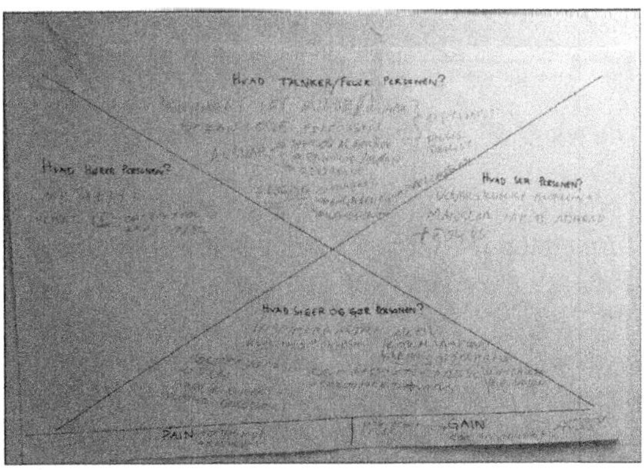

Figure 11.16. Empathy map

To obtain this in-depth understanding of the object, the student group first asked the participants to work out a persona, based on the theory of Osterwalder and Pigneur's (2010) Empathy Map (see Figure 11.16). The next step was for the participants to further categorise the different types of Green Agents, in a hierarchical triangle model, visualizing the different levels of commitment to the project. By doing this the group hoped to be able to identify whom to target, in order to generate more user commitment among the citizens of Aalborg.

The first exercise provided an overall understanding of the characteristics of a Green Agent. The method worked well as an initial exercise in the workshop, as it helped the participants in articulating their opinions to each other, and in reaching a common understanding of the user group.

The second exercise worked out well, as the method was easy to understand for the participants. By making them fill out each section of the model separately, they gradually filled out the sections, building on their acquired knowledge of the previously worked-out sections. The visual qualities of the model helped to ensure that, at all times, they had an overview and understanding of the process.

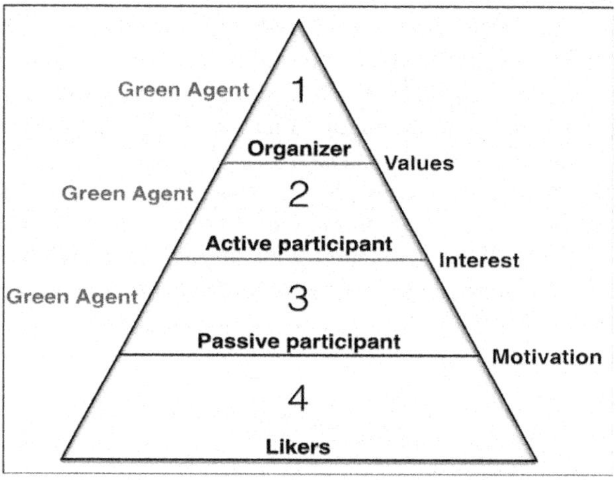

Figure 11.17. The pyramid with the green agent types

The workshop resulted in an in-depth understanding of the object. The student group's findings formed the foundation for the future approach in creating a service design that would engage the citizens of Aalborg.

(3) Later co-design meeting. At this stage, the student group had created a prototype on the basis of the knowledge obtained in the activities with the client. In order to refine the design, they wanted to test and evaluate it with the users. The user feedback gave the group an opportunity to create a redesign and a new prototype that included their input. First of all, the group wanted to ensure that the

participants had a clear understanding of the process. To make the agenda clear, the student group used the framework I *DO ART*. The tool is developed by IDEO and is used to visualise and articulate creative processes. In this way, they sought to ensure that the participants were aware of the purpose and activities of the workshop at all times.

Later during the workshop, an evaluation matrix (Rebernik, 2008 and see Figure 11.18) was worked out with the purpose of having the participants rank to what extent they found the listed requirements for the service design fulfilled. To make the participants generate new ideas on how the concepts could best support the listed requirements, they used De Bono's (1989) well-known *six thinking hats* approach. The method ensured that the participants adopted different perspectives, when focusing on the service design.

Figure 11.18. The matrix evaluation based on design criteria

The participants' assessment and evaluation helped to lead the direction and development of our service design. Their interaction with the concept meant that the criteria had changed. Therefore the group needed to do another iteration, where they identified the needs of the service design and established new requirements (Rogers et al., 2011).

(4) Final meeting and handover. Until now the student group had used different co-design tools in the design process, which was vital for reframing the case and for exploring and eliciting tacit knowledge from the stakeholders (Polanyi, 1962). This made them able to design a low-fidelity prototype that could be tested and evaluated on a small group of people representing the main target group.

Further on, the student group found it interesting to develop a physical high-fidelity prototype to test if it could act as intended. The student group wanted to examine if it met the Green Agents' expectations with respect to their activities. The group arranged a meeting where the service design was presented to the Green Agents with three other representatives from the Environmental Department. Before presenting the prototype of the service design, they introduced the stakeholders to the entire design process up till that point. The aim of the presentation was specifically to get their feedback and opinions to include in a new iteration.

The project manager and communication employee liked the fact that the student group had challenged the specific frame and reframed it to provide a significantly different solution to the case. The meeting resulted in specific ideas that could improve the service design and take it from a theoretical idea towards a realistic service design.

For instance, the stakeholders mentioned that the surprise would be ruined when people observe other people using the machine and what would happen. Therefore they suggested a foreclosure to hide the experience. They wanted to know if it could be developed from sustainable materials, if it should be manual or automatic, if it was suitable for outdoor use and what the costs would be in use.

To answer the above-mentioned questions and to get a professional evaluation, the student group decided to arrange a meeting with a marketing bureau known for playful and experiential approaches. This meeting meant a new diverging approach and functioned as a new iteration towards a final design. Based on the meeting with the business case owner, the group worked out the questions that the marketing bureau could perhaps give some further insights into.

First, the student group wanted to introduce them to the designed service and receive their overall feedback of the concept. Secondly, the group also wanted to get an estimate of the production cost and wanted to know if and how the installation could be produced in a sustainable way, to ensure the authenticity of the concept. Finally, there was a need to get their feedback on how appealing the concept would be, targeting a broad user group.

Overall, the marketing bureau owner was able to provide concrete answers to what the student group could do differently and what to focus on in a final design.

The marketing bureau owner was initially introduced to the concept, in the form of a small pitch containing renderings of the service design, helping to visualise it and secure an understanding of how it creates value for the users.

> *Bureau Owner*: "I really like this concept! It reminds me of how we work with digital experiences here. The most important thing about it is, in my opinion, that it allows the user to be curious and to gain new experience and knowledge through play and activation of the senses."
>
> *Student 1*: "Do you think it could be used as a part of a marketing campaign, supporting increased awareness about sustainability among citizens?"
>
> *Bureau Owner*: "I am positive that a design like this would play an effective part in reaching that goal. My experience tells me that it is important that you activate the users, when you communicate complex messages and want to change people's behaviour."

The second thing on the agenda was to get an estimate of the production cost. The group wanted to avoid neglecting cost concerns especially because they were working with a small organisation. This insight was used to give the client a precise understanding of the expense of the design.

> *Student*: "Can you give me an estimate on the production cost of this design?"

> *Bureau Owner*: "Hmmm. It really depends on how technical you want it to be. If you just want it to be able to flash lights on and off, install a small motor that can make it shake and allow users to interact on a simple interface on a tablet, we have made similar installations costing around 20,000 kr. But if you want a more detailed version with more features, which allows the users to do more complex interaction, it would mean more hours coding. Then it would be around 50,000 kr."

> *Student*: "Okay – so prices would start at around 20,000 kr. for a simple version, that would still allow the users to interact with the design?"

The last question on the agenda was whether the design was appealing enough to a broad target group as desired by the client.

> *Bureau Owner*: "This design would definitely appeal to a wide audience! The most important thing about it is that it allows the users to experience something new and gives them the opportunity to play and be curious. My experience tells me that even grown ups want to play. It is not just something that children do. We have often made installations that we thought were for children, but then we discover that men in their 40's and 50's find them just as amusing."

Based on the meeting, the student group found themselves with a more specific and validated solution and knowledge. This new knowledge was, as mentioned before, used to inform the client about the practical approach of the realisation of the design.

CROSS-COMPARISON DISCUSSION & TENTATIVE CONCLUSIONS

In this design case comparison we take a cross-perspective look at the cases to discuss interesting elements and nuances.

Strategic Co-Design Tools

In the early meetings all the groups chose to use the BMC. Even though the business model canvas are simple in its nature and cannot contain a more detailed view on an upcoming business model, the BMC helped the groups and the business case owners to reach mutual understanding and – perhaps even more importantly – shared communication. Therefore we can argue that understanding each other's professional terminology is a first step towards a positive and constructive collaboration and that the broad scope of the BMC supports this. This has also been documented in earlier participatory design research and dubbed a 'third space' platform (Greenbaum & Loi, 2012; Müller, 2003). However, in these strategic co-design projects it is harder to establish such a third space, because of the increasing complexity of the projects and the wider circle of stakeholders with varying professional expertise. It seems that the Domino mapping set-up helped the group in case two to achieve an understanding on the process before they entered the project, and a first reflection from the stakeholders in the project, that is, that they might have left out the user perspective along the way. The Domino mapping set-up enabled a fruitful dialogue through playful interaction by proposing a perspective and inviting the stakeholders to adjust and elaborate further.

In the middle meetings the student groups worked with various stakeholders to further frame and reframe ideas and concepts. They all used visual tools to bring conversations to a concrete mode. Group one created a very transparent design process through which the stakeholders could monitor the design choices from interview to 'the three opportunities', which became a starting point for ideation and further exploration of requirements and issues to consider. Group two and three created a design game with the overall goal of getting a specific framing narrowed down to fewer options, but without closing it to a specific solution. With the design games the groups succeeded in inviting the stakeholders to be an active part in the framing of the design directions. Design games as such can be used both as an exploration tool and a convergent tool to qualify ideated options (Gudiksen, 2015).

In the later meetings the student groups presented various prototypes, again using strong design arguments to support their solutions. Prototyping helps stakeholders to imagine and to some degree experience what a potential solution might look and feel like. Even though this is more sense-giving than sense-making, it might help to still think of them as participatory prototypes (Sanders & Stappers, 2014) because the feedback from the stakeholders still implies a need to be part of the later stages of the development.

As could also be observed, the student groups had solid and vital arguments through their human-centred design focus in general, that is, a fresh attention to the customers, users and clients in the projects. In the banking case, the interviews with potential customers and the clustering of insights provided design criteria for the group to evaluate ideas and concepts against, as well as data to support choices and arguments for certain directions in the meetings with the stakeholders.

Stakeholder Involvement and Constraints

In the development process, all the groups had meetings in which new stakeholders were brought in, who naturally introduced new perspectives or 'constraints' to the table. Within creativity research, constraints are sometimes thought of as a positive thing that leads to specific directions (Stokes, 2005) in an otherwise endless world of possibilities. Design briefs from clients to design agencies are commonly used by many companies, however, in the above perspective, such a document cannot be thought of as a 'static' document that is only established at the beginning. In the banking case with group one, the final presentation included more people from the management of the bank. They had not been part of the process and the student group therefore had had no chance to elicit arguments from these stakeholders. Through their human-centred design process and focus, the student group seemed to leave out typical managerial concerns such as resources and cost, which were not part of their original design brief. Group two, through their pre-handover presentation at the conference, received feedback that led them to improve the presentation with additional clarification of the concept. It might be that prototyping in strategic co-design also means testing with stakeholder archetypes, perhaps with a manager in a similar position, but who is not part of the bank in case one. In an ideal situation and from a strategic perspective, the best way forward would be to include managers with higher decision-making possibilities from the very beginning, but this is rarely possible.

The proposition is, therefore, that strategic co-design implies an increased focus on the stakeholders at the table e.g. what background they have and what kind of terminology is used, as well as when and how they enter into the project. Rather than arguing strongly for new perspectives and ideas to begin with, the students in a sophisticated manner continuously opened up and improved arguments until they had a stronger supported argument through a fully fleshed concept and initial prototype. As course organisers we have seen, through the years, how potentially good ideas fall flat when brought in too early. Possible ways forward for the student groups would be to clearly indicate where in the process they are at each meeting and to provide strategic design arguments, addressing specific stakeholders' likely concerns. This can be further nurtured in upcoming courses. We can detect through these cases that, more often than not, stakeholders bring new 'constraints' to the table along the way – constraints that the groups need to consider and work around. Based on this, we can also argue that it is not only the decision makers who are important to address in these interventions. As Brown and Martin (2015) mention, it is equally important to consider other stakeholders.

The Use of Experienced 'Peers'

All the groups chose to involve experienced peers, but at different moments of the process and for varying reasons. In the first case, a design agency helped the group to collect interviews and arrive at central opportunity insights. In case two, a design agency was brought in between middle and later meetings to give the student group feedback on the current ideas and possible next steps. And in the last case, the group received feedback from a marketing bureau on the realisation of the concept with elements such as resources, technical concerns and implementation. We can see that the use of experienced peers also becomes a design argument in its own right to qualify both process and concept solution. Verganti and Öberg (2013, p. 93) argue that peers are not only experts, but also 'critics of the current domain'. Bringing in interpreters from outside the project will introduce fresh perspectives and challenge both process and potential solution. In this sense, it is a valuable asset for the students' learning, because it requires preparing for new feedback by engaging in meta-reflections on their ongoing project – in a sense, stepping out of the project for a while and applying a more holistic perspective. This enables students to adapt to new perspectives, but also to be critical towards feedback given. The new stakeholders and the experienced peers should not be thought of as oracles with all the right answers, as they, too, might be caught up in a routine way of thinking in a current domain. We see the inclusion of extra-project experienced professionals as a further argument for the need to consider all types of knowledge that can be beneficial to a specific co-design project and also as a key ingredient in the idea of Engaged Scholarship.

FUTURE SUGGESTIONS

The following suggestions can be seen both as potential new concerns to be addressed explicitly in upcoming courses, and as new research topics. In this chapter we have described the design process of three student groups, with a focus on how the students manage to get across design ideas, concepts and, in general, suggestions to decision makers and stakeholders. The projects were carried out as part of an Engaged Scholarship course called BizChange, with the aim of creating synergy between the students, stakeholders (case partners) and academics involved. In this article, we have first described how the students developed competences within design facilitation as part of their design process, and secondly how local companies can receive conceptual designs that are tailor-made for them.

(1) Based on these cases, co-design tools – e.g. design games – have a clear potential for gathering stakeholder perspectives and interest in order to reach mutual understanding and discuss future directions. For the educated or trained designer, this becomes a necessary tool for involving, exploring and convincing stakeholders with very different attitudes, working styles and professional language. We argue that a series of interventions with ongoing negotiation is better than a single pitch at the end of a project. The groups learn to negotiate and have patience, rather than delivering 'all-in' suggestions. They also see their own blind spots and pay attention to the professional expertise the stakeholders have and express. With the involvement of experienced peers they get to see their project from different angles, although student groups should also be critical in a constructive way of these approaches. We suggest bridging theories from co-design with basic negotiation theories, to arrive at strong, decisive, design intervention tools. Tools like that can combine the strong learning styles in the visual and tactile language with the power of negotiating in stages.

(2) In all three group processes, we have described how new stakeholders entered the project along the way, which meant attention to new constraints. Also, some of the stakeholders brought in new perspectives. The groups' ability to work with these

constraints in a constructive way – even though this can be frustrating – advances them to a state where they become quality design negotiators. In a reality where complex problems require collaboration within a circle of diverse stakeholders, this, we argue, is a vital 21st century skill. In upcoming courses and research we will further look into how co-designers can nurture 'what lies beneath' stakeholders' approaches and working procedures, including routines and habits.

We consider this chapter to be an example in itself of how Engaged Scholarship activities can feed into research, as one of the research contributions derived from the BizChange course. The student groups have taken part in the writing and, through this, added another level of reflection-on-action on the case they had and compared with other cases. We have, with the students reflections, described how they engage in early reflection of how the activities were carried out, how the participants were involved, how the activities contributed to their design process etc. The result in relation to the students' learning is that, at the end of the course, they are capable of developing and running very different co-design activities that are directed to the specific ongoing case. In short, they become better co-design negotiators.

REFERENCES

Archer, B. (1995). The nature of research. *Co-Design Journal, 2*(11), 6–13.

Argyris, C., Putnam, R., & Smith, D. M. (1985). *Action science*. San Francisco, CA: Jossey-Bass.

Argyris, C. (2010). *Organizational traps: Leadership, culture, organizational design*. OUP Oxford.

Brandt, E. (2006). Designing exploratory design games a framework for participation in participatory design? *Proceedings Participatory Design Conference*, 57–66.

Brinkmann, S., & Tanggaard, L. (Eds.). (2010). *Kvalitative metoder og tilgange: En grundbog*. Hans Reitzels Forlag.

Brown, T. (2008). Design thinking. *Harvard Business Review, 86*(6), 84.

Brown, T. (2009). *Change by design*. HarperBusiness.

Brown, T., & Martin, R. (2015). Design for action. *Harvard Business Review*, September, 55–64.

Buur, J., & Matthews, B. (2008). Participatory innovation. *International Journal of Innovation Management, 12*(3), 255–273.

Buxton, B. (2007). *Sketching user experiences: Getting the design right and the right design*. Morgan Kaufmann.

Bødker, S. (2000). Scenarios in user-centred design—setting the stage for reflection and action. *Interacting with computers, 13*(1), 61–75.

De Bono, E. (1989). *Six thinking hats*. London: Penguin.

Dorst, K. (2015). *Frame innovation*. MIT Press.

Ehn, P. (1993). Scandinavian design: On participation and skill. *Participatory design: Principles and practices*, 41–77.

Flyvbjerg, B. (2006). Five misunderstandings about case-study research. *Qualitative inquiry, 12*(2), 219–245.

Frayling, C. (1993). *Research in art and design*. London: Royal College of Art.

Gioia, D. A., & Chittipeddi, K. (1991). Sensemaking and sensegiving in strategic change initiation. *Strategic management journal, 12*(6), 433–448.

Greenbaum, J., & Loi, D. (2012). Participation, the camel and the elephant of design: an introduction. *CoDesign, 8* (2–3), 81–85.

Gudiksen, S. (2014). Game feedback techniques: Eliciting big surprises in business model design. *Design research society proceedings*.

Gudiksen, S. (2015). *Co-designing business models: Engaging emergence through design games* (Ph.D Dissertation). Aalborg University.

Gudiksen, S. (2015). Designerly influence on politics and the press: Changing a deadlocked relationship. *Nordes, 1*(6).

Gudiksen, S., Poulsen, S. B., & Buur, J. (2014). Making business models. *CoDesign, 10*(1), 15–30.

Houde, S., & Hill, C. (1997). What do prototypes prototype? In M. Helander & T. K. Landauer (Eds.), *Handbook of human-computer interaction* (2nd ed.). Amsterdam, the Netherlands: Elsevier Science.

IDEO.org. (2015). The field guide to human-centered design.

Junginger, S., & Sangiorgi, D. (2009. Service design and organizational change: Bridging the gap between rigour and relevance. In *Proceedings of the 3rd IASDR Conference on Design Research* (pp. 4339–4348). Seoul, South Korea: Korean Society of Design Science.

Kelley, T., & Littman, J. (2006). *The ten faces of innovation: IDEO's strategies for defeating the devil's advocate and driving creativity throughout your organization.* Crown Business.

Kelley, T., & Kelley, D. (2013). *Creative confidence: Unleashing the creative potential within us all.* Crown Business.

Kim, A. J. (2000). *Community building on the web.* San Francisco, CA: Peachpit Press.

Kolb, D. A. (1984). *Experiential learning: Experience as the source of learning and development* (1). Englewood Cliffs, NJ: Prentice-Hall.

Koskinen, I., Zimmerman, J., Binder, T., Redström, J., & Wensveen, S. (2011). Constructive Design Research-1.

Muller, M. J. (2003). Participatory design: The third space in HCI. *Human-computer interaction: Development process, 4235*, 165–185.

Osterwalder, A., & Pigneur, Y. (2010). *Business model generation: A handbook for visionaries, game changers, and challengers* (2nd ed.). UK: John Wiley & Sons, Inc.

Pestoff, V. (2012). Co-production and third sector social services in Europe. *New public governance, the third sector and co-production*, 13–34.

Polanyi, M. (1966). *The tacit dimension.* Routledge.

Prahalad, C. K., & Ramaswamy, V. (2004a). Co-creating unique value with customers. *Strategy & Leadership, 32*(3), 4–9.

Rebernik, M., & Bradač, B. (2008). Idea evaluation methods and techniques. *Institute for Entrepreneurship and Small Business Management.* Slovenia: University of Maribor.

Rogers, Y., Sharp, H., & Preece, J. (2011). Interaction design: Beyond human-computer interaction.

Roos, J., & Roos, M. (2006). *Thinking from within: A hands-on strategy practice.* Palgrave Macmillan.

Rosted, J. (2005). *Brugerdreven innovation: Økonomi- og erhvervsministeriets enhed for erhvervsøkonomisk forskning og analyse.*

Ritzer, G., & Jurgenson, N. (2010). Production, consumption, prosumption the nature of capitalism in the age of the digital 'prosumer'. *Journal of Consumer Culture, 10*(1), 13–36.

Rousseau, D. (1995). *Psychological contracts in organizations: Understanding written and unwritten agreements.* Sage Publications.

Sanders, E. B. N., & Stappers, P. J. (2014). Probes, toolkits and prototypes: Three approaches to making in codesigning. *CoDesign, 10*(1), 5–14.

Schön, D. A. (1983). *The reflective practitioner: How professionals think in action* (Vol. 5126). Basic books.

Schön, D. A. (1987). *Educating the reflective practitioner.* San Francisco, CA: Jossey-Bass.

Simon, H. A. (1976). The business school: A problem in organizational design. In H. A. Simon (Ed.), *Administrative behavior: A study of decision-making processes in administrative organization* (pp. 335–356). New York, NY: Free Press.

Spool, J. M. (2004). The KJ-technique: A group process for establishing priorities. *User interface engineering Newsletter.*

Stokes, P. D. (2005). *Creativity from constraints: The psychology of breakthrough.* Springer Publishing Company.

Toffler, A. (1980). *The third wave.* New York, NY: Bantam.

Toffler, A. (1984). *Future shock.* New York, NY: Bantam.

Verganti, R., & Öberg, Å. (2013). Interpreting and envisioning—A hermeneutic framework to look at radical innovation of meanings. *Industrial marketing management*, *42*(1), 86–95.

Sune Gudiksen
Department of Communication & Psychology
Aalborg University

Søren Bolvig Poulsen
Department of Communication & Psychology
Aalborg University

Mads Kunø
Department of Communication & Psychology
Aalborg University

Søren Iversen
Department of Communication & Psychology
Aalborg University

Joakim Glerup
Department of Communication & Psychology
Aalborg University

Klaus Greve True
Department of Communication & Psychology
Aalborg University

Emilie Holst
Department of Communication & Psychology
Aalborg University

Nanna Schmidt
Department of Communication & Psychology
Aalborg University

Helle Tetzchner
Department of Communication & Psychology
Aalborg University

Klaus Gregersen
Department of Communication & Psychology
Aalborg University

TURID NØRLUND CHRISTENSEN

12. TEACHING CO-CREATION

Paradoxes in Rock and Pop Ensemble Classes

> In the domain of arts-based rock and pop music, co-creative processes are essential in the formation of the artistic expression.
>
> (Behr, 2015, p. 18; Green, 2006, p. 106)

INTRODUCTION

All musicians intuitively know and understand the experience of co-creation in a band, but we have yet to develop awareness in Higher Education (HE) of the tacit knowledge and practices linked to these experiences. When teaching rock and pop ensemble playing in HE, we often limit ourselves to focusing, during classes, on the music tradition and the domain-specific technical skills. This frequently results in a retrospective product characterised by variations of reproduction (Christensen, 2013, p. 35) or merely a cover version, instead of an original and authentic art-based product and performance. Meanwhile, the same students can be capable of creating excellent, creative and authentic concerts with their own bands.

Today, it is often the degree of perceived authenticity of the performer (Moore, 2002, p. 210; Behr, 2014, p. 18) and originality of the performance (Hebert, 2011, p. 13) that separates the experience of pop and rock as entertainment (expectation affirmative in a closed form) or art (unpredictable in an open form). It could be considered paradoxical that we often end up reproducing originals, instead of teaching how to create an original expression and sound (Christensen, 2013, p. 35) – which is essential for the genre as an art form (Anthony, 2015, p. 142; Behr, 2015, p. 18; Hebert, 2011, p. 13).

There seems to be a lack of codified knowledge and methodology for working with these parameters in relation to rock and pop music as an art form. The purpose of this chapter is to map out an educational design structure for working dynamically towards authentic, co-creative and original performances in rock and pop ensemble classes in HE, while granting musical and personal autonomy to the students.

Institutional Background

The Royal Academy of Music, Aarhus (RAMA) is a music conservatoire providing HE in music. Achieving a high level of artistic performance skills is central to the

T. Chemi & L. Krogh (Eds.), Co-Creation in Higher Education, 205–223.

coursework of both the performance and the teaching degrees. Student admission is audition-based, focusing on artistic performance skills, and no secondary degree or prior formal academic training is required. Since 2003 RAMA has followed university models, with graduate and postgraduate levels (Bachelor and Master degrees) as part of implementation of the Bologna process.

The Rhythmic Music Department at RAMA has existed since 1991. The Danish term *rhythmic music* covers music genres characterised by having pulse and an element of improvisation at their core, such as jazz, rock, pop, folk, and world music. The main objective of the curricula in the Rhythmic Music Department is to:

> ...help students develop their musical and artistic personalities without forgetting the all-important aspect: to be able to work with others in a creative and dynamic manner... emphasis is placed on the individual student's creative and independent development as a musician, an artist, and a communicator. (RAMA, 2011, p. 3)

The learning objectives for ensemble playing in the RAMA Music BA (2011, p. 11) mention general, domain-specific crafts in the field such as:

- musical and technical skills at a level that supports working professionally;
- artistic skills are described as the ability "to make relevant artistic choices and assessments, especially with regard to developing his/her artistic expression";
- co-creative skills are emphasised as being "able to work in a creative, investigative, and analytical manner in a musical and artistic context" (p. 11).

Limitations of the Aesthetic Learning Tradition

RAMA traditionally provides ensemble classes largely based on aesthetic learning (Christensen, 2013, p. 35) formed by the professional skills and personal knowledge (Eraut, 2000, p. 114) of the instructors and the professional performance traditions in their domains. The strength of aesthetic learning, as with all apprentice ship-style learning, is that students learn the domain-specific technical skills and traditions (Eraut, 1994, p. 6) through social learning (Marquardt & Waddill, 2004, p. 188). Aural copying also leads to enhancement of the ability to listen to music and thus appreciate and understand more (Green, 2006, p. 115) on a tacit knowledge level (Eraut, 2000, p. 118). However, the traditional focus on aesthetic learning leads to several challenges in the educational setting of a rock and pop ensemble class:

- the focus on a pre-defined aesthetic product leads the students to replicate what is around them (Christensen, 2013, p. 35) and thus the result is reproductive instead of creative and authentic. Acquiring technical skills and traditional knowledge through aesthetic learning does not necessarily lead to developing artistic competencies;
- focussing on the musical text or inherent meanings may suggest that these are the only 'real' or 'important' aspects of music, thus ignoring the social and cultural

influences on both the production and reception of that text (Green, 2005, p. 190), as well as the importance and relevance of frames and obstructions for creativity to occur (Lehmann, 2012, p. 152);
- the assessment and student feedback refer to a pre-set but not explicit product influenced by instructor preferences (Christensen, 2013, p. 35). The format is closed, yet invisible;
- a structure or method for working with the creative process is not clearly stated (Christensen, 2013, p. 35) and hence is not part of the learning outcome;
- a lack of contextual understanding and limited methodological and practical abilities lead students to doubt their competence (Rønnestad, 2008, p. 283);
- fear of failure can become a stifling factor in the student's performances, artistic as well as educational.

It appears that the aesthetic learning tradition (Christensen, 2013, p. 35) can lead, for the students, to an imbalance between the learning objectives in curriculum and the actual learning outcomes of the coursework. Research and educational design development in similar domains of education, such as design (Sanders & Stappers, 2008) and dramaturgy (Lehmann, 2012), have shown that incorporating codified knowledge (Eraut, 2000, p. 113) from other domains can be beneficial for the development of propositional knowledge (Eraut, 1994, p. 43) and educational design. A similar development is still in its very early days at RAMA.

The Aesthetic Paradox in Ensemble Playing Classes

This leaves us with the paradox in rock and pop ensemble playing classes: the tradition of aesthetic learning leads to variations of reproduction instead of to creative and original artistic expressions, or creative structures that the students can benefit from in their future professions (Christensen, 2013, p. 35). New approaches, structures and methods for teaching the domain-specific tacit knowledge must be developed and applied to achieve the curriculum-defined artistic and co-creative learning objectives.

This leads to the research question for our pedagogic development project: What could be an appropriate design structure from an instructor's point of view for facilitating a learning process focusing on the co-creative artistic competencies in rock and pop ensemble playing classes in HE?

MATERIALS AND RESEARCH METHODS

In order to investigate this research question, the author conducted a pedagogic development project at RAMA with an ensemble class for one semester. Due to the performance orientation of the pedagogic development project with a focus on "problem-finding creativity" (Getzels & Csikszentmihalyi, 1976, p. 79; Sawyer, 2003, pp. 104–106; 2007, p. 45; 2012a, pp. 90–93) and process as the product, the aim was not to study "what is true", but "what is worth doing" (Gergen & Gergen, 2012, p. 49).

The general aim of the pedagogic development project at RAMA was to:

- qualify teaching rock and pop ensemble playing in HE by focusing on the co-creative artistic competencies and collaborative perspectives;
- develop teaching methods for unarticulated tacit knowledge in this field;
- test co-creation as a conscious learning strategy and teaching method in rock and pop ensemble classes.

"To embrace co-creativity requires that one believes that all people are creative" (Sanders & Stappers, 2008, p. 9). Thus the main hypothesis in the development project in relation to working with co-creation in an arts educational setting is: creativity is not a special innate talent, but rather cognitive abilities and a lot of hard work within a framework that enables this (Sawyer, 2007, p. 124). The right approach and attitude for creativity to occur can be identified, managed, trained, and learned (Bono, 1970, pp. 11–13).

Socio-cultural definitions of creativity include the concept that the product or process must be novel and appropriate to the domain (Sawyer, 2012a, p. 214). "Creativity in bands is socially constructed" (Behr, 2015, p. 9) and, in particular, the result of a group effort (Sawyer, 2003, pp. 4–5), which in this pedagogic development project was sought during classes by taking into account the design of the structure and the facilitation of the coursework. In order to describe creativity and the related co-creative artistic competencies in a rock or pop band performance, theory and research from a broad range of related academic fields were applied, in an attempt to identify the co-creative artistic learning objectives, and reveal the underlying didactics and methodology of this pedagogic development project. The deriving educational design was tested with a RAMA ensemble class.

Class notes, class conversations, feedback from participating students and recordings of the student course evaluation were included in the analysis of the potential and limitations of the co-creative educational design approach.

Description of the Case Studied

The ensemble class consisted of 7 students, from Denmark (3), Finland (3) and Ireland (1), representing three different educational programmes in the Rhythmic Music department (Rhythmic Music, Rhythmic Music and Dance, and Global Music) and all study levels, from second year Bachelor students to final year Master students, playing drums, bass, guitar, plus four vocalists. Their previous experience in arts-based rock and pop ranged from some performance experience, to comprehensive performance experience and identity. The instructor participated on keyboards, and two of the vocalists occasionally played additional keyboards and piano. Each student had chosen this particular course from a range of ensemble class options. This freedom of choice in what to learn and when during their education is hoped to be an enhancing factor with regard to the students' intrinsic motivation (Amabile, 1998, p. 79). The course comprised 10 x 2-hour lessons (process) during one semester and ended with a 20-minute public concert performance (product), followed by an evaluation of the course with the students.

General Course Structure

The primary idea behind the educational design was to mimic the work process of co-creative bands, as a similar learning environment "is essential to the tertiary popular music student's real world Knowledge" (Anthony, 2015, p. 144). The students at RAMA are already very competent on their instruments, and several other classes focus on developing technical skills. The group identity of bands is rooted in concrete actions, entangled in socialisation and creativity (Behr, 2014, p. 18). So our development project attempted to facilitate the co-creation of an artistic expression by designing "a conducive environment" (KEA, 2009, p. 32) for exploratory behaviour in rock and pop ensemble classes in "an atmosphere where people trust each other" (Ind & Coates, 2013, p. 89). This was inspired by the fundamental belief of action learning that "we learn best when undertaking some action upon which we reflect" (Marquardt & Waddill, 2004, p. 190), combined with a dialogic experience-based learning process.

Parallel to the role of co-designing researcher (Sanders & Stappers, 2008, pp. 12–13) and of action-learning coach (Marquardt & Waddill, 2004, pp. 197–198), the instructor conducted the workshop-based ensemble classes as a facilitator, actively and equally involved in the interactive musical co-creation process, while stepping in and out of the facilitating role. The task for the facilitating instructor was to bring the students into the co-creative process "in the ways most conducive to their ability to participate" (Sanders & Stappers, 2008, p. 14) by setting the right framework and defining tasks that enabled the students to have relevant co-creative experiences through group improvisations. "This means leading, guiding, and providing scaffolds, as well as clean slates" (Sanders & Stappers, 2008, p. 14) depending on the student's levels of creativity. "The students must be given freedom to explore" (Anthony, 2015, p. 143) as "individuals create through exploration, dialogue and experimentation" (Ind & Coates, 2013, p. 91).

Torunn Kjølner's general structure for *Conceptual Devising* (Kjølner, 2009) as a theatre production method was applied for a theoretical understanding of structuring the co-creative workshop process during the ensemble course. In brief, the group of students worked through three production phases during the semester:

- Phase 1: Create/generate material; through an open and improvisational approach the students work with stripped-down songs as a framework, exploring the potentials and different options of the material, while building a set of mutual co-creative concepts, values and trust.
- Phase 2: Composition and dramaturgy; students select the songs to be used at the concert and find an overall characterising concept/theme/atmosphere for devising their concert.

- Phase 3: Tests of concept/staging; this phase is the final concert and the way it is executed and evaluated.

Though all three phases are experienced in the development project, the emphasis in this chapter is on studying phase 1.

IDENTIFICATION OF THE DOMAIN-SPECIFIC CO-CREATIVE SKILLS

An attempt to identify the domain-specific aesthetic and educational characteristics in rock and pop formed the basis for the development of the co-creative educational design. The theoretical background and the deriving didactics and methodology in the course design will be presented in the following section.

Aesthetic Features of Arts-Based Rock and Pop

Post-modern rock and pop music can be regarded as a kind of modern folk music (Behr, 2015, pp. 1–6; Moore, 2002). There is an interaction between the music, the performer and the audience that can create identity-confirming recognition, as well as pose identity-evolving questions to the recipient. According to Behr (2014) rock can be understood as "a social construct of a particular way of making music" (p. 18), a set of practices that are subject to authentication in relation to a genre-specific methodology (p. 18) favouring interactions between band members (p. 16), group creativity (p. 6), and originality (Hebert, 2011, p. 13).

The co-creative process in the ensemble performance of a rock band seems to be a crucial element in the shaping of the artistic expression (Behr, 2015, p. 18; Green 2006, p. 106), and is arguably more important than the instrumental skills of each individual musician. History has provided a long list of brilliantly creative rock and pop bands formed by musicians with average technical skills, as well as brilliant rock bands where, after the band broke up, the solo careers and performances of the band members have not nearly lived up to the band's former level. This point of view is supported by contemporary systems-based theories of creativity that suggest creativity is not a singular effort, but rather a group process (Jones, 2014; Sawyer, 2007).

From an aesthetic point of view the borders between rock and pop are "open to question and dependent on both their context and the listener's position" (Behr, 2014, p. 5), and "distinctions between jazz and popular music are ill-defined at best" (Hebert, 2011, p. 15). This is especially the case in Europe, where the genres have been adopted from outside the culture and transformed into artistic expressions unattached to the cultural heritage, but with an added and integrated European cultural dimension. There is no distinction between jazz and popular music genres in the educational settings of the Rhythmic Department at RAMA. Still students and instructors tend to identify themselves as belonging more to one tradition than the other.

Though jazz and popular music are both originally rooted in blues music and have pulse and an element of improvisation at their musical core, numerous aesthetic and educational differences also exist. While competencies in rock and pop music are primarily based on "socially acquired informal knowledge" (McPhail, 2013, p. 45), competencies in jazz build on "socially developed but formally acquired disciplinary knowledge" (McPhail, 2013, p 45). Jazz ensembles have a tradition to build from. The jazz standard songs with similar harmonic structures provide a common frame with a corresponding well-developed set of musical tools and improvisation rules (Sawyer, 2003, p. 31, pp. 50–54). These can be taught formally (Green, 2006, p. 106), and applied by the individual musician when playing in a jazz ensemble (Sawyer, 2003, p. 31). However a similar formal learning tradition is lacking in rock and pop music, where the aesthetic and educational tradition is much more anarchistic in its nature. The musicians are primarily self-taught through informal learning, which takes place in groups, "involving discussion, watching, listening to and imitating each other" (Green, 2006, p. 106). Their primary task is to find the group's unique sound and ground rules for playing together in a co-creation of the vision, form and content (Hauen, 2011, p. 688) with an "emphasis on creativity and 'cutting edge' practices rather than cultural heritage" (Hebert, 2011, p. 13). The musicians "perform more than just musical functions. They are intrinsic to the 'character' of the band" (Behr, 2015, p. 11). While jazz ensembles are often defined and named by the bandleader, rock and pop bands are often defined as a collective with a group name.

The element of group improvisation, also called jamming, is a common and basic principle in the co-creative work process of most rock bands, but unlike in jazz ensembles, it happens without a common tradition and frame of standard songs and improvisation rules. Instead, the sum of the individual band members' musical taste, experience, skills, informal tacit knowledge and creativity (Green, 2006, p. 106) defines the frames for the group improvisations. The improvisatory elements in rock and pop are heavily based on factors such as energy, sound and personal characteristics in the playing style, and the musicians need "experience to gain the confidence to explore music and follow their instincts" (Anthony, 2015, p. 143). Improvisations are more often expressed as group improvisations of the song, rather than as an instrumental soloist with an accompaniment. The emphasis is on interpreting and performing the song, prior to any instrumental solos that might only be added to enhance the energy and expression of the song. The joint achievement is the focal point, but each musician and vocalist has a major responsibility for managing his/her personal role and contribution to it. It is a group performance with a broad management structure. This co-creative approach calls for more than the cooperative competencies of merely supporting and working through a general idea defined by an instructor or a bandleader (Hauen, 2011, p. 688).

An attempt to sum up the differences in the educational and aesthetic tradition of jazz and rock/pop ensembles is shown in Tables 12.1 and 12.2. The derived educational (Table 12.1) and aesthetic (Table 12.2) characteristics for arts-based rock/pop ensembles formed the basis for the co-creative educational design (Table 12.3) and the corresponding structural elements (Table 12.4) in the educational development project.

Table 12.1. Educational differences in the tradition of jazz and rock/pop

Jazz	*Rock and pop*
Formal educational tradition based on: • Socially developed but formally acquired disciplinary knowledge • Formal education + organised jam sessions • Standard songs	Informal educational tradition based on: • Socially acquired informal knowledge • Self-taught through informal learning in bands • Original songs and radical interpretations
Improvisational rules & tools	Improvisation based on sound, energy, and personality
Task: Build on/from tradition	Task: Find the group's unique sound and ground rules for playing together

Table 12.2. Aesthetic differences in the tradition of jazz and rock/pop

Aesthetic characteristics in jazz	*Aesthetic characteristics in rock and pop*
Cultural heritage	Creativity and cutting edge practices
Excellence in performance	Perceived authenticity in performance
Build from tradition	Break with tradition, no common tradition
Musicians perform musical functions	Musicians intrinsic to the 'character' of the band
Individual improvisations over the chorus/ theme	Interpreting the song through group improvisations
Individual soloists + accompaniment	Group improvisation prior to individual solos
Bandleader defining vision, form and content	Joint group co-creation of vision, form and content
Named after the bandleader + number of musicians	Defined as a collective with a group name

CO-CREATIVE CONSIDERATIONS FOR THE EDUCATIONAL DESIGN STRUCTURE

Playing in a band is a highly complicated co-creative group performance with multiple factors in play (Sawyer, 2003, pp. 4–5), where the self-directed improvising band members reach "insights and direction through the process of interaction and mutual self-commentary" (Ind & Coates, 2013, p. 91). Co-creation occurs in communities centred around voluntariness, confidence, desire and interest, where all community members contribute to the co-creative process with a focus on the common good while constantly seeking innovation (Hauen, 2011, p. 691). "Co-designing requires creative initiative on the part of the entire team" (Sanders & Stappers, 2008, p. 9). Hence group creativity involves distributed cognition when integrating individual contributions in the formation of the collective product (Sawyer, 2012a). "People will be most creative when they feel motivated by the interest, satisfaction, and challenge of the work itself – and not by external pressure" (Amabile, 1998, p. 79). By giving individuals space to be themselves, while using their creative power in favour of the group (Hauen, 2011, p. 691), co-creative communities obtain not only better ideas – as collaboration over time is the best way to distinguish good ideas from bad (Sawyer, 2007, p. 124) – but also very inclusive results (Hauen, 2011, p. 691).

These co-creative aspects were integrated into the educational design by making group improvisation the foundation of class activities. All songs were approached as frames for improvisation and playful co-creation, instead of as a preconceived end point. "Play provides the freedom to do things differently on each occasion" (Ind & Coates, 2013, p. 90), and thus emphasise the creative element of co-creation in rock and pop ensemble playing. To avoid musical habits of thought and to encourage exploration, the songs chosen by the instructor were either supposedly unfamiliar to the students, or original compositions by the instructor, presented in an open, basic version that was easy to learn and remember, but did not provide straight answers as to how it should be played. The intention was to have the students work in a format closer to the aesthetic tradition of the musical genre. Also, inspired by co-design methodology, we aimed to change the students' role from passive consumers to expert adaptors of their knowledge and experience (Sanders & Sstappers, 2008, p. 12), whilst enhancing the level of motivation in the process and authenticity of the product through group improvised student contributions. However, in order for the students to do so, "they must be given appropriate tools for expressing themselves" (Sanders & Stappers, 2008, p. 12).

Problem-Finding Creativity

Most studies in creativity focus on fixed end products that can be analysed. But in the case of art-based rock and pop music, the process during the performance *is* the actual product (Sawyer, 2003, p. 5). The high level of improvisation in the group performance challenges the way we look at it in an educational context, as there is no fixed end product or defined end goal, bar the one "intrinsic to the performance itself – to perform well and to entertain the audience" (Sawyer, 2007, p. 45). The improvising artist must find ways to allow this to happen by taking advantage of ideas and accidents as they occur (Ind & Coates, 2013, p. 90) from the moment-to-moment contingency (Sawyer, 2012b, p. 72). The type of creativity involved in an improvised aesthetic product is called "problem-finding creativity", as opposed to "problem-solving creativity" (Getzels & Csikszentmihalyi, 1976, p. 79; Sawyer, 2003, pp. 104–106; 2007, p. 45; 2012a, pp. 90–93). While problem-solving creativity has a defined goal – a problem that needs to be solved – problem-finding creativity seeks to find and define the problem, or challenge, while solving it (Getzels & Csikszentmihalyi, 1976, p. 83; Sawyer, 2007, p. 45). Improvising musicians notice small emerging musical ideas, motifs, patterns, possibilities, and contrasts, explore them and build upon them, use them as a frame or an obstacle, while playing. In order to find a creatively significant problem, "changing elements and introducing new combinations… is more likely to contribute to an original solution" (Getzels & Csikszentmihalyi, 1976, p. 92).

Three dimensions are important in problem-finding creativity, according to Getzels and Csikszentmihalyi (1976):

- "openness to the problem" (pp. 90–91), in this case the song or frame given for the musical improvisation and performance, as well as the length of time the problem remains open;
- "exploratory behaviour" (p. 91) while playing;
- added "changes in the structure and content of the initial problem" (p. 91).

These actions delay the problem-solving process and prevent premature fixation on an unoriginal problem that might lead to unoriginal solutions (pp. 91–92). This is suggesting a very different approach in the ensemble classes from the traditional aesthetic learning processes based on teacher instruction and reproduction. "Early fixation on a melodic line or other musical decisions might influence the subsequent outcome" (Kleinmintz, Goldstein, Mayseless, Abecasis, & Shamay-Tsoory, 2014, p. 7). Instead, keeping the form of the song open and for as long as possible, while exploring it through improvisation and different added obstructions (e.g. a change of instrumental roles, tempo, rhythm, groove, harmonies, key, dynamics, sound effects, emotions, lyric interpretations), should enhance the level of creativity and originality in the performance. Conscious structural thinking triggers other opportunities for approaching elements in art production than a merely aesthetic approach, opportunities you would hardly have come up with through purely aesthetic entrances (Christensen, 2013, p. 35).

Affirmation and Openness to Problems

An open-minded affirmative approach and communication (Lehmann, 2012, pp. 151–152) is arguably the most important mindset and attitude for students to adopt. Exploring open formats while changing perspectives and structures demands an affirmative communication and mindset for options and stimuli to keep emerging.

The facilitating instructor articulated this competence as a ground rule for communication in the class. Statements were commented and rephrased when critical, vertical-thinking mindset and communication took over. So "I don't like that chord" (critical and closing) was rephrased as "that's an option" (affirming the idea), "what if we played another chord there?" (generative and open). This demonstrated effectively the difference in mindsets and modes of communication, and the subsequent responses and reactions. Affirmative communication generated options instead of rejections. The effect of the change was instant, liberating and motivating for the students. A similar affirmative approach was sought in the musical communication, and additionally taught and conceptualised through applied theatre and drama exercises.

Action Learning and Problem-Finding Creativity

An educational parallel to problem-finding creativity is found in action learning, where open-ended problems, project tasks or challenges of importance to the group or individual are used "to excite the interest of the participants in what they cannot see already" (Marquardt & Waddill, 2004, p. 190). The problem "creates a hook for experimentation using stored knowledge" (Marquardt & Waddill, 2004, p. 190), in a process that emphasises questions and reflection.

In group improvisations, the identity of a creative problem does not exist until musically expressed and communicated in some way. "Problems only 'exist' when declared by social agreement" (Jones, 2014, p. 97). Other band members finding and reacting to the problems already available in the music, offered by their improvising peers, is what distinguishes musical problems as creative hooks for experimentation from noise in the music. A musical statement needs a reply, to become conversational and acquire meaning through this retrospective interpretation (Sawyer, 2012b, p. 72). Hence another ground rule for playing in the ensemble class was to seek problems to build on, and focus on "taking in", listening and responding, prior to "sending out". The instructor articulated this in the ground rules "make the others sound good", and "make it possible" (by adding interactional meaning to or offering ways out of musical statements). These proved to be simple, efficient and creatively more generative tasks than the stifling idea of having to come up with something interesting on the spot. Also, they assisted in building a safe, conducive environment for improvisatory explorations, as any impulsive musical statement was likely to be picked up and built upon, enhanced and made better by the others, if they stuck with their idea long enough for anyone to be able to notice and respond.

APPLICATION OF THE EDUCATIONAL STRUCTURES IN CLASSES

Examples of how the educational design was facilitated during classes will be presented in the following section.

Tuning into a common group 'breath' and impulse: The frame for the first ensemble playing exercise was to improvise collectively, starting by exploring one single note (A). A pulse was not to be added before an impulse for it derived naturally from the improvisation. Same rule was applied (but not directly expressed) for adding other notes. The group improvisation evolved naturally and showed the students had good improvisational skills and listened attentively and responded accordingly to each other's ideas. When a common pulse and groove was established, the instructor added a very simple, melodic three-note line based on an A major triad and a short lyric consisting of 8 three-syllable phrases for the vocalists to elaborate on and improvise from. The group improvisation went on for about 15 minutes before finding a natural ending. The instructor then opened the class discussion by asking: "What did you experience?" This facilitated an experienced-based discussion about some of the basic co-creative competencies in rock and pop music:

- fear as a stifling factor in co-creativity. Fear of rejection and fear of the space a completely open improvisation provides;
- how the pulse and introduction of a simple melodic structure provided frames for improvisation and scaffolding for a direction in the co-creation of a more song-based and rock/pop sounding group improvisation;
- roles in the music: taking the lead through clear initiatives and musical statements or backing up the lead by supporting and enhancing it or adding contrasts to it musically. These lead/supporting roles were mutable and impulse-driven during the improvisation;
- frames and limitations as an idea-stimulating and fear-diminishing factor in creativity;
- an introduction to the CSP-zone model (Allan, Kingdon, Murrin, & Rudkin, 2009, p. 176) introducing the concepts of the comfort/stretch/panic zones, identification of the corresponding emotions, and the importance of stretch zone behaviour in creativity.

The ensemble playing exercise was repeated, followed by a class discussion adding recognition of and further perspectives to the themes listed above.

Song introduction. After this exercise, the instructor introduced the students to the song "Squares" (The Beta Band) by singing and playing the three basic parts of the song. Each part consists of one melodic line that is repeated with variations in the lyrics. The harmonic base for all three parts was presented as one chord (F minor) with an optional descending chromatic four-note bass line. The groove was presented as shuffle. These elements provided the scaffolding for the next group improvisation.

The themes in the class discussion that followed were:

- the amount of information downloaded in relation to traditional ensemble playing classes and originality in the performance;
- the comfort zone provided by the shuffled groove and the style indicating musical roles, and at the same time how stifling these musically ready-made roles were for coming up with original ideas;

This was followed by a new group improvisation of "Squares", but this time with even notes as the groove. The enhancement of originality in this performance was noted in the class discussion and the importance of keeping the format open for creativity to occur was confirmed. Thus, in one session, the students had identified the impact of rules and frames on creativity, experienced and articulated both panic zone, stretch zone and comfort zone behaviour and how these impacted their co-creativity in ensemble playing.

Action Learning through Co-Creation

From a social constructionist perspective, knowledge production and social action go together (Burr, 2015, p. 5). In addition to co-creation of music, the students also co-create tacit and propositional knowledge as individuals and as a group while revealing new realities through musical and verbal dialogue (Camargo-Borges & Rasera, 2013, p. 4; Green, 2006, p. 106). The instructor-facilitated conversational approach (Iversen, Pedersen, Krogh, & Jensen, 2015, pp. 5–6) to experience-based reflections and class discussions, and the informal social interactions of the students (Eraut, 2000, p. 120), are important factors in the transformation of tacit and codified knowledge into propositional knowledge (Eraut, 1994, pp. 107–116; Rønnestad, 2008, p. 290), as language gains its meaning through experience (Burr, 2015, pp. 9–12). Thus social experience and language both play a vital part in the learner-led co-creation of new perspectives and propositional knowledge of creativity in ensemble playing, as well as in the collaborative development of the emerging artistic expression (Sawyer, 2012b, p. 72).

It is common for trained musicians to think of music as a language due to the inherent meaning of the musical syntax of sounds and silences, and socially and culturally delineated meaning (Green, 2006, p. 102). Hence, for trained musicians, music also gains meaning through experience and dialogue. "Most improvisation practice is conversational and takes place in a group setting" (Kleinmintz et al., 2014, p. 7). Conversations lead to flow, emerging "from the successive individual contributions of the participants" (Sawyer, 2012b, p. 63) and flow leads to creativity (Sawyer, 2007, p. 43). Realities are created "through language, in its varied forms of presentation, stimulating a process of continuous creation" (Camargo-Borges & Rasera, 2013, p. 3). By making equal participation (Sawyer, 2012b, p. 72) in musical improvisation, instead of instruction, the centre of the social action of the ensemble class, the students are freed through spontaneity to relate and act in the moving, changing world around them (Spolin, 1999, p. 4), and empowered to co-create an authentic artistic expression through the collaborative emergence (Sawyer, 2012b, p. 72) of the musical communication.

Instructor Facilitation of Reflection

Meaning emerges while creative impulses and ideas are being used, and "in the conversations that recipients have with each other" (Ind & Coates, 2013, p. 91). So the co-creative activities were followed by the instructor posing unbiased, open-ended questions, thus allowing the students to reflect, express their experiences and emotions. In this way they developed a domain-specific language and acquired experience-based propositional knowledge through the co-creative work with the music. To avoid a sense of approval/disapproval of their artistic expressions and thus enhance artistic authenticity (Spolin, 1999, pp. 6–9), the instructor's feedback and evaluation focused on their problem-finding exploratory behaviour and co-creative approaches (process), rather than on their aesthetic and musical choices (product), and was based on the students' own wordings and experience-based reflections.

The facilitating instructor assisted in condensing themes and concepts, topics and challenges from the experience-based class discussions, and related these to codified knowledge and applicable domain theories (Sanders & Stappers, 2008, p. 14) when relevant. "The degree to which teachers can create links between informal and formal knowledge" (McPhail, 2013, p. 43) and thereby extend students' understanding and conceptual abilities, can be "a key factor in student engagement" (McPhail, 2013, p. 43).

By extending the time of reflection-in-action during ensemble classes through experience-based class discussions, and thus including a reflection-on-action, the desired functional closure of the reflection-in-action leading to a professional co-creative approach and competent behaviour (Rønnestad, 2008, p. 288) could be facilitated. Time is a factor in knowledge creation, and a similar extension of the time in musical exploration and reflection-in-action through improvisation in an open-ended format of the song is desirable in co-creative ensemble playing, as "systems inquiries require the learning and re-integration of new thinking that occurs over successive explorations and exchanges" (Jones, 2014, p. 125).

RESULTS

Two main contributions were derived from the pedagogic development project:

- structures for a co-creative educational design (Table 12.3) inspired by the informal educational tradition in rock and pop ensembles (Table 12.1), incorporating the educational characteristics and corresponding learning objectives (Table 12.3).
- a mapping of the structural elements of the educational design and corresponding co-creative competencies (Table 12.4), derived from the aesthetic characteristics of rock and pop ensembles (Table 12.2).

The Co-Creative Workshop-Based Teaching Process

The facilitating instructor has three possible threads of interaction: structure, content and process. By changing perspective of the content from product to process and thus incorporating the aesthetic and educational tradition of art-based rock and pop ensembles (Table 12.1 and 12.2) in the educational design (Table 12.3), other competencies and structural elements of the co-creative group process are revealed (Table 12.4). By including these in the educational design (Table 12.3), genre-relevant structural framework for facilitating the co-creative process is provided, enabling "conceptualisation and operationalisation of co-creation challenges and opportunities" (Degnegaard, 2014, p. 104) by the design. Generative, empathetic and

Table 12.3. Co-creative learning objectives and corresponding co-creative educational design approach in rock and pop ensemble classes

Informal educational tradition in rock and pop based on:	*Corresponding co-creative learning objectives*	*Corresponding co-creative educational design approach*
Socially acquired informal knowledge	Intrinsic motivation, engagement, interest	Task and term clarification, change of structures
Self-taught through informal learning in bands	Participation and experience-based reflection, respect, affirmative communication, voluntariness	Facilitation of an affirmative, conducive environment for group exploration and reflection, openness to problems
Original songs and radical interpretations	Lateral thinking skills, aesthetic sensitivity, desire	Using original material or unfamiliar songs as frames
Improvisation based on sound, energy, personality	Use of emotions, courage, trust, readiness, confidence	Exploration through added obstructions, use of emotions, lyrics interpretation
ARTISTIC TASK Find the group's unique sound and ground rules for playing together	ARTISTIC COMPETENCE Authentic performance, co-creating an original artistic group expression	INSTRUCTOR TASK & COMPETENCE Facilitate an art-based conducive environment for artistic co-creation in rock and pop ensemble classes

trans-disciplinary methods (Jones, 2014, p. 99) can assist the instructor in facilitating the complex bottom-up processes of collaborative emergence (Sawyer, 2012b, pp. 71–72) in improvisatory musical co-creation, the action learning on which the rock and pop ensemble class is based. Hence the educational design practices of the co-creative process become more systemic, transparent, and in accordance with the learning objectives of the RAMA curriculum.

DISCUSSION

Creativity research has found "it takes a minimum of ten years of hard work and practice before attaining the high level of performance that results in great creativity" (Sawyer, 2007, p. 124). Thus, in an educational setting, rather than focusing on the quality of the current end product, it may be preferable to study the process and structures enabling development that qualify the student to reach this level of artistic competence in the future. The creative paradox that the goal is achieved through abandonment of target steering (Lehmann, 2012, p. 153) is very much in place here and is fundamentally different from the reproductive aesthetic learning tradition. Lehmann's (2012) two other creative paradoxes – that proactivity occurs through reactivity (p. 152), and that freedom is won through limitations (p. 153) – are telling us something about how this can be achieved

Table 12.4. Corresponding co-creative competencies and structural elements of the educational co-design approach

Aesthetic characteristics of rock and pop	*Corresponding co-creative competencies*	*Corresponding structural elements of the educational co-design approach*
Creativity and cutting edge practices	Openness to problems, exploratory behaviour, changing perspective	Facilitate a conducive environment and scaffolding for problem-finding creativity and exploratory behaviour
Perceived authenticity in performance	Group improvisation, presence and spontaneity at the centre	Group improvisation and spontaneity at the centre, process prior to product
Break with tradition, no common tradition	Stretch zone behaviour, playful co-creation, flow	Match challenges with competencies, songs perceived as frames for playful co-creation
Musicians intrinsic to the 'character' of the band	Sharing personal knowledge and experience	Enable students to apply and share knowledge and experiences
Interpreting the song through group improvisations	Open approach, affirmative communication, suspend judgement, understand and nurture ideas, change perspectives, reactivity	Keeping the format open, feedback beyond approval/disapproval, nurture ideas, change perspectives, apply frames, add obstructions.
Group improvisation prior to individual solos	Contingency preparedness, readiness, let go of control	Focus: Joint achievements, make the others sound good
Joint group co-creation of vision, form and content	Achieving results by abandonment of pre-conceived endpoints, letting go of personal baggage	Equal participation in music making, facilitation of experiences and group reflection, pose questions, relate experiences to codified knowledge
Defined as a collective with a group name	Working as a band, not an ensemble class	Approach students as competent peers

through training of reactivity and readiness in improvisational explorations, in an affirmative, conducive environment of frames and rules, enabling the dissolution of an ultimate goal into concrete tasks.

Instructors tend to teach the way they have been taught, in this case, meaning informal learning or methods inherited from classical or jazz music education, with a formal educational base and different aesthetic learning outcomes. To change this, the instructors have to be creative, too, in their role as facilitators, and develop new approaches to the way they teach and what they teach. Moving focus from a fixed product to an open process may feel like a radical, unsettling change of paradigm, challenging the instructor's self-confidence. However "if the conclusion of the process was already evident, there would be no creation" (Ind & Coates, 2013, p. 91). This supports the importance of the development of a theoretical and methodological basis clarifying the relevant qualifications for rock and pop musicians. In other words, theoretically grounded, arts-based teaching practice as the foundation for reflection on personal and group competencies in the field.

Students already possess tacit knowledge about creative processes from their professional experiences outside HE. Transforming this tacit knowledge into codified and propositional knowledge through experience-based reflections can strengthen their contextual understanding and experience of professional competence. In the aesthetic learning tradition of rock and pop ensemble classes at RAMA, the students are generally left to reflect on their experiences by themselves. This might indicate some of the reasons why this learning tradition does not lead to developing the required co-creative competencies. They are neither being experienced nor articulated.

Looking at the learning outcomes articulated by the students during the class evaluation, it is noticeable that the majority of the responses were related to lateral thinking, while Amabile (1998) argues that this is a hard skill and slow process to develop (pp. 79–80). However, the responses do not tell to what degree these lateral thinking skills have been developed by the students, but merely that they have gained an awareness of them and articulated their tacit knowledge in this area and thus transformed it to codified and propositional knowledge (Eraut, 1994, pp. 107–116). The language they used indicates that the knowledge has been primarily produced through action-based reflection, rather than transferred as codified knowledge.

Each class is a unique group of students who will develop a unique construction of knowledge. However, multiple studies of the co-creative educational design structure and how various groups of students behave in it might reveal some patterns of general learning outcomes and general limitations of the educational design and didactics. Research into the long-term effects on students and how the co-creative methods have been incorporated in their further artistic development may show how dependent students were on the facilitator and whether they can apply the knowledge independently without facilitation in future processes.

CONCLUSION

Lehmann's three paradoxes of creativity, together with the three dimensions of problem-finding creativity, suggest some reasons why the traditional aesthetic learning approach is not helping us to develop artistic co-creative competencies in class. They also suggest alternative approaches.

Social constructivist theories hint that we cannot pinpoint what knowledge the students will produce during these classes. However, a general design structure for the process management and facilitation of the classes might be a more relevant focus point for figuring out "what is worth doing". We can identify relevant competencies, mindsets and approaches enabling the students to navigate in such a structure, and facilitate options for experiencing and learning these through the educational design. However, the outcome of other competencies and skills they will develop, creative as well as artistic, will be highly dependent on the unique sum of people in the actual class, what shared experiences they will produce, and what language, mindset and culture they will develop and adopt.

ACKNOWLEDGEMENTS

The author would like to thank the participating students at RAMA for bringing their talent, courage, fear, trust, creativity, reflections and open minds to the ensemble classes, and for giving frank and honest feedback to the instructor and classmates. The author would also like to thank Julie Ørnholt Bøtker, Søren Bolvig Poulsen, Dorina Gnaur, and Maija Hansen, for giving constructive feedback on the content of this chapter, and Anita Graugaard for help with the layout.

REFERENCES

Allan, D., Kingdon, M., Murrin, K., & Rudkin, D. (2009, April). *Sticky wisdom: How to start a creative revolution at work.* Oxford: Capstone Publishing Limited.

Amabile, T. M. (1998, September-October). How to kill creativity. *Harvard Business Review, 76*(5), 77–87.

Anthony, B. (2015). Creative conceptualisation: Nurturing creative practice through the popular music pedagogy of live recording production. *Journal of the International Association for the Study of Popular Music, 5*(1), 139–156. doi:10.5429/2079-3871(2015)v5i1.9en

Behr, A. (2015). Join together with the band: Authenticating collective creativity in bands and the myth of rock authenticity reappraised. *Rock Music Studies, 2*(1), 1–21. doi:10.1080/19401159.2014.969976

Bono, E. de. (1970). *Lateral thinking.* London: Penguin Books.

Burr, V. (2015). *Social constructionism* (3rd ed.). Devon: Routledge.

Camargo-Borges, C., & Rasera, E. F. (2013, April-June). Social constructionism in the context of organization development: Dialogue, imagination, and co-creation as resources of change. *SAGE Open, 3*(2), 1–7. doi:10.1177/2158244013487540

Christensen, M. (2013). *Musik under huden: Struktureret kreativitet i undervisningen.* Tarm, Denmark: Dansk Sang, Musiklærerforeningens forlag.

Degnegaard, R. (2014). Co-creation, prevailing streams and a future design trajectory. *CoDesign, 10*(2), 96–111. doi:10.1080/15710882.2014.903282

Eraut, M. (2000). Non-formal learning and tacit knowledge in professional work. *British Journal of Educational Psychology, 70*, 113–136.

Eraut, M. (1994). *Developing professional knowledge and competence.* Hong Kong: Routledge, Taylor & Francis Group.

Gergen, M. M., & Gergen, K. J. (2012). *Playing with purpose.* Walnut Creek, CA: Left Coast Press.

Getzels, J. W., & Csikszentmihalyi, M. (1976). *The creative vision: A longitudinal study of problem finding in art.* New York, NY: John Wiley & Sons.

Green, L. (2005). Musical meaning and social reproduction: A case for retrieving autonomy. *Educational Philosophy and Theory, 37*(1), 77–92. doi:10.1111/j.1469-5812.2005.00099.x

Green, L. (2006). Popular music education in and for itself, and for 'other' music: Current research in the classroom. *International Journal of Music Education, 24*(2), 101–118. doi:10.1177/0255761406065471

van Hauen, E. (2011). Fra køn til co-creation. *CHARA – Journal of Creativity, Spontaneity and Learning, 2*(1), 687–692. Retrieved 16th October 2016 from http://www.chara.dk/artikler/20110112.pdf

Hebert, D. G. (2011). Originality and institutionalization: Factors engendering resistance to popular music pedagogy. *Music Education Research International, 5*, 12–21.

Ind, N., & Coates, N. (2013). The meanings of co-creation. *European Business Review, 25*(1), 86–95. Emerald Group Publishing Limited. doi:10.1108/09555341311287754

Iversen, A. -M., Pedersen, A. S., Krogh, L., & Jensen, A. A. (2015, October-December). Learning, leading and letting go of control: Learner led approaches in education. *SAGE Open*, 1–11. doi:10.1177/2158244015608423

Jones, P. (2014). Systemic design principles for complex social systems. In G. Metcalf (Ed.), *Social systems and design: The translational systems science series* (Vol. 1, pp. 91–128). Tokyo: Springer Japan. doi:10.1007//978-4-431-54478-4_4

KEA European Affairs. (2009). *The impact of culture on creativity.* Retrieved 7th June 2014 from http://www.keanet.eu/docs/impactculturecreativityfull.pdf?4f4eb7&4f4eb7

Kjølner, T. (2009) Devising og konceptuel devising. In L. Kobbernagel (Ed.), *Skuespilleren på arbejde*. København: Frydenlund.

Kleinmintz, O. M., Goldstein, P., Mayseless, N., Abecasis, D., & Shamay-Tsoory, S. G. (2014). Expertise in musical improvisation and creativity: The mediation of idea evaluation. *PLoS ONE, 9*(7). doi:10.1371/journal.pone.0101568

Lehmann, N. O. (2012). Mentale sideværtsbevægelser: Kunstfagene og den generaliserede kreativitet. In B. Eriksson, J. Lund, H. K. Nielsen, & B. S. Pedersen (Eds.), *Æstetisering: Forbindelser og forskelle* (pp. 147–156). Aarhus: Klim.

Marquardt, M., & Waddill, D. (2004). The power of learning in action learning: A conceptual analysis of how the five schools of adult learning theories are incorporated within the practice of action learning. *Action Learning: Research and Practice, 1*(2) 185–202. doi:10.1080/1476733042000264146

McPhail, G. (2013). Informal and formal knowledge: The curriculum conception of two rock graduates. *British Journal of Music Education, 30*(1), 43–57. Cambridge University Press. doi:10.1017/S0265051712000228

Moore, A. (2002). Authenticity as authentication. *Popular Music, 21*(2), 209–223. Cambridge University Press, United Kingdom. doi:10.1017/S0261143002002131

RAMA. (2011), Curriculum, BA of music, rhythmic department. Aarhus, Denmark: The Royal Academy of Music. Retrieved 4th August 2016 from https://www.musikkons.dk/fileadmin/pdf_musikkons.dk/Uddannelser/Rytmiske/Studieplaner_2016/Studieplaner_engelsk/160226_BMus_RM.pdf

Rønnestad, M. H. (2008). Profesjonell utvikling. In A. Molander & L. I. Terum (Eds.), *Profesjonsstudier* (pp. 279–292). Oslo: Universitetsforlaget.

Sanders, E. B. -N., & Stappers, P. J. (2008). Co-creation and the new landscapes of design. *CoDesign, 4*(1), 5–18. doi:10.1080/15710880701875068

Sawyer, R. K. (2003). *Group creativity: Music, theater, collaboration.* London: Lawrence Erlbaum Associates Publishers.

Sawyer, R. K. (2007). *Group genious: The creative power of collaboration.* New York, NY: Basic Books, Perseus Books Group.

Sawyer, R. K. (2012a). *Explaining creativity: The science of human innovation* (2nd edition). New York, NY: Oxford University Press.

Sawyer, R. K. (2012b). Extending sociocultural theory to group creativity. *Vocations and Learning, 5*(1), 59–75. doi:10.1007/s12186-011-9066-5

Spolin, V. (1999) *Improvisation for the theater.* Evanston, IL: Northwestern University Press.

Turid Nørlund Christensen
Rhythmic Music Department
The Royal Academy of Music, Aarhus

DORINA GNAUR AND INGER MARIE LARSEN-NIELSEN

13. DESIGNING LEARNING FOR CO-CREATION

Conceptual and Practical Considerations

In this chapter, we explore the practical implications of the concept of co-creation in a professional context from an educational point of view. The question we are posing ourselves is: how can higher and further education (HE) educate for co-creation, that is, provide educational frameworks that respond to the societal demand for co-creation, particularly within the public welfare sector?[1] More specifically, we focus on which organisational and individual requirements a HE learning design should take into account in order to support the diffusion of co-creation competences within the public welfare sector. In order to address this question in a qualified way, we will first investigate the conceptual inferences of the notion of co-creation and some methodological implications. We will do this in relation to a 10-ECTS Process Consultant and Co-creation course in a Danish post-graduate university college context. We then argue for the need to integrate these considerations into the learning design of such programmes and we demonstrate a practical application of such an attempt in the form of a particular educational design that the aforementioned course is built upon. We call this a hybrid learning design, in that it takes advantage of technological developments to mediate co-creative learning in multiple learning environments.

A study among all Danish municipalities (Esbersen Hygum, & Ibsen, 2016) has shown that co-creation in practice is marked by certain paradoxes. On the one hand, there is already a comprehensive collaboration between municipalities and citizens. On the other hand, it is uncertain how close this collaboration is, as it often involves concrete, commissioned tasks rather than policy development, planning and prioritisation. It is thus debatable whether this form of collaboration can be termed co-creation. Furthermore, two out of three functional managers doubt that municipal workers possess the necessary co-creation competences, while admitting that they do not know how to support the development of such competences. The study concludes that "there is a need for knowledge on how the quality and the democratisation of municipal work can contribute to solving complex problems, and which competences and organising forms are required within the municipal organisation in order to nurture these values, together with civil actors" (Esbersen Hygum & Ibsen, 2016, p. 81). This confirms our perception of a pressing need for educational incentives to support the development and diffusion of co-creation competences. We will elucidate this challenge within

T. Chemi & L. Krogh (Eds.), Co-Creation in Higher Education, 225–246.

a Danish understanding of public welfare from the point of view of further education of welfare professionals.

Theoretically, we base ourselves on Luhmann's systems thinking, particularly his conceptualisation of trust. Our theoretical discussion runs throughout the article as we search for conceptual implications for practice. Initially, these point to the need to develop organisational trust and learning competences, which are related to the capacity to navigate and operate in the open spaces of potentiality. This capacity, we argue, is required in order to explore and pursue opportunities for co-creation that can leverage innovative solutions in the field, in our case, the social welfare sector. We advocate a particular focus on the creative aspect of co-creation, which has the potential to continually renew practice. Methodologically, our learning design relies on an action-research approach where teachers and participants act as co-researchers as they explore ways to validate and develop knowledge on co-creation, thereby advancing their fields of practice. To guide these processes, we introduce a specially developed operational framework called "re-innovation". It consists of three steps: discovery, adaptation and integration.

The learning design supports these methodological considerations and is organised around the re-innovation model. In this respect, the learning design is exemplary, as it is organised as an action-research project based on participants' investigations regarding affordances for co-creation in their respective environments. Similarly, the didactical organisation is exemplary with respect to the re-innovation framework, being organised around the three steps of discovery, adaptation and integration. Each of the three steps involves sets of action that mobilise knowledge, skills and competences in relation to co-creative processes in context. These processes are dynamically facilitated by the hybrid-learning environment that contains online resources, procedural support and learning in multiple environments, as well as feedback mechanisms that perpetuate learning. The learning that takes place is continually assessed through activities of sharing of experiences, reflection and feedback. In the vein of action research, the final assessment is designed as a conference, where participants share their findings and insights in the field of co-creation.

The chapter is organised as follows: we first present a theoretical perspective on co-creation and the overall methodological implications, after which we discuss the methodological consequences for a learning design in the context of an educational programme within process consultancy and co-creation. We then concretise these considerations within the context of a hybrid learning design for a process consultant programme based on co-creation. The chapter concludes on the main contributions we bring regarding the theoretical and methodological considerations that may influence how to design an educational programme on co-creation.

THEORETICAL DISCUSSION OF THE CONCEPT OF CO-CREATION

Below we will introduce the concept of co-creation in a Danish public sector context and argue for the need to transcend the productive and reproductive levels of co-creation that can be associated with the New Public Management (NPM) paradigm, for the developmental and creative forms of co-creation found within the New Public Government (NPG) paradigm. The NPM paradigm is market- and customer- oriented and relies on economics of efficiency regarding the production of welfare services (Gouillart & Hallet, 2015). NPM-inspired co-creation can involve rather instrumental approaches to citizen involvement, as a form of extended collaboration (Brandsen & Pestoff, 2010). The NPG paradigm, on the other hand, is mainly network-oriented and has an explicit focus on democracy, trust, problem solving and involvement in decision making (Runya, Qigui, & Wei Si, 2015).

In this section we will explore the creative potential of co-creation and discuss some methodological implications for supporting NPG co-creation through a hybrid conceptualisation of the learning environment.

The Co-Creation Continuum

Co-creation is, in a Danish context, a rather diffuse and liquid notion (Hulgaard, 2016). It draws on international concepts such as collaborative innovation (Sørensen & Torfing, 2011), co-creation (Prahalad & Ramaswamy, 2004) and co-production (Pestoff, 2009). Common for all these concepts is that co-creation is different from cooperation in several ways (Agger & Tortzen, 2016, p. 8), such as:

- there is active citizen involvement based on partnerships and common responsibilities between the public sector and the citizens
- each party contributes with resources, particularly knowledge
- the basic assumption is that "common citizens" possess worthwhile knowledge, which can contribute to developing the quality of public services.

The difference between these various concepts is the purpose with which the parties are involved and the way in which the knowledge that the parties contribute is utilised. Thus, the goal of collaborative innovation is to create an organisational space and managerial prerequisites for leading co-creative activities that involve various learning and motivational processes (Sørensen & Torfing, 2011). It is generally agreed that the main purpose of co-creation is to improve outputs, i.e. products and services in the private sector (Prahalad & Ramaswamy, 2004) as well as in public welfare areas (Bason, 2010). According to this view, co-creation can indeed serve normative purposes in terms of creating cheaper and better welfare by involving citizens, volunteers and private companies to actively contribute to finding new solutions within regular formats for welfare production. To the extent that this form of extended cooperation will replace or relieve pressure on public employees, it might arguably support NPM goals through what we might call a kind of NPM co-creation, as the intention in NPM philosophy is the liberalisation and privatisation of the public sector (Klausen, 2001).

Within the co-production understanding, the normative goal is that co-creation should take place in an equal partnership, where the parties are involved as co-producers of new welfare solutions, having an active share in the processes of decision making, planning and implementation. Subsequently, the outcome of the joint efforts will either supplement or replace regular welfare solutions, but the framework of welfare production will have changed. The goal of co-production rests on a vision of empowered citizenship and, through that, increased quality of life, the formation of new social relationships and empowerment of underprivileged social groups. In this perspective, co-production invites a re-thinking of the democratic welfare paradigm perspective that may break through invisible constraints into a more flowing, network-oriented distribution of power. In this case, one may invoke the NPG perspective and speak about NPG co-creation.

This enhanced form of co-creation – NPG – presents certain organisational and participation challenges. The organisation may not be geared to double loop learning, which requires a change in the governing variables for welfare production (Argyris, 2000). Similarly, the participants may not have the competences necessary to change the ruling variables through democratic participation. The practical implication of any co-creative learning design within NPG co-creation should take into account organisational requirements, as well as the individual competences necessary for double-loop learning.

In his research on organisational learning and innovation, Per Erik Ellström (2001) has described a continuum of learning levels, which display various degrees of freedom and restrictions depending on whether the task, the method and the outcome are open or predefined. They range from relatively restricted reproductive and productive forms of learning to the more enhancing processes found within developmental and creative types of learning (see Table 13.1). While all these levels are legitimate expressions for learning in organisations, Ellström

Table 13.1. A learning taxonomy of co-creation

Types of learning / Learning levels —— *Aspects of learning*	*Reproductive learning*	*Productive learning: method driven*	*Developmental learning: problem driven*	*Creative learning*
Problem	Given	Given	Given	Not given
Method	Given	Given	Not given	Not given
Result	Given	Not given	Not given	Not given

[the co-creation continuum in relation to degrees of creative freedom]

→---→---------------------------------- →----

NPM co-creation (extended cooperation) ----------→-----------(creative) NPG co-creation points to the necessity of paying special attention to the innovative, double loop learning connected to developmental and creative levels that imply higher degrees of freedom. If we relate the aforementioned distinction between NPM and NPG co-creation to this taxonomy, we find a similar continuum between the more restricted re-/productive NMP co-creation forms, and the more developmental and creative forms that we will place at the NPG end of co-creation. The increase of freedom (depicted by the arrow below Ellström's taxonomy in Table 13.1) is related to the degrees of creativity that promote the re-creative or transformative learning potential of NPG co-creation. The model can be used, e.g. by process consultants, to identify co-creation opportunities and indicate the learning conditions that support a progression towards the developmental and innovative forms of NPG co-creation.

Exploring the Creative Potential of Co-Creation

The need for a learning design for co-creation is motivated, in our case, by a paradigm shift, from NPM contained achievements to more enhanced forms of learning within NPG co-creation. NPM is based on reliance upon contractual agreements and control to ensure that these are followed through against evidence of expected results (Lerborg, 2009). Within NPG, on the other hand, co-creation is based on trust that welfare can be evolved and reinvented by enhancing co-creation across organisational and sectorial boundaries (Sørensen & Torfing, 2011). From a policy perspective, NPG is justified by the fact that the production of welfare, as we know it today, is about to become socio-economically unaffordable, as the population requires longer and better education and gets older and older (Hood & Dixon, 2015). But NPG does not produce anything by itself, just because individuals are invited to share in a joint responsibility (Allentoft, 2015). Jacob Bundsgaard, mayor of the municipality of Aarhus, puts it this way:

> If we are to meet the expectations of the citizens and contribute to solving their everyday problems and help them reach out to their dreams and ambitions, then we need to employ our efforts to change the welfare. (Mandag morgen, 2016, our translation)

For employees in the welfare sector, the NPG paradigm has the practical consequence that they must be able to initiate and lead co-creation processes across professional, sectorial and organisational borders in ways that enhance the production of new welfare solutions (Sørensen & Torfing, 2011). In this context, five city managers and five educational directors signed a manifesto on "Kommune 3.0" (municipality 3.0) for an extended collaboration to provide educational programmes for this purpose:

> Municipality 3.0. is sustained by the value that the municipality is a community of active citizens, where the employees strive to find resources everywhere and to bring people together in meaningful communities. We

> have a burning ambition to re-think welfare, community, tasks, roles and professional competence. We will only succeed if the employees mobilise their professional and personal competences in new ways. We endorse and underwrite today the principle of helping other players into a better position and setting each other free. In the current conception of a municipality, we deliver, serve and provide services to the citizens. In the municipality of tomorrow, we are playmakers bringing our competences into play in order to develop a local community. We call this principle "Playmaker – the 3.0 Competences Manifesto". (Playmakerdogme, 13th January 2014, our translation)

Loose and Tight Couplings in a Systemic Perspective on Organisational Functioning

From a systemic point of view (Luhmann, 1995), organisations can be regarded as living systems, whose survival depends on their capacity to interpret and integrate complex information from their surroundings in meaningful ways (Thyssen, 2004). In order for welfare professionals to act as 'playmakers', i.e. spot and enhance opportunities for co-creation, they need to be able to 'play' across organisational, sectorial and professional boundaries in favour of new organisational formations. That is, they need to operate in loosely coupled, flexible organisational environments where they can exercise their capacity to explore meaningful interpretations regarding new ways to conceive of welfare. A loosely coupled organisational set-up is necessary if we want to support emergent processes of organising among individuals, departments, hierarchical orders, between the organisation and the surrounding world, between various activities, ideas, intentions and actions (Borum, 2013). Meanwhile, installing new organisational processes will not alone suffice to promote the NPG vision to re-think welfare, but must be powered by an organisational drive that is predominantly creative (Majgaard, 2013).

It might be tempting to simplify the transition to new welfare by continuing to lean on known organisational decision patterns. This might reduce complexity and safeguard against the uncertainty that follows with any new demands, but at the same time risks dragging the organisational past into the future (Andersen & Pors, 2014). This will hardly enhance the rethinking of welfare. Rather it might fall back on a single loop re-/production of various solutions.

Contrarily, re-thinking entails that an organisation engages in internal interpretations against unknown conditions that can lead to new possibilities for organising the production of welfare. Certainty and predictability are no longer the governing variable, but are replaced by emerging ways of organising joint efforts that can tolerate uncertainty. We thus operate within the realms of contingency and potentiality moving into an unknown future of potential solutions, where there are no predetermined expectations, but an exploration of multiple possibilities. The methodological implication of maintaining several concomitant options open would be to practise management of potentiality (Andersen & Pors, 2014). The challenge for the organisation will then be to support the management of emerging processes. A way to address this is through creative process leadership, where the process consultants take the role of learning partners. Their role is to orchestrate the many voices, ideas and professional competences available that can engage in co-creative learning processes with the purpose of exploring new welfare solutions.

We use the notion of process leadership to denote ways in which process consultants engage with promoting and sustaining co-creation in their respective organisations. When understood as a learning partnership, leading such processes entails paying full attention to the concrete situation in terms of uncovering and pursuing learning affordances (Billet, 2001), i.e. the invitational qualities for learning in any work-related situation. In order to capitalise on the potential for co-creation, the partners need to respond in a learning, explorative attitude. Together, the partners learn to recognise and realise potentiality for co-creation. It also involves learning to trust the process, one another and one's own capacity to partake of unknown, emergent scenarios. This can be termed as a hybrid state as it combines several elements into emergent solutions, which however cannot be retraced to its components (Bhabha, 1990). In this way, the parties can be said to assume a hybrid identity that allows them to embark on a journey of learning, leading and re-defining themselves in relation to emergent states (Andersen, 2012).

The building of trust is thus decisive in letting go of familiar ways of handling tasks related to habitual organisational demarcations. Trust entails a reassuring effect on individuals while making their way through uncertainty and, in that sense, trust can be said to reduce complexity (Luhmann, 1973). Thus, in order for an organisation to make sense as loosely coupled system, the subjective systems within it need to be met with trust in their capacity to differentiate themselves through creative interpretations and integration of external complexity. The outcome of co-creation cannot be defined or decided beforehand, otherwise actual re-thinking might not be possible. The greater the trust that the agents involved can use their freedom creatively, the better they may be able to navigate within what Luhmann calls social contingency (1995).

ORGANISATIONAL METHODOLOGICAL IMPLICATIONS REGARDING TRUST

Creativity involves some degree of extended latitude to play and explore without aiming at a certain output. Arguably, this increases the range of potential outcomes and the possibility of worthwhile innovations. Nevertheless, the processes involved in the transition state of internal re-interpretation in relation to the context require trust as opposed to control and pre-defined expectations to allow for the contingent character of potentiality, i.e. that something else might be possible, and at the same time that the outcome might not necessarily be the best possible one

(Andersen & Grønbæk, 2014). How can an organisation accommodate the trust requirement, and how might this be capitalised upon by its members?

Organisational Trust Strategies

Trust is constructed when individual systems are given a fair share of latitude for manoeuvre while aiming at rethinking welfare as well as rethinking themselves within the contingency of co-creation. In this way, the range of potentiality is more fully mobilised and so the probability of worthwhile co-creative scenarios for sustained welfare solutions will arguably increase. For the process consultant, leading co-creative processes means encouraging the parties to learn from and with each other, as a means to redefining themselves in the process of rethinking new welfare solutions. The ability to learn implies that the subjective systems learn to navigate as loosely coupled systems that are capable of integrating the increased complexity related to rethinking welfare. In this way, they will be able to partake of co-creative processes that are premised by contingency.

Creating such a learning environment has implications for the strategies that organisations use to inculcate trust in order to encourage the subjective systems to employ creativity despite the uncertainty of entering into new working constellations entailed by co-creation. What kind of trust strategy are organisations in need of in order to support contingent processes of co-creation of new welfare? The close and loose coupling principles can serve to differentiate between tightly coupled and loosely coupled types of trust in organisations (Borum, 2013).

A tightly coupled trust strategy implies providing guidelines and directions for co-creation to replace usual procedures within prevalent organisational and professional compartmentalisation. The advantage of this approach is that it may reduce the risk for interpretation breakdown. It may, however, also reduce the creativity of the system in that it limits the co-creative range to fit into given expectations and regulations to the extent of re-/productive forms of co-creation.

A loosely coupled trust strategy, on the other hand, presupposes that individual subjects are capable of managing the increased complexity that arises in an open space without closing their system off. This implies that the strategy should provide a space for experimentation without requirements to produce a certain output, although the risk of the co-creating parties not producing any valuable outcome is also present (cf. contingency). A third way of looking at trust strategies is through the lens of a learning partnership, which affords learning-oriented freedom to explore and pursue creative potentiality. We might call this a loosely coupled creative trust strategy that opens up an explorative, experimental space to conduct co-creative processes in creative ways. One may still not be able to guarantee tangible outcomes, but it promotes a mutually enhancing commitment towards rethinking welfare. A loosely coupled creative trust strategy may not remove the uncertainty in entertaining co-creative processes, especially as new welfare solutions must be affordable and must increase, rather than limit, the range of welfare services.

Leading Potentiality in Learning Partnerships – Some Implications for a Learning Design

To Luhmann, trust is not about knowing. Nobody can know everything in the world. Trust cannot be obtained from one's surroundings, but is rather something one builds through action: "...one must act without adequate knowledge and involve oneself actively" (Luhmann, 1973, p. 79). External complexity is reduced, as the individual system consolidates its own internal structures and processes to deal with expectations and trust in own processing capacity. When contingency is translated into potentiality, the individual internal systems of trust in own capabilities need to be strengthened, so that the subjective system can benefit from increased tolerance to uncertainty.

> Expectation is secured from external refutation, in that it incorporates a contradiction within itself, but it must then, however, be able to maintain and deal with the contradiction internally. The problem of the stabilization of the expectation is thus shifted from the environment into the system, because other, more effective, forms of problem-solving are available there. Trust is then nothing other than a type of system-internal 'suspension' (Aufhebung) of this kind of contradiction in expectation. The possibility of disappointment is not simply ignored, but anticipated and dealt with internally (...) The problem of readiness to trust, accordingly, does not consist in an increase of security with a corresponding decrease in insecurity; it lies conversely in an increase of bearable insecurity at the expense of security. (Luhmann, 1973, p. 79)

As no system can ever reflect the complexity of the entire world internally, the effort to absorb complexity must increasingly comprise structures to cope with ambiguity and the paradox of trust and uncertainty. This absorbent capacity cannot be taught, but is built gradually from within through repeated internal learning processes of interpretation and sense making. Any learning design aiming at supporting potentiality must support incentives that spur such learning processes.

Thus, the learning design should support the process consultant and the co-creative parties in exploring and pursuing potential opportunities for co-creation in authentic situations, such as re-thinking welfare, as a part of the educational incentive. In this way, the subjective systems find themselves in situations where they learn to structure internal processes in contingent ways, at the same time as they develop tolerance with regard to the relative increase in uncertainty that is part of exploring new terrain in more than one way. The work of the process consultant being thus to lead potentiality, makes the leading of co-creation a porous business, since its very basis is uncertainty (Andersen, 2012). There are no guaranties that the learning processes will be reciprocal since the learning process is self-referential (Andersen & Grønbæk, 2014). Through agreeing to a learning partnership, one only agrees to a promise to potentially engage in joint learning processes. This promise can only be fulfilled when participants agree to involve themselves in learning how to learn through co-creative learning processes.

As the trust and uncertainty paradox represents the potentiality of co-creation, we need didactical approaches that allow participants to train their own capacity to handle and tolerate this paradox. Problem-based learning might be a viable approach as long as it involves the creative spectrum of problem work, i.e. where participants identify and define their own working problems and methodologies. Within the educational context of co-creation, the participants are prompted to involve their work practice in new, creative ways, so that the learning takes place in relation to a familiar, meaningful context, yet on completely different terms. This will not only expand individual creative capacity, but also open up for a dissemination of co-creation competences in the organisation.

The implications for a learning design for co-creation involve, in our view, merging and integrating learning and work processes into a hybrid learning environment that capitalises on leveraging the learning potential through realistic experiences of the learned in one's own work and organisational context (Zitter & Hoeve, 2012). A hybrid learning environment accommodates knowledge and work- and practice based learning through scaffolding reciprocal processes of informing work through knowledge and validating and advancing that knowledge through practice. This requires the ability to move between and across various action and learning spaces, in the form of a digitally mediated hybrid learning environment consisting of the physical and digital setting in which learners engage with learning activities, including the organisational, socio-cultural setting of their work.

CO-CREATION AND THE LEARNING DESIGN

A learning design for co-creation will, in our view, have to take into account organisational conditions for supporting co-creation and co-creative competence development and include this dimension in the didactical set-up, e.g. in the form of an operational methodology to support the initiation of co-creation projects in organisations as a part of the learning design. In our case, we have found the methodological framework of re-innovation to be immediately applicable at both pedagogical and organisational didactical levels. The re-innovation framework thus serves both as an approach to initiate co-creation in practice and as the bearing framework for the learning design aiming at developing co-creation competences in the participants, i.e. the process consultants. As will be shown, this learning design involves a more fluid, hybrid learning trajectory that connects work and knowledge, training of new skills and active experimentation in context, discussion and reflection spaces, within and across multiple learning and action spaces. It also implies an expanded view of the role of the teacher, which embodies various functions that fit best within an action research approach, where both teachers and participants act as co-researchers aiming at evolving practice through theoretically and methodologically informed co-creation processes.

Re-Innovation as a Way to Diffuse Co-Creation Competences in the Organisation

The notion of re-innovation originates from the multifaceted practice field, as well as from research and development fields that focus on innovation. As a concept, re-innovation addresses those particular aspects of the innovation field that deal with spreading or diffusion of innovation (Roger, 2003). A report from the Danish Centre of Public innovation with the title: *Diffusion of public innovation – what can we learn from research?* (Hansen, 2015), contains recommendations based on research contributions from the fields of innovation theory, network theory and behavioural science about re-innovation, i.e. the diffusion of innovation, which involves various forms of translation processes. Thus, *adoption* denotes pure imitation of an innovative solution in a new context, whereas *adaption* implies certain processes of adaptation and reforming so it better serves the purposes of the new context. In our use of the concept, re-innovation is understood as adaption and requires a reorganisation or reinventing of the innovative solution through processes of discovery, adaptation and integration, which covers our didactical approach of re-innovation.

The translation metaphor is also used regarding the diffusion of process leadership approaches, where the translation can either assume a reproduction, a modification, or a radical translation mode. Reproduction implies a copying mode, with a minimum of conversion. Modifications involve moderate forms of adjustments so the solutions are made to fit. A radical translation mode implies considerable adaptations in terms of both form and content and can either entail a re-presentation or a re-creation process, with the translator as entrepreneur (Røvik, 2007, p. 307).

Re-innovation is, in our case, the diffusion of co-creation (as a form of innovation) and co-creative competences, and this diffusion can assume various degrees of freedom depending on how the innovative potential is translated. This resonates with Ellström's organisational learning continuum, ranging from the re-/productive to the developmental/creative levels (Table 13.2). Furthermore, re-innovation contributes to the spreading of co-creation and co-creative competences at both micro-, meso- and macro-level, i.e. among individuals, groups of individuals and organisations/ divisions. In this respect, the diffusion of co-creation will rely on the range of the translation fluency, which reflects the interplay between organisational trust and individual abilities to handle the trust and uncertainty paradox. The translation modes can be displayed on the same continuum, between re-/productive and creative learning (see Table 13.2). The more creative translation/learning/co-creation modes, e.g. within the NPG paradigm, are associated with a wider impact of the re-innovation approach on the diffusion of co-creation and co-creation competences in organisations.

Table 13.2. Translational degrees of re-innovation versus degrees of freedom in learning (Ellström, 2001)

Types of learning	*Reproductive learning*	*Productive learning, method driven*	*Developmental learning, problem driven*	*Creative learning*
Re-innovation mode	Reproduction (imitational; repetition of known knowledge)	Modification (moderate adaptation; identifying knowledge)	Radical translation (considerable adaptation; knowledge utilisation)	Re-creation of content (knowledge creating)
Aspects of learning				
Task	Given	Given	Given	Not given
Method	Given	Given	Not given	Not given
Result	Given	Not given	Not given	Not given

The role of concepts is to sustain currents of thought and stimulate them creatively so that society can be continually recreated (Deleuze & Guattari, 1991). By connecting the concept of re-innovation with the organisational learning levels, the way is paved for NPG co-creation to do just that. It is particularly worth noting that the organisational learning taxonomy involves the training of progressively higher levels of tolerance with regard to uncertainty in order to match the intentionality of changing current organisational variables of welfare production. While NPM co-creation would be mainly concerned with the re-/productive organisational learning (cf. Table 13.1), NPG co-creation will allow for a wider grasp of potentiality in the ongoing knowledge creation. That which will spread throughout the organisation will then be a continual flow of patterns and mutual responsiveness in relation to a joint effort to further co-creative organisational processes. The gate is opened for new welfare models arising out of people co-employing their reflexive and discerning capacities to navigate through the paradoxes of everyday, spanning in the area of tension between predictability and unpredictability (Stacey, 2001).

These being some of the qualities pertaining to co-creative competence, a learning design must be supported by methodologies to bring these to the fore of learning. Organisationally, double-loop learning is a widely acknowledged, yet scarcely employed framework for rethinking the bearings of organisational practice (Argyris, 2000). How might a learning design for co-creation then support the diffusion of NPG co-creation competences and creative re-innovation in practice?

Designing for Co-Creation and the Learning Design

We are now moving to exemplify a particular re-innovation approach to designing for co-creation, which also serves as the bearing framework for the learning design aiming at developing co-creation competences with process consultants in Danish municipalities. This methodology was developed in a research and development project involving seven Danish university colleges, to form a Competence Hub[2] to promote re-innovation competences in the Danish welfare sector. The re-innovation framework consists of three steps, which are: discovery, adaptation and integration. These steps have been employed to carry the pedagogical didactical design in the same way that it might be employed in an organisation, as an organisational didactical design for co-creation.

Our learning design can thus be said to be exemplary in more than one way. Firstly, it demonstrates in itself a re-innovation methodology, which the process consultants may take into use during and after the programme, when involved in co-creation. Secondly, because it is co-creative in its development, in that it continually invites the participants to 'translate' or co-design the way each of the three steps is effectuated. Finally, it invites co-creative knowledge creation in the spirit of action research, where teachers, participants and organisations have a say in feeding back their own enriched perspective into the process of co-constructing knowledge. This is expected to take place both during the course, through various ways of validating knowledge in action and shared reflections, as well as at the end of the course when participants will share their co-created knowledge through practice in a day-long exam conference.

The re-innovation framework invites participants on a learning journey through the three stages of discovery, adaptation and integration. From a pragmatic learning theory perspective (Dewey, 2009), the learning journey is initiated by a perceived gap, ambiguity and even wonder in relation to a problem field, in this case within the participants' workplaces. Learning is thus situated within the confines of everyday work situations and implies the utilisation of knowledge as an integral part of experience-based learning processes. The pragmatic learning theory allows for knowing through experience in practice and this requires didactically involving different contexts and situations in the learning design. With a model of experiential learning, such as the re-innovation inspired framework, we can afford a meta-analytic perspective on the progression in co-creative learning, as the process passes through each stage, without pre-determining the elements of the learning process. That is, each one will make a unique discovery, adapt it according to a specific context and seek ways to integrate findings in various organisational settings. Such a pedagogical approach echoes systemic theoretical perspectives on education where the individual learning system and its internal processes are seen as loosely coupled to teaching (Qvortrup, 2004), which fits the pragmatic view of learning, where the learner's experiential knowledge processes are proven empirically. As part of a learning partnership, a re-innovation inspired learning design enacts a promise to support the creative learning freedom in co-creation contexts at three levels: (1) the didactical setup accommodates the need to ensure continuity between the various stages of exploring knowledge, skills and competences in relation to co-creation; (2) pedagogically, the learning approach promotes creative learning in capitalising on contextual affordances for co-creation; (3) tactically, the learning progression is enhanced by a hybrid, digitally mediated learning environment that affords multiple communication and feedback facilities as well as continuous learning transactions, e.g. individual and group action and reflection along the learning journey.

Lastly, the pragmatic learning tradition supports an empirical socio-psychological perspective (Mead, 1934/2005) on how we can strengthen individuals in handling the trust and uncertainty paradox in a functional way, through the capacity of the self to perceive its own perceptions. This capacity can be promoted with the support of a learning design that creates connections between various spaces of action, learning and reflection. Hence, experience-based learning implies learning experientially across various learning spaces.

A Hybrid Learning Environment for Co-Creation

The basic pragmatic method, learning-by-doing, translates for us into learning-by-co-creating, and so the learning design must assist our learners in transposing them between various situations, places and modalities that allow them to identify and mobilise potentialities for co-creation. Our learning design involves a more fluid, hybrid learning trajectory that connects work and knowledge, laboratory practice of new skills and active experimentation in context, discussion and reflection spaces, personal, with colleagues, with one another and with teacher/co-researcher.

Thanks to modern communication and digital learning means, this learning journey can potentially take place within the confines of an educational programme. Our learning design consists of a hybrid learning environment, which interweaves educational and workplace learning components combining digitally supported learning elements with face-to-face activities, in such a way that it mediates between various learning, action and reflection spaces. In our case, the hybrid learning environment accommodates learning at three levels, and is supported virtually through an online interaction platform, which ensures continuity, actuality and human presence. Here, the digitally mediated resources and interaction modes coexist and complement each other, both in physical and in online environments. The three levels display knowledge through (1) common sharing and presentation, (2) processing in relation to the practical context and finally through (3) problem solving and creation of new knowledge. To support the metaphor of the journey, we introduce an extended terminology including learning stations, where we get new supplies with regard to each of the three main steps on the re-innovation/co-creation journey, which are marked by so-called boot camps, i.e. face-to-face meeting days, where we get ready for the journey ahead.

Thus, at the first level of interaction, the focus is on communication of central knowledge content and introduction to methods used, and is organised around so-called learning stations, i.e. digitally mediated knowledge presentation with integrated interaction. From the point of view of the content thus presented, the passage through the learning stations qualifies participants in initiating the learning journey into NPG co-creation, in that they find the theoretical and methodological provisions that they may require in order to initiate and design for co-creation. During the boot camps, they will learn how best to fuel or facilitate these processes on the way, as we here train central skills, e.g. communication, sensitivity training and facilitative competences that are associated with co-creation competences. At the second level of interaction, participants are organised in (net)working groups in order to explore knowledge and skills in their respective contexts, as well as design and plan their real life co-creation projects. Although open ended, these activities are carefully designed to spur participants' inquiries into their respective fields of action as they undertake so-called group missions. The interaction is peer-facilitated with assistance from the teacher, each group displaying their findings, in a variety of modalities (e.g. text, graphics, pictures, voice/ sound, video) and receiving feedback from one or more groups and the teacher. The third level of interaction involves workplace learning, where the participants accomplish informed action in their respective work environments, where they initiate and sustain processes of NPG co-creation. These are organised on the basis of the re-innovation approach, along the three steps of discovery, adaptation and integration, and involve unique sets of action in relation to each context situation. From this, new knowledge can be shared on the online platform in the form of multimedia generated real field stories or reality cases that substantiate examples of co-creation process leadership in real life situations. During the final boot camp, the exam conference day, the participants will share their analysis and reflections on their experience contributing their lessons learned to the knowledge field.

Thus the teacher has in no way a monopoly over what counts as knowledge. Rather, she acts as a supporter during the learning journey and her role is rather to re-think and mobilise knowledge to satisfy participants' needs regarding their respective projects. Learning can no longer be ruled by a curricular view on knowledge, but is in itself subject to co-creative learning processes. Knowledge becomes multifaceted and evolves along the open-ended problems brought to the fore by the participants, and distributed among participants as well as validated through action, as practice-oriented knowledge.

Figure 13.1 shows the various elements involved in the suggested learning design as well as their internal interplay. Thus, our learning design for co-creation is shaped within an overall action learning approach, where participants/action co-researchers embark upon a learning journey that leads through the three progressive stages of discovery, adaptation and integration of a re-innovation inspired didactical framework. At each stage, learners are invited to partake of knowledge work at three levels, i.e. through presentational, framing and re-framing processes.

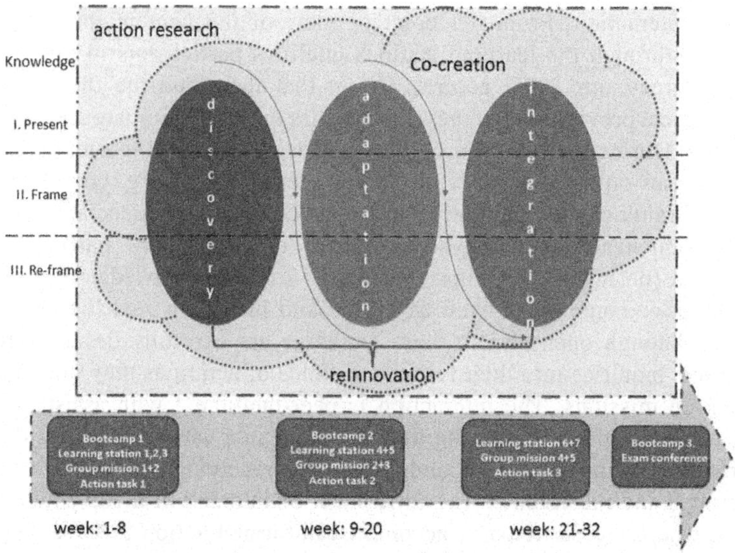

Figure 13.1. A learning design for co-creation: within an overall action learning approach, the learning journey is guided through the three progressive stages of a re-innovation inspired didactical framework

At the first, presentational level, central theoretical and method-related knowledge is exposed online in various digital formats. Then, at the framing level, participants make sense of this knowledge respective to their contexts as well as acquire skills and competences related to co-creation, being guided by practical exercises, both online and during boot camps. Finally, at the third level, participants transform this knowledge through pro-active utilisation of knowledge, skills and competences in a co-creation project, where the potential for a new solution is discovered, adapted and integrated in practice. At the concluding meeting (cf. the time frame at the bottom of Figure 13.1), each participant shares valuable insights from their learning for and through co-creation. The learning design is hybrid in that it accommodates learning in mixed virtual and face-to-face spaces, across multiple school and work based environments and diverse modalities. The online learning milieu works as a meeting and mediating platform that facilitates the learning journey.

Action Learning in Learning Partnerships

Pedagogically, the learning design can benefit from being based on an action research approach, as the aim of action research is to act in emancipatory ways as well as to develop practice. In our case, the participants act as co-researchers aiming at evolving their practice through theoretically and methodologically informed co-creation processes. With aims similar to those of co-creation, action research is by no means a neutral scientific project, rather a socially empowering, democratic change project with regard to practitioners' impact on their own practice (Nielsen, 2014). This matches the normative intention in NPG co-creation with regard to the societal need to advance welfare production. From an ontological perspective, action research operates based on the assumption that the not-yet-accomplished already exists in the form of 'frozen' action tracks, which can thaw through performative communication, social participative and sustainable actions (Nielsen, 2014).

Epistemologically, action research views knowledge as emerging out of hermeneutical cycles of continual interpretative processes through which meaning and identity are created, and the emergent rises out of pre-existing formations. Thus, action research aims both at changes in the social system, e.g. the organisation, as well as at supporting system internal processes, e.g. within the individual. Action research marks a break with the objectifying and objectified views on knowledge as well as the means to attain it, in that dialogue is given a pivotal role in what counts as knowledge and how it can be made sense of in relation to the specific context (Nielsen & Nielsen, 2015). This allows for a certain sense of awe in front of the complexity of the world, which the action research participants strive to open up to, with courage and curiosity.

The action researchers and co-researchers are thus engaging in a learning partnership, which is practically oriented towards uncovering learning and development potentialities as well as, through continual dialogic processes, capitalising on epistemological questions that serve practice-related purposes (Nielsen, 2014). The re-innovation approach to a learning design for co-creation offers a framework for triggering the learning partnership, i.e. between participants and their organisations on the one hand, and teachers and institutionalised education on the other hand, towards systematic interpretive cycles of explorations, action and knowledge creation. Within the learning partnership, members are free to form networks to inspire and support the diffusion of co-creation in their respective organisations (see Figure 13.2).

Subsequently, the role of the teacher as provider of knowledge becomes marginalised by the imperative to promote the participant's own examination of learning needs in order to make sense in relation to both external social systems and internal systemic landscapes that are activated when engaging in potentiality and process leadership and diffusion of NPG co-creation. In order to support epistemological dialogues, it is helpful to use a meta-theoretical frame of understanding, which can grasp this explorative inquiry mode as the ability to learning-to-learn in the world. This is a necessary meta-competence when entering a learning partnership, which has been defined as a promise of a promise (Andersen, 2012), i.e. a declared intention to embark upon a journey of potentiality or learning discovery together. We have found such a meta-theoretical framework in the pragmatic learning philosophy, where learning can be interpreted as a co-creative endeavour that is perpetuated through action and reflection in the world.

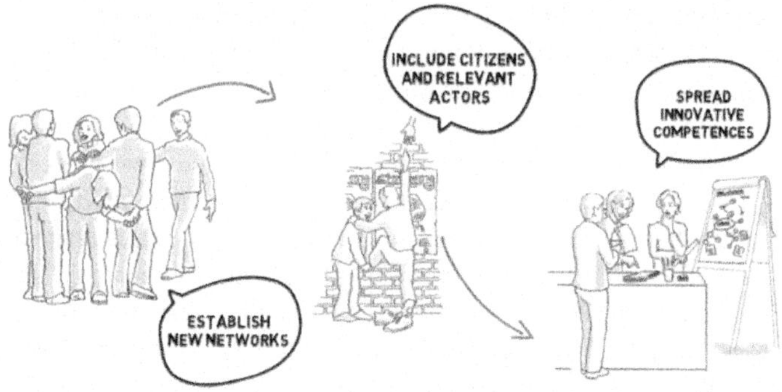

Figure 13.2. Action research for co-creation: Participants and teachers in a learning partnership establish networks, to inspire and support the initiation and diffusion of co-creation

A hybrid learning environment can support learning partnerships and the participants' learning explorations by providing actuality, continuity and feedback through the online platform and the digital learning means, so that one is continually partnered either by the system, the peers or the teacher. Through the continual feedback mechanisms, the participants strengthen their own analytical skills and co-creative learning competences as they traverse the hybrid learning landscape. The process consultants thus produce valuable knowledge on co-creation and potentiality management in practice, and through that they spread NPG co-creation and co-creation competences in their respective organisations – which is the intention behind our re-innovation based learning design.

In the light of the double aim in action research to integrate critical analysis and practice change, education and organisations enter learning partnerships, to declare a 'joint venture' between theory and practice (Nielsen, 2014). The learning partnership between participants and teachers as co-researchers triggers epistemological dialogues on questions that arise from exercising potentiality and process leadership in 'real-life cases'. The outcomes of knowing through co-creation are unique and validated through practice. These findings are a worthwhile contribution to the field of knowledge on co-creation. Although non-transferable, these findings are analytically generalisable (Yin, 2003, pp. 31–33), i.e. to the principles of a phenomenon and as such much wider applicable than the particular real-life case reported. In other words, this particular knowledge on co-creation may aptly be subjected to creative re-innovation in new contexts to spread NPG co-creation.

CONCLUSION

Danish municipalities have a great demand for co-creation as an innovative approach to maintaining high levels of social welfare in the public sector. Meanwhile, co-creation holds certain paradoxes related to new ways of organising and new professional competence needs. Current research agrees that co-creation involves a certain degree of normativity. There are thus differences in the values associated respectively with NPM and NPG co-creation. When linked to levels of quality of learning in organisations, co-creation is more fully manifested in relation to the higher degrees of freedom in learning with regard to defining the scope of co-creation, the methods and approaches to be used, as well as to the openness in terms of expected results. A learning design for co-creation would arguably aim at uncovering the full potential of co-creation, which we find at the higher end of the degrees of freedom scale, i.e. within NPG.

Working with NPG co-creation in practice requires that the organisation is able to interpret itself in the light of a trust-based governing variable so that the creative potential for co-creation can come into play. The practical implications of a learning design for NPG co-creation include organisational requirements as well as individual competences necessary for double-loop learning. Learning partnerships can provide higher degrees of freedom to learn creatively and explore potentiality. The learning partners proceed in ways that increase their tolerance to uncertainty by increasing their internal complexity or absorbent capacity through repeated processes of interpretation and sense making. A learning design that supports the potentiality of co-creation is in need of didactical approaches that allow participants to train their own capacity to handle and tolerate the uncertainty and trust paradox. We suggest a learning design that provides a hybrid learning environment by combining learning in both educational and workplace settings, based on the pragmatic view of learning occurring as participants explore, apply, reflect on, revise and share knowledge in practice. We believe that this will increase the relevance of the educational incentive and fuel interpretation and meaning creation processes as the learners operate within a mutually enhancing interplay between knowledge and practice to perform informed action in the world. This may not only sustain individual creativity, but also enhance the diffusion of co-creation competences in the organisation

Within the framework of a re-innovation inspired didactic design, the participants are thus encouraged to embark upon a learning journey that interweaves theory and practice. The progressive qualification of participants' approaches is supported through an action research methodology of systematic turns of theory-action-reflection cycles that are mediated through a carefully designed hybrid learning environment. Here, digitally supported materials and ways of interaction are intertwined with face-to-face activities, while the digital platform ensures actuality, connectivity and continuity of various types of learning across multiple environments and situations. The emancipatory, practice-oriented, empowering approach in action research creates a dialogic inquiry space for knowing through being and acting in the world, paying particular attention to learning how to learn within the perpetual co-creative learning processes of a learning partnership aiming at the diffusion of NPG co-creation.

The notion of hybridity is highly relevant to a learning design in co-creation in several respects. At the conceptual level, co-creation implies a hybrid, emergent structure that, although intentionally initiated, needs to be set free in order to work. In the same vein, hybridity reflects the bridging into something unknown, creating communication and making new couplings (Andersen, 2016). Moreover, the learning partnership organisation that makes this possible is also a hybrid in the sense of promising a promise or learning how to learn as the qualitative promoter of NPG co-creation. With respect to the implementation of a learning design, hybridity reflects the need to create new connections and initiate cross-functional configurations merging action and learning throughout educational and various workplace contexts. This is adequately mediated in digitally enhanced hybrid learning environments that include physical and virtual meeting, learning and communication spaces. Finally, the requirement inherent to the pragmatic view on higher education, i.e. to promote research-based knowledge combined with learning-by-doing, in our case learning-by-co-creating, is aptly realised through an action research approach, which arguably represents a hybrid knowledge mode.

Within this new hybrid learning design, the pragmatic philosophical claims of learning as the continuous, concrete and mutual forming between the subject and the world are supported by a digitally mediated exploratory learning environment for learning to co-create.

NOTES

1. http://ufm.dk/uddannelse-og-institutioner/videregaende-uddannelse/universiteter/styring-og-ansvar/udviklingskontrakter/udviklingskontrakter-2015-2017/via-university-college-udviklingskontrakt-2015-17.pdf
2. www.kompetetencehub.nu

REFERENCES

Allentoft, N., & Pedersen O. K. (2015, December 21). Velfærdsdebatten er løbet af sporet, *Den offentlige*.

Andersen, T. K., & Reiermann, J. (2016, February). Sammen skal vi gentænke velfærden, *Mandag Morgen*.

Andersen Åkerstrøm, N. (2012). To promise a promise: When contractors desire a life-long partnership. In N. Andersen Åkerstrøm & I. –J. Sand (Eds.), *Hybrid forms of governance: Self-suspension of power*.

Andersen Åkerstrøm, N., & Pors Grønbæk, J. (2014). Playful membership: Embracing an unknown future. *Management & Organizational History*, *9*(2), 166–183. doi:10.1080/17449359.2014.891796

Andersen Åkerstrøm, N., & Pors Grønbæk, J. (2014). *Velfærdsledelse: Mellem styring & potentialitet*. København: Hans Reitzels forlag.

Argyris, C. (2000). *Organisatorisk læring – single- & double-loop*. In K. Illeris (Ed.), *Tekster om læring*. Roskilde: Roskilde Universitets forlag.

Bason, C. (2010). *Leading public sector innovation: Co-creating for at better society*. Bristol: Policy Press.

Bhabha, H. (1990). The third space. In J. Rutherford (Ed.), *Identity, community, culture and difference* (pp. 207–221). London: Lawrence and Wishard.

Billett, S. (2001). Learning through work: Workplace affordances and individual engagement. *Journal of Workplace Learning*, *13*(5), 209–214.

Borum, F. (2013). *Strategier for organisationsforandringer*. København: Handelshøjskolens Forlag.

Deleuze, G., & Guattari, F. (1996). *Hvad er filosofi*. København: Gyldendal.

Dewey, J. (2005). *Demokrati & uddannelse*. Århus: Klim.

Dewey, J. (2009). *Hvordan vi tænker*. Århus: Klim.

Elstrøm, P. E. (2002). Integrating learning and work: Problems and prospects. *Human Resource Development Quarterly, 12*(4), Winther 2001.

Esbersen Hygum, H., & Ibsen, I. (2016). Kommunernes samarbejde med civile aktører – forskelle & ligheder i forventninger, praksis, samarbejdspartnere & oplevet udbytte. *KORA Det Nationale institut for Kommuners & Regioners Analyse & Forskning, 2016.*

Hansen, D. m.fl. Spredning af offentlig innovation: Hvad kan vi lære af forskningen? *Center for offentlig innovation, COI*, 2015.

Hood, C., & Dixon, R. (2015). *A government that worked better and cost less?* Oxford: Oxford University Press.

Hulgård, E. (2016). Socialt entreprenørskab, innovation & samskabelse. In E. Hulgård, E. Nielsen, & M. Juul-Olsen (Eds.), *Samskabelse & socialt entreprenørskab – en casebaseret grundbog til professionsuddannelserne*. København: Hans Reitzels Forlag.

Klausen, K. K. (2001). *Skulle det være noget særligt*. København: Børsens Forlag.

Lerborg, L. (2011). *Styringsparadigmer i den offentlige sektor.* København: Jurist- & Økonom forbundets Forlag.

Luhmann, N. (1973). *Trust and power: Two works by Niklas Luhmann*. Great Britain: Pitman Press.

Luhmann, N. (1995). *Social systems*. Stanford, CA: Stanford University Press.

Majgaard, K. (2013). *Offentlig styring – simpel, reflekteret & transformativ*. København: Hans Reitzels forlag.

Mead, H. G. (1934/2005). *Sindet, selvet & samfundet*. København: Akademisk Forlag.

Nielsen Aagaard, K. (2014). Aktionsforskningens videnskabsteori: Forskning som forandring. In L. Fuglsang, P. Bitch Olsen, & K. Rasborg (Eds.), *Videnskabsteori i samfundsvidenskaberne – på tværs af fagkulturer & paradigmer*. Frederiksberg: Samfundslitteratur.

Nielsen, K., & Nielsen, B. (2015). Aktionsforskning. In S. Brinkmann & L. Tanggaard (Eds.), *Kvalitative metoder: En grundbog*. København: Hans Reitzels Forlag.

Pestoff, V. (2009). Towards a paradigm of democratic participation: Citizen participation and co-production of personal social services in Sweden. *Annals of Public and Cooperative Economics, 80*(2), 197–224.

Prahalad, C. K., & Ramaswamy, V. (2004). Co-creation experiences: The next practice in value creation. *Journal of interactive marketing 18*(2), summer 2004.

Qvortrup, L. (2004). *Det lærende samfund: Hyperkompleksitet & viden*. København: Gyldendal.

Roger, E. M. (2003). *Diffusion of innovation* (5th ed.). New York, NY: Free Press.

Runya, X. U., Qigui, S., & Wei, S. (2015). The third wave of public administration: The new public governance. *Canadian Social Science, 11*(7), 11–21.

Røvik, K. A. (2007/2014). *Trender & translasjoner: Ideer som former det 21: Århundrets organisasjon.* Oslo: Universitetsforlaget.

Sørensen, E., & Torfing, J. (Eds.). (2011). *Samarbejdsdreven innovation – i den offentlige sektor.* København: Jurist- & Økonomiforbundets Forlag.

Stacey, R. (2001). *Complex responsive processes in organizations*. New York, NY: Routledge.

Thyssen, O. (1997). *Værdiledelse – om organisationer & etik*. København: Gyldendal.

Yin, R. (2003). *Case study research* (3rd ed.). Thousand Oaks, CA: Sage.

Zitter, I., & Hoeve, A. (2012), Hybrid learning environments: Merging learning and work processes to facilitate knowledge integration and transitions. *OECD Education Working Papers* (81). OECD Publishing.

Weblinks

https://www.mm.dk/aarhus-borgmester-sammen-skal-vi-gentaenke-velfaerden

http://www.danskekommuner.dk/Artikelarkiv/2014/Magasin-04/Kommuner-sender-playmakeren-pa-banen/

www.kompetencehub.nu

Dorina Gnaur
Department of Learning and Philosophy
Aalborg University

Inger Marie Larsen-Nielsen
School of Further and Continuous Education
VIA University College

ABOUT THE AUTHORS

Annie Aarup Jensen, PhD, Associate Professor in 'The acquisition and development of intercultural competence in practice' at Department of Learning and Philosophy, Aalborg University, Denmark. Her research interest is primarily adults' learning processes and the development of teaching, learning and assessment forms to support the process, in particular in relation to Problem Based Learning. She has many years' experience in creating, implementing and evaluating problem-oriented, project-organised and group-based study programmes and has done extensive pedagogical research into the university's study programmes. She is furthermore interested in the international and cultural aspects of teaching and learning and is the co-founder of the research group I.C. Learning (research into international, intercultural, interdisciplinary culture learning). She has published a number of articles and the latest co-edited anthologies are *Visions, Challenges and Strategies for Problem Based Learning* (2013) and *Teaching and Learning Culture: Negotiating the Context* (2013).

Julie Borup Jensen, PhD in 'Innovation and knowledge use in teacher practice', Associate Professor at Department of Learning and Philosophy, Aalborg University, Denmark. She is a long-term member of the research group FIU, Forskning i undervisning og uddannelseskulturer (research in education and the culture of education). Her two professional backgrounds of classical violin and nursing are channelled into her cross-disciplinary research field of creative learning. Here, she brings artistic and academic tools into play in arts-based research on professional development in public sector-professions. Her publications include a range of articles and book contributions in Danish and English, on themes such as public sector innovation, innovative professional development and action research – all with a focus on creativity as part of learning, innovation as a social exchange of knowledge and practices, and arts in teaching and learning settings.

Tatiana Chemi, PhD, Associate Professor, Department of Learning and Philosophy at Aalborg University, Denmark. Chair of Educational Innovation, where she works in the field of artistic learning and creative processes. She is the author of many published articles and reports and is also the author of *Artbased Approaches. A Practical Handbook to Creativity at Work*, Fokus Forlag, 2006, *Kunsten at integrere kunst i undervisning* [The art of integrating the arts in education], Aalborg Universitetsforlag, 2012, *In the Beginning Was the Pun: Comedy and Humour in Samuel Beckett's Theatre*, Aalborg University Press, 2013, and *The Art of Arts Integration*, Aalborg University Press, 2014. In 2013, Aalborg University Press named Tatiana Chemi Author of the Year. Her latest work focuses on distributed creativity, artistic creativity and artistic partnerships published in the following contributions: *Behind the Scenes of Artistic Creativity*, with Julie Borup Jensen and Lone Hersted, Frankfurt, Peter Lang, 2015; 'Distributed Problem-Solving: How Artists' Participatory Strategies Can Inspire Creativity in Higher Education', in C. Zhou (ed.). *Handbook of Research on Creative Problem-Solving Skill Development in Higher Education,* IGI global. 2016; 'The Teaching Artist as Cultural Learning Entrepreneur: An Introductory Conceptualization', in *Teaching Artist Journal*, Vol. 13, 2, 2015. She is currently involved in research projects examining artistic creativity cross-culturally, arts-integrated educational designs in schools and theatre laboratory.

Turid Nørlund Christensen is an associate professor at the Royal Academy of Music, Aarhus, Denmark (RAMA), department of rock/pop/global music, teaching vocals, ensemble playing, and songwriting. Her research and pedagogic development work is focused on creative learning processes and art-based music didactics. She is an internationally acclaimed songwriter and recording artist with several tours in Europe, Canada and the U.S.A., holding a Danish Music Award, a nomination for a Danish Grammy, as well as being a three-time finalist in the Danish Eurovision Song Contest. She has received numerous art grants, and is currently a board member of The Danish Association of Composers and Songwriters DJBFA, and the SPOT Festival. Latest publications include with Lenora Helm Hammonds et. al., Jazz, Constructionism and Music Composition: Building Cultural Competencies in a Global Classroom Through the Performing Arts, in Globally Networked Teaching in the Humanities, chapter 16, 218–230, Routledge (2015).

Lotte Darsø, PhD, Associate Professor in Innovation, Department of Learning, The Danish School of Education, University of Aarhus, Denmark is researcher, author and an acknowledged conference speaker both nationally and internationally. Her main areas of interest are innovation, creativity and artful approaches in educational and organisational settings. As one of Denmark's leading experts in creativity and innovation her distinct focus is on the 'human factor' and its significance for leading and succeeding with innovation. Lotte Darsø is one of the founders of the executive master programme: Leadership and Innovation in Complex Systems (www.laics.net). Lotte Darsø received The Industrial PhD Fellowship Prize 2000 for her research on innovation ('Innovation in the Making', 2001). In 2004 she published the book 'Artful Creation: Learning-Tales of Arts-in-Business', which led to her being invited to the World Economic Forum in Davos as workshop leader and panel discussant. She has published several books, articles and book chapters in both Danish and English.

Xiangyun Du (杜翔云), PhD, Professor at the Department of Learning and Philosophy at Aalborg University, Denmark, and at the College of Education, Qatar University. Her main research interests include innovative teaching and learning in education, particularly, problem-based and project-based learning methods in fields ranging from engineering, medicine and health, and foreign language education, to diverse social, cultural and educational contexts. She has also engaged with educational institutions in over 10 countries in substantial work on pedagogy development in teaching and learning. Dr. Du has over 140 relevant international publications including monographs, international journal papers, edited books and book chapters, as well as conference contributions.

Henrik Find Fladkjær, MSc in Economics and Business Administration. Associate Professor and head of study board at the Department of Business and Management, Aalborg University, Denmark. Henrik Fladkjær's research and teaching activities are primarily focused on complex issues within theoretical business economics, which include concrete and potential business opportunities. His research and teaching topics include: Activity-based Costing, Contribution Costing, Internal and External Accounting, Full-Cost, Balanced Scoreboard, Strategic Budgeting, HR Systems, Production Management and Project Management. Solutions within topics relating to business economics are always combined with relevant IT, particularly within Enterprise Resource Planning (ERP), relational database technology and business intelligence. In addition to his activities in the fields of research and teaching, Henrik Fladkjær has, for a number of years, maintained close contact with the business world though his involvement in various development and consultancy projects and his role as a guest speaker.

Joakim Glerup is a user-centred experience designer focussing on experiences as value-creating activities in marketing. Furthermore he believes that experience design and the underlying processes can contribute in the value chain of innovative companies. In the last couple of years he has worked with co-design and co-creation and how they can be effective in developing design processes related to service, business models and organisational progress. Some of his recent projects have covered these subjects where they have contributed in the development of digital concepts in marketing-related cases. These cases include The Green Agents in Aalborg Municipality and Friis Shoppingcenter in branding purposes to create an overall commitment and participatory culture through experiential marketing activities.

Dorina Gnaur, PhD, Associate Professor, Departments of Learning and Philosophy, Aalborg University, Denmark. Her current research and development activities concern teaching and learning in higher education including competence development of university staff, as well as course development and learning designs. She is particularly interested in the way digital technologies can support learning in context, and in how learning is impacted upon by technology.

Klaus Gregersen started out with a BSc in Communication and Digital Media from Aalborg University, and continued his studies at AAU to get an MSc in Interactive Digital Media. Here – amongst other projects – he has focused on creating engaging, immersive and innovative user-experiences using interactive digital media. During his last semester, before writing his master thesis, he worked as a project assistant at one of the largest communication agencies in Denmark, where he helped develop, produce and test interaction design, UX-design and service design on several different digital products, for some of the biggest companies and organisations in Denmark.

Sune Gudiksen, PhD, Assistant Professor in Co-design and game tools. He has worked extensively with co-design, co-creation and game tools for development and change primarily related to service design, business model innovation and organisational development. He is one of those rare designer-researchers who both design the game tools and do research into how they work. He has published several articles and papers in leading international design and innovation journals and conferences.

Emilie Holst, while studying for her MSc in Interactive Digital Media, Emilie has had the opportunity to collaborate with external stakeholders on developing interactive digital media concepts. It has given her great insights in how important it is to engage and motivate the members of a project group in order to reach the shared objectives. Through these collaborations she has obtained insights and great interest in how to convert theoretical and methodological approaches in practical working environments while keeping track of both time and budget and constantly keeping the values and strategies of the current business in mind. She is particularly interested in how to ensure that members of staff or a given project group are collaborating across fields of work in the best possible way to ensure that the work in the process is as efficient as possible.

Ann-Merete Iversen, Assistant Professor, PhD fellow of University College of North Denmark. Formal education: BA in Danish, MA in Psychology (cand. mag.). Specialises in: didactic design, innovation and creativity, educational research and development, co-creation in education and social work. At present: writing a Ph.D. thesis on co-creation in social work (01.11.2013). Publishing areas: creativity in education, teaching and evaluation, didactic design and educational development, learner-led approaches in Higher Education. Latest publication: *Learning, Leading, and Letting Go of Control: Learner-Led Approaches in Education,* Sage Open, Oct.–Dec. 2015, DOI: 10.1177/2158244015608423 (co-writers: Anni Stavnskær, Annie Aarup Jensen & Lone Krogh).

Søren Iversen is completing an MSc in Information Technology, Interactive Digital Media primarily aimed at user experience design and the value of UX-design in different design processes and with a background as a Graphic Designer. Focus throughout university projects has been on a combination of user-centred design, early stages of design processes, stakeholder involvement through participatory innovation, problem setting vs. problem solving, Design Thinking and concept development.

Lone Krogh, Associate Professor and Head of Higher Education Research Group at the Department of Learning and Philosophy, Aalborg University, Denmark. Her main areas are academic staff development, well-educated adults' learning processes, higher education didactics and development of education and teaching. Her interests also include evaluation/accreditation/assessment, as well as educational politics and development in a globalised setting, framing higher education institutions. She has experiences in implementing PBL strategies nationally and internationally. Writing about Gross National Happiness (GNH) in Bhutanese education is related to a collaborative research project between researchers from Aalborg University and The Royal University of Bhutan where data has been gathered 2012–2014. She has published a number of articles, and the latest co-edited anthologies are *Visions, Challenges and Strategies for Problem Based Learning in a Danish and Global Perspective* (2013), Aalborg Universitetsforlag and articles in *University Teaching & Learning* (2015), eds. Rienecker et al, Samfundslitteratur.

Mads Kunø is, with his graphic design background, an unconventional graduate student on the MSc course in Interactive Digital Media. His approach is based on Design Thinking through a creative and design oriented mind-set, combining practical and analytical skillsets. Through a graphical and theoretical under standing of design as an approach, he seeks to implement design on a strategic level, as a means of organisational growth. Alongside the master's programme he works as a digital consultant at one of Denmark's leading digital marketing agencies, consulting for companies about the possibilities and implementation of digital media and technologies.

Inger Marie Larsen-Nielsen is Associate Professor at the diploma programme in management at VIA University College for higher education and competence development, Denmark. She participated in a national research and development project between university colleges and municipalities in Denmark in 2015–2016. In addition, she has been working on the further development and design of a new learning design, through which the facilitation of co-creation can be professionalised and research in professions can become innovative.

Kathrin Otrel-Cass, PhD, Professor MSO at the Department of Learning and Philosophy, Aalborg University, Denmark. She is a classroom-based researcher, working primarily with visual data collection and analysis. She founded VILA, the video research laboratory at Aalborg University (vila.aau.dk) and recently opened with colleagues a laboratory teaching and innovation classroom called XLab. In this project, Kathrin was intrigued working together with Henrik to contribute with her ideas and explore new facets of university teaching through Henrik's insights.

Anni Stavnskær Pedersen, BA in communication, MA in Psychology (cand.mag.), Master in Leadership and Innovation in Complex Systems (LAICS), Associate Professor at University College of North Denmark. Publishing areas: didactic development of professional and innovative higher education, development of innovativeness and transferability in students, innovative teaching and evaluation, didactic design and educational development, learner-led approaches in Higher Education, user-driven processes and organisational development. She is currently involved in research projects examining innovative evaluation and assessment in higher education, and how to facilitate self-efficacy in students in an entrepreneurial environment. Finally, one research focus is, which interdisciplinary innovation pedagogy has the best potential to stimulate the development of innovation and transferability competencies in students? Latest publication: *Learning, Leading, and Letting Go of Control: Learner-Led Approaches in Education,* SAGE Open, Oct.-dec. 2015 (co-writers: Anni Stavnskær, Annie Aarup Jensen & Lone Krogh).

Pierangelo Pompa has studied theatre history (with a thesis on the influence of Asian body techniques on the training of Western actors and theatre laboratories) and foreign languages and literature at Rome University, with a thesis in Chinese language and translation, specialising in traditional Chinese theatre and Mei Lanfang's writings, after various stays of several months in China and Taiwan. He has been assistant director for Eugenio Barba at Odin Teatret from 2008 for several performances by Odin Teatret and numerous other projects.

He founded in 2008 in Italy the international theatre group Altamira Studio Teater, which later moved to Denmark. With Altamira Studio Teater, Pierangelo Pompa has created performances presented in several countries, such as *I look at the sea, The Garden, Twelve Good Words, Don Giovanni, The Last Night, The Clinic of the Blinded, The Staggering Circus, The World in a Song, The River – Dream of a Poet, By Heart, Boudu tager til Danmark, Playroom* (in progress) and the work demonstration *Style Exercises.* For Holstebro Festival Week 2014 he directed the opening performance *Prologue to the Future* and the intercultural ceremony *The Empty Chair*, which was produced also in Amsterdam, in the frame of the European Project 'Caravan Next'.

He regularly leads workshops and pedagogical projects on actor training and dramaturgy, invited by international academies, universities and festivals in Denmark (Danish National School of Performing Arts, Aarhus University, Aalborg University), Italy (Rome University, Ferrara University), China (Beijing Central Academy of Drama, Shanghai Theatre Academy), Iran (International Festival of University Theatre). He has published articles, translations and reviews on Chinese theatre and his work with Altamira Studio Teater and Eugenio Barba.

Søren Bolvig Poulsen, PhD in User-Centred Design, Associate Professor in Design Thinking at InDiMedia, Aalborg University, Denmark. He has explored the boundaries of User Centred Design in practice and later through his Ph.D. A desire for innovating with-and-for users led to exploration of Strategic Design and Design Thinking, which are his current key areas of interest, together with continuous development of the affiliated educations.

Ole Ravn, PhD, Associate Professor in educational and philosophical studies at Department of Learning and Philosophy, Aalborg University, Denmark. His research is focused on problem-based learning in university education – its foundation and different practices as well as the general design of university educations based on problem-based and project-oriented learning models. Another focal point is philosophical and cross-disciplinary perspectives on mathematics and science. In particular, his research has addressed the philosophy and education of mathematics, emphasising the post-modern conditions for knowledge production and the socio-cultural construction of mathematics in general. In the area of problem-based learning, contributions evolve around the issue of interdisciplinarity, PBL in mathematics and engineering disciplines, as well as the construction of knowledge in collaborative learning processes.

Nanna Schmidt is writing her master thesis on how to implement systematic design methods in large companies in Denmark, and at the same time she works as a project manager in a Danish IT-consultancy company. Here, she is particularly interested in ensuring that time and budget are allocated to conducting UX processes in order to promote successful products and a sustainable business model. Furthermore, she is interested in implementing UX processes in all projects as a systematic method. She has been working on developing interactive, digital concepts for several stakeholders, considering both UX and project management in the process.

Claus Springborg, PhD, is owner and founder of CoCreation (cocreation.dk) where he provides managerial development through workshops and individual sessions. Claus is also an international meditation teacher (sensingmind.com). He has a background as a choral conductor and musician with an MA in Musicology and as a dancer/teacher of tango and contact improvisation with extensive international experience. He continues to enjoy practicing these art forms. He did his doctoral work on art-based methods in management education at Cranfield School of Management 2010–2014. His research interests include art, embodied cognition/neuroscience, and managerial development. He has published a number of book chapters and articles in academic journals on these topics. In his work with managers, he emphasises development of self-knowledge and embodiment of leadership qualities, and he draws on his research findings and his extensive experience with dance, music, and meditation.

Helle Tetzschner has a background based on a BSc in International Business Communication, Helle is now studying for an MSc in Interactive Digital Media at Aalborg University. She focuses on a user-centred design approach and on co-creation as being a part of the design process, while working with concept development. The most recent projects, along with the upcoming master thesis, follow these design and process approaches, together with a focus on creating or supporting customer and business value through interactive digital media.

Klaus Greve True has a specific focus on design concepts that can be used by both private and public organisations, in order to create value for the end-user. He is interested in creating valuable user experiences that are based on genuine user needs. He has been involved in different projects focusing on the design of digital concepts to be used in marketing-related cases. These include *The Green Agents* (Municipality of Aalborg) and the *Sailing World Championships 2018* (Municipality of Aarhus). Both projects have had the overall aim to raise awareness and create commitment, through experiential marketing activities.

Charlotte Wegener, PhD, Associate Professor at Department of Communication and Psychology, Aalborg University, Denmark. She is passionate about writing and has explored the art and craft of writing in several ways. She seeks to expand academic writing as both process and product by involving fiction, music, dreams, and everyday life experiences. She has published blog posts on the London School of Economics Impactblog and Review of Books. She is co-editor of *Cultivating Creativity in Methodology and Research: In Praise of Detours* and co-author of *The Open Book: Stories of Academic Life and Writing* or *Where We Know Things*. Together with her long-time writing friend, Ninna Meier, she has developed the concept of "Open Writing"—a project devoted to the creation of a new research field and writing practice that explores the role of writing in achieving impact and innovation. Specifically, the aim is to make academic knowledge production more democratic, open, and joyful. Follow Open Writing on https://twitter.com/open_writing

She is involved in the Open Writing Community on https://www.facebook.com/OpenWritingCommunity/

Chunfang Zhou, PhD, is a lecturer at the Department of Learning and Philosophy and the Department of Planning, Aalborg University, Denmark. In 2012, she finished her PhD study on *Group Creativity Development in Engineering Education in Problem and Project-Based Learning (PBL) Environment* in Denmark. Chunfang locates her research in the area of Science, Technology and Society (STS), with a particular focus on creativity study and its relations to organisation innovation, STEM education, group learning, organisational learning and management, Problem-Based Learning (PBL), engineering and technology design, and Information Communication Technology (ICT). She has especially contributed to cross-cultural studies on creativity in higher education between Denmark and China. In 2007, her master thesis *Core Competence Development in Science and Technology Groups in Universities in Liaoning Province* was awarded the Best Master Thesis by Northeastern University (NEU), China. In 2009, her published journal article *Research on the Research Group's Structure and Creative Climate of Universities in Liaoning Province, China* won the Annual Article Award of Japan Creativity Society. She is the editor of the *Handbook of Research on Creative Problem-solving Skill Development in Higher Education*, published in 2016, by IGI Global.

CPSIA information can be obtained
at www.ICGtesting.com
Printed in the USA
BVOW06*2126271017
497495BV00009B/20/P

9 789463 511186